PENGUIN BOOKS

Melba

John Hetherington, born in 1907, began his newspaper career as a copy boy and gained international
acclaim as a war correspondent. In 1968 he retired
from daily newspaper work to write full-time until
his death in 1975. He is survived by his widow
Mollie. Of his 14 published books, his biographies of
Melba, Blamey, and Norman Lindsay are most
notable. His memory is honoured by the John
Hetherington Prize for biography, to be awarded in
the Bicentennial year.

OTHER BOOKS BY JOHN HETHERINGTON

Airborne Invasion (1943)
The Australian Soldier (1943)
The Winds Are Still (1947)
Blamey (1954)
Australians: Nine Profiles (1960)
Forty-two Faces (1962)
Australian Painters (1963)
Witness to Things Past (1964)
Uncommon Men (1965)
Pillars of the Faith (1966)
The Morning was Shining (1971)
Blamey: Controversial Soldier (1973)
Norman Lindsay: The Embattled Olympian (1973)

Melba

a biography by

JOHN HETHERINGTON

'. . . wherever human nature is to be found, there is a
mixture of vice and virtue, a contest of passion and
reason . . .'

Dr Johnson

'One owes respect to the living, but to the dead one
owes nothing but the truth.'

Voltaire

PENGUIN BOOKS

Penguin Books Australia Ltd,
487 Maroondah Highway, P.O. Box 257
Ringwood, Victoria, 3134, Australia
Penguin Books Ltd,
Harmondsworth, Middlesex, England
40 West 23rd Street, New York, N.Y. 10010, U.S.A.
Penguin Books Canada Ltd,
2801 John Street, Markham, Ontario, Canada L3R 1B4
Penguin Books (N.Z.) Ltd,
182-190 Wairau Road, Auckland 10, New Zealand

First published by Faber 1967 and F.W. Cheshire 1967

Offset from the F.W. Cheshire edition
Made and printed in Australia by
The Book Printer, Maryborough, Victoria

CIP

Hetherington, John, 1907-1974.
Melba.
Bibliography.
Includes index.
ISBN 0 14 009785 6.
1. Melba, Dame Nellie, 1861-1931.
2. Singers – Biography. 3. Opera –
Biography. I. Title.
782.1'092'4

AUTHOR'S NOTE

Acknowledgement by name of people who helped me with information about Dame Nellie Melba, and a list of my chief printed sources, will be found at the end of this book. References in the narrative to 'Rosenthal' denote Mr Harold Rosenthal, the historian of Covent Garden. His absorbing and scholarly *Two Centuries of Opera at Covent Garden* (London: Putnam, 1958) was invaluable to me in reconstructing the salient events of Melba's career at the Royal Opera House.

J.H.

CONTENTS

MORNING

1861-1886

1

THE child who was to become Dame Nellie Melba was born in Melbourne on an otherwise unremarkable day of 1861. The date was 19 May, which was a Sunday, and as the mother, Isabella Mitchell, lay with her baby daughter on her arm the sound of church bells floated through the open windows of the bedroom on the evening air. The autumn day had been mild and serene, with nothing to foreshadow the tempests as well as the triumphs in store for the infant sleeping against her mother's breast.

For Isabella Mitchell and her husband, David, anxiety tempered the joy of their daughter's birth; this was their third child in four years of marriage, and each of the two earlier children – a girl and a boy – had died at eleven months. The Mitchells sometimes wondered if they were fated not to see a child of their bodies survive the rigours of infancy, but their fears were groundless. The baby born that day was the first of a line of eight children, seven of whom were to reach maturity; she was also to win fame as the greatest soprano singer of her own time, perhaps of all time, and one of the greatest singers the world has known.

Melbourne, though hardly more than twenty-five years old in 1861, was already a substantial city. Having landed on the shores of Port Phillip with their livestock and stores in 1835, the first white settlers ran up their wattle-and-daub huts and, after hustling the peace-loving and childlike Aborigines away into the bush with no more force than was absolutely necessary, set about taming the wilderness. They did it to such purpose that twenty-five years later the population was nearing 140,000. Such was the colony into which Helen Porter Mitchell was born, in Doonside, a bow-fronted two-storey house, stucco on brick, with a squat yellow tower, standing in Burnley Street, Richmond. Her father had built the house himself, as he built many of the most distinguished buildings in the Melbourne of his time; some of these, including Scots Church, one of the city's loveliest churches, still stood a century later, and looked solid enough to stand for another century or two.

David Mitchell was well off in 1861, and the foundations of his future wealth were already laid. He was a building contractor with a growing business, and a reputation for doing work of high quality; he had also begun to buy farm and grazing land within easy distance of Melbourne, and was to graduate as a significant, if never a major, primary producer, particularly of cattle and wine. Although a man of small formal education, he was intelligent, resourceful, shrewd, ruthless in driving a bargain, careful with money, a perfectionist, and unflaggingly diligent—qualities which he passed on to his daughter Nellie. Both he and Nellie were born knowing that the world is a jungle and must be met and mastered as such, if necessary claw to claw and tooth to tooth. David Mitchell was all his life a practising Presbyterian and a God-fearing man, but he never accepted the doctrine that the meek shall inherit the earth; nor did Nellie.

It is unlikely that he had any prevision of the worldly fame his new-born daughter was to win when he stood looking down at her on that evening of Sunday 19 May 1861. Having come to the Australian colonies to find the material success which Europe did not offer to a poor man's son, he could hardly foresee that a child of his would grow up and go back to the old world that he had forsaken, seeking her own success. The opera houses of Europe were at most only names to him, and the idea that his daughter would one day rule over them like an empress could not have entered his head.

At the time of Nellie's birth he was thirty-two years old, a shortish man with stout limbs, powerful shoulders and strong workman's hands; his golden hair and beard were crisp, with a tendency to curl. He had a quizzical sense of fun, and this made his eyes, which showed hazel or green depending on the light, take on a glinting twinkle when something amused him. He was born in Forfarshire (now Angus), one of the eastern maritime counties of Scotland, on 16 February 1829, a son of William and Ann Mitchell. His father worked a small farm named North Meathie, as a tenant-farmer, and David, at seventeen, entered upon four years' apprenticeship to a master stonemason in the town of Kirriemuir, nine or ten miles away.

Seeing little hope of a prosperous future as a journeyman stonemason in Scotland, he decided to try Australia, and set out from Liverpool on 6 April 1852 in the three-masted sailing-ship *Anna*. She carried two hundred-odd passengers, and he was one of seventy-two travelling steerage. Many of the passengers were young men who, having read glowing newspaper reports of the Australian gold discoveries, were burning to get to the diggings and make themselves rich, but David Mitchell, who all his life distrusted the idea of easy money, had other plans.

The legend is that he landed in Australia with no money at all except a single gold sovereign, but he had unbounded faith in himself. Melbourne was still a smallish colonial city then, with thick bush surrounding it. After getting together a few pounds by working as a stonemason, he found his way to Richmond, one of the embryo suburbs, a mile or two from the centre of Melbourne. There he established himself in a makeshift shanty on a piece of vacant land, which he bought cheap, and went into business as a building contractor. The shanty was to become a mansion, but he was to live most of his remaining sixty-odd years on the same piece of land. The only interlude came about a year after his arrival. He went to the Bendigo goldfields, some ninety miles north of Melbourne, to work as a builder, but soon met difficulties. His money ran low, so, having spent his last few pounds on a digger's tools of trade and a Miner's Right, he became a gold-seeker on his own account. He found a little gold, though not much, but did not like the life, and after some weeks left his claim and returned to Melbourne. Back on his own land at Richmond once again, he settled down to make his way as a builder. He was soon favourably known. If he undertook to build a house or an office block or a factory or anything else by a given time, he did it; and workmen found him a satisfactory employer even if they grumbled that he was a slave-driver who wanted full value for wages paid and sometimes a little more.

He was doing well enough to marry in 1857, and he and his bride, Isabella Ann Dow, settled in to Doonside. She was four years younger than David Mitchell, and one of the four daughters of James Dow, a Forfarshire man, who had emigrated to Melbourne in 1842, and become an engineer in a large foundry company. David Mitchell had met the Dows a few weeks after landing from the *Anna*, and Isabella had taken his eye from the first.

Although Nellie Mitchell inherited many physical characteristics from her mother (who was said to have Spanish blood), she was pretty well a temperamental replica of her father, and all through her life no other human being exercised more influence on the way she thought and acted. Among the things they had in common was a healthy respect for money and what it could buy. Neither of them ever made any pretences about that, and if Nellie really did inherit a few drops of fiery Spanish blood from her mother these were drowned in the canny Scottish blood she took from her father.

From the time she became a professional singer she was as businesslike a diva as any that ever trod the operatic stage, who understood to a farthing her value to an impresario and took care to get it. Most famous singers hire a business manager, but Melba managed herself; she could not have found a business manager with a sharper eye than her own for the small print in a contract.

2

THE Mitchell family grew apace. A baby was born every two or three years. Two girls, Ann and Belle, came after Nellie, and while their father accepted these gifts from heaven with gratitude he did not hide his eagerness for a son. He had his wish; two boys, Frank and Charlie, were born in succession. After them came Dora, and then Ernest, and last of all another girl, Vere.

David Mitchell's business concerns were thriving and he had no worries about finding the money required to bring up his children in the best style available. He wanted them all to have a good education, and his daughters responded rather better than his sons. Frank and Charlie Mitchell were outlaws, and made one school after another too hot for them; then their father engaged private tutors, but the Mitchell boys drove these poor men away as fast as they came. Nellie Mitchell probably envied her brothers the male privilege they enjoyed of defying authority without putting themselves outside the pale. Even in childhood she liked boys' company rather than girls'; this preference strengthened in adolescence, and as a woman she was always happier with men than women, although she had a few women friends to whom she was as staunch as they were to her.

As a girl she was strong-minded, a tomboy, something of a hoyden. But she liked dressing up in filmy frocks for any special occasion, such as a concert at Richmond, in which she appeared when she was eight and not only sang such ditties as *Comin' thro' the Rye* and a number called *Shells of ocean*, but also accompanied herself on the piano. *Shells of ocean* disappeared from her repertoire, but *Comin' thro' the Rye* stayed in it to the end of her life; like two other great stand-bys, *Home, sweet home* and Tosti's *Good-bye!*, she knew it to be a song that could always be depended on to round off a concert and send the audience home reeling with nostalgia.

Although never an infant prodigy she was convinced, even as a young girl, that she had musical genius and told her schoolfellows so. In childhood she was more interested in the piano and the pipe-organ than in learning to sing, however. She had her early schooling, beginning when she was five, from two of her mother's sisters. The four Dow girls were all women of some education. Isabella Mitchell, who sang a little (it was an age when most gently-bred young women sang a little, even if badly), was a fairly talented pianist, organist and harpist, so Nellie's first music teacher was her mother. One of Mrs Mitchell's sisters, Lizzie Dow, had a soprano voice which her niece described long afterwards as possessing 'extraordinary beauty'. This might suggest that Nellie inherited her voice entirely from her mother's side—if a thing of such freakish wonder can be considered an inherited property rather than a genetic miracle—but musical appreciation and talent came to her with the Mitchell as well as the Dow blood; her father had a resonant bass voice, and was also a self-taught violinist.

Three of the Mitchell children as well as Nellie had fine singing voices; Belle had a soprano of professional quality, and the youngest child, Vere, had already given the first infant glimpses of a phenomenal voice when she died at four and a half, while the last of the boys, Ernest, in young manhood developed a lyric tenor of splendid timbre and a natural trill equal to Nellie's. At one time Melba said, perhaps with sisterly exaggeration, that Ernest had 'the sweetest, most divine tenor voice that ever came from mortal lips', and announced her intention of launching him on a professional career, but she later lost her enthusiasm for the idea; she had evidently come to agree with Ernest himself who once said, 'One prima donna in the family is enough'. Or perhaps she concluded that, while vocally equipped to be a professional singer, he was temperamentally unsuited to the life, for he had none of her business acumen, her readiness to obliterate any dangerous rival, her inexhaustible toughness of mind and spirit. A friend once urged him to back a racehorse on the ground that it was a brother of Carbine, the 1890 Melbourne Cup winner, and he said, 'That means nothing! I'm Nellie Melba's brother, but nobody would pay a guinea to hear me sing.'

The schoolgirl Nellie Mitchell was always humming, so incessantly that her mother used to beg her to stop; she did not know she was developing her voice but she said in after years that humming was as good an exercise as a young singer could practise. The three singing Mitchells, Nellie, Belle and Ernest, were also enchanting whistlers. At home and at school Nellie was forever being told that whistling was vulgar, unladylike, a pastime for butcher boys, but she went on whistling. All through her life she did exactly what she pleased, indifferent to censoriously raised eyebrows, unless to do it threatened her social standing or business interests.

After her aunts had given her the rudiments of an education she was for some years a boarder at a private school in Richmond, Leigh House; then in 1875 she went as a day-girl to the newly opened Presbyterian Ladies' College. The elocution master, George Lupton, counted her as his most promising pupil, which is surprising considering the views many critics were to express about her histrionic shortcomings when she became a prima donna. At the Presbyterian Ladies' College she also did her first singing studies under a professional teacher, Mary Ellen Christian, an English contralto, who had come to Melbourne and set up as a teacher after training at the Royal Academy of Music under the younger Manuel Garcia. Nellie Mitchell possibly had irons in too many musical fires at that time to profit much by Madame Christian's teaching, for she was simultaneously studying the piano with Alice Charbonnet and the organ under Otto Vogt. Her life was not all music, though. According to Joan Sutherland's biographer, Russell Braddon, Nellie 'promptly at the end of her organ lesson would gallop down to the Yarra River, strip off and swim nude with the local boys'. The banks of the narrow winding Yarra near her home were one of her favourite childhood haunts, and among her companions there was a boy named Billy Neilson, who later developed a good tenor voice and became known in Australia and New Zealand as a singer in oratorio, grand opera, Gilbert and Sullivan opera, and concerts. David Mitchell did not like his daughter to play beside the Yarra with the tough neighbourhood boys, and whenever he came in sight one of her companions would cry, 'Look out, Nellie! Here comes your old man!', and she would bolt for home.

At school she evidently gave more energy to music and elocution than to routine studies. She was poor in mathematics and no better than average in most other subjects but English, for which she showed particular aptitude. She also wrote a strong and legible hand. This was to grow even stronger when she reached womanhood, and to match the thoughts, often dogmatic, prejudiced and intolerant, which she set down in the personal letters she wrote at high speed with reckless indifference to discretion or diplomacy, and oftentimes to the recipient's feelings.

Nothing about her environment as a child or a young woman was peculiarly conducive to a prima donna's career. The Melbourne of her youth was like a rather raw English provincial city of the era. Built on a flat and uninteresting site beside a large and uninteresting port, it was well populated with earnest gentlemen having a respectful eye to the main chance, whose influence was to make it, as the influence of their spiritual descendants was to keep it, the financial capital of Australia. Melbourne was even stuffier then than it is today, which is saying something. It looked askance at its older sister, Sydney, which derived an air of cheerful defiance from the knowledge that it had been founded as a penal settlement, while Melbourne walked in a glow of conscious rectitude, knowing it had been spared that birthstain. Even to this day something of that spirit lingers in each city—the be-damned-to-you attitude of Sydney and the faintly snuffling self-righteousness of Melbourne.

Although Nellie Mitchell's professional career was made and most of her adult life was lived in cities she always preferred the Australian country to the Australian town. If she had been condemned to live always in the country she would have groaned with frustration, but in girlhood she discovered a love of the Australian bush in reasonably small doses—the bush which had been tamed and softened, not the harsh bush of the pioneers—and this stayed with her. It was no less genuine even though she dramatized it at times.

While she was a little girl her father took over a grazing property, Dalry, on gentle river flats thirty-odd miles east of Melbourne. The journey to Dalry by horsedrawn coach and waggonette took seven or eight hours in those days of poor roads, and once she was there she could indulge her love of the bush. The men and boys working on Dalry understood her language and she understood theirs, and it was probably then that she fell into the habit of using one or two of the casual male oaths; in later life these often stood her in good stead in some crisis in which a polite term was inadequate. A few of her old friends say that Melba never in their hearing uttered a word stronger than 'Botheration!', but the weight of evidence is against them. A Melbourne artist, Cyril Dillon, who was a close friend of Melba in her later years, once noticed a photograph of Queen Victoria hanging on the wall.

'You know, Nellie,' he said, 'you look very like the old Queen.'

'Don't say that!' she exclaimed, with a frankness about her feelings for a British royal personage which she would have shown only to an old and trusted friend. 'I hated the bloody woman!'

3

WHATEVER thoughts the young Nellie Mitchell might have had of making a career in music, her idea of the life lived by the darlings of Europe's grand opera houses and great concert halls must have been sketchy. To an Australian of the 1860s and 1870s such matters were mere hearsay, and hardly more real than imaginative tales of events on another planet.

Although steamships had cut the sea journey between Britain and the Australian colonies to between six and seven weeks, Europe was still a remote place to Australians; they might visit it once in a life-time if their parents were well-to-do or if they grew rich by their own efforts, but not otherwise. While most Australian-born girls and boys of Nellie Mitchell's generation heard their elders speak of the British Isles as 'Home', with a misting of the eyes for times remembered, the self-exiles had no thought of going back to live in the land they had left; they were only casting a sentimental glance over a shoulder while driving roots deeper into their adopted soil.

At that time music in even the larger Australian cities, Melbourne and Sydney, was not exciting. Every upper-class and middle-class household owned a piano, and in most such homes the soirée or musicale was a regular event, with amateur singers warbling ballads, amateur instrumentalists performing on piano, violin, flute or harp, and amateur elocutionists reciting, while well-behaved guests patiently listened, with their thoughts fixed on the punch and jellied eels to come. Most of Australia's resident professional musicians then were of modest talent and had to work hard for a living, eking out meagre theatre and concert earnings by teaching; the music-starved colonies were a potentially rich field for overseas singers and instru-mentalists of celebrity, but such people had only just begun to see the possibilities and visits were infrequent.

This state of musical backwardness was not surprising. No opera had been staged in Australia until 1834, when *Clari*, or *The Maid of*

Milan, by Sir Henry Bishop, was produced in Sydney. Nellie Mitchell owed a special debt to *Clari*, for in that opera Bishop introduced the most famous of all his songs, *Home, sweet home*. Probably nobody—unless perhaps Patti, whose audiences always clamoured for it—sang *Home, sweet home* as often as Nellie Mitchell did when she became Melba, and not even Patti sang it with more success. Even those who winced when they heard the opening bars of the accompaniment had to admit that her seemingly artless singing of it was impeccable.

No grand opera performance approaching international standard was heard in Australia until a versatile Irishman named William Saurin Lyster brought a company from the United States of America in 1861. Lyster opened in Melbourne, on 9 March, with Donizetti's *Lucia di Lammermoor*, an opera in which the child born at Doonside two months later was to score many triumphs. Lyster was unchallenged as Australia's leading grand opera impresario for nearly twenty years, until he died in 1880, and his influence long outlived him. One of his staff was his nephew, a young man named George Musgrove, who sold tickets, ushered patrons to their seats, pasted up playbills, and learned to do all the other things which go to the making of a successful theatrical enterprise. Within a few years he was one of Australia's leading theatre and concert managers.

A man associated with the Lyster opera companies was to play a major part in turning Nellie into a singer of world renown. This was Pietro Cecchi, an Italian tenor. Cecchi, who came to Australia in 1871, and joined Lyster to sing leading roles, retired after two years or so, and presently settled down to teach in Melbourne. One of his pupils was Nellie Mitchell. Notwithstanding the accepted story, which the great Melba herself often told and even affirmed in print, Cecchi, not Mathilde Marchesi, did more than any other teacher to make of her the singer she became.

When she left the Presbyterian Ladies' College at the end of 1880 she was eighteen years old, dark-haired and strongly made, but slim, although she grew stocky later. She stood not more than five feet six inches, but always managed to appear tall on the stage or concert platform because she carried herself well and had a trick of lifting her chin high. She moved briskly, as if never in doubt where she was going, and surveyed the world with direct and challenging reddish-brown eyes, which seemed to dare anyone to stand in her way. She was not beautiful, but dominated nearly any gathering, small or large, in which she found herself; this was a matter of personality, which lasted all her life, and had nothing to do with any quality so evanescent as youthful charm or beauty.

The lines of her future seemed to be clearly marked. The daughters of moneyed parents in the Australian colonies, as in the England of the time, had no paid career readily open to them; the idea that they should do any kind of work, except to supervise the servants and arrange bowls of mixed flowers, while occupying their spare hours with tapestry, pen-painting or some other genteel pastime, was nearly unthinkable. Every well-bred young woman's true destiny, as both men and women saw it, was to make a good marriage, then settle down and produce eight, nine or ten children, as her mother had done before her.

Nellie Mitchell knew that all the conventional advantages of being a rich man's daughter were hers for the taking. Her father was no longer merely a substantial man but now a moderately wealthy one. Quarries which he had opened in 1878 at Cave Hill, on the outskirts of the little town of Lilydale, twenty-three miles east of Melbourne, had been particularly successful. He had started these to provide the lime he needed as a building contractor, but other people also wanted his lime, and his quarries were soon Melbourne's chief source of lime for building; modernized, they were still flourishing nearly ninety years later, and so, as a business enterprise, were David Mitchell's most lasting monument. The Mitchell children were always proud of Cave Hill, even though some of them pretended to deplore it as a physical blot on the landscape, with the scars cut into the green hills by the quarrying operations and smoke staining the sky overhead. When Nellie was a prima donna she sometimes spoke of Cave Hill as 'Mess, muck and money!', but she never despised it; she was too practical to despise any successful business undertaking.

In her first two or three years out of school she did not trouble herself much with thoughts of a career. Isabella Mitchell had been ailing for some years, and Nellie, as the eldest daughter, took over some of her mother's duties for a time, but most of these soon passed to Annie, the sister next in age. This suited Nellie; she was going on with her music studies, especially of the piano and singing, and these took time and concentration. While still at school she had started taking singing lessons from Pietro Cecchi, who had become the most fashionable teacher in Melbourne; he was so well regarded that two or three promising pupils made weekly journeys of a hundred miles or more, in a time when railway travel was slow and uncomfortable.

Cecchi, short, plump, and dark, with a heavy black moustache, was a mercurial man given to sweeping enthusiasms and uncontrolled excitements. He was rising fifty when Nellie Mitchell first went to him, and had been in Australia for nearly ten years. A native of Rome, where he first trained and worked as an architect, he took up arms under Garibaldi in 1848. Finding Rome too hot for him after Garibaldi's defeat, Cecchi turned to singing, and in the next few years sang leading tenor roles in Italian and other European opera houses, and toured the United States of America before arriving in Australia. On retiring from the stage, Cecchi worked in Melbourne, first as an architect for about three years, and then as a singing teacher. As well as Nellie Mitchell (and her one-time riverside playmate, Billy Neilson) he trained a large number of young Australian singers.

Cecchi believed from the start that Nellie could make a great name as a singer. Another of his pupils, Margaret Laidlaw, a contralto, was early for her lesson one day and, while waiting, listened to a soprano of superb quality singing one of the great arias. When Miss Laidlaw went in to Cecchi she said:

'What a glorious voice that girl has!'

'Yes,' Cecchi replied. 'It's going to enthrall the world.'

The young soprano was the future Melba.

If David Mitchell had known that his daughter had thoughts of a professional singer's career he would have been horrified. To his rigidly Presbyterian mind a woman who flaunted her grease-painted face on the stage of a theatre was a hussy. He was not at all impressed by the popular acclaim won by famous musicians who, in those early years, made the time-consuming journey to and from Australia, in the expectation–rarely disappointed–that rich pickings were to be had by playing or singing to the unsophisticated but warmly receptive colonials. Indeed the antics of the Hungarian prima donna, Ilma Di Murska, who had arrived in Australia in 1873 and stayed for two years, had confirmed his belief that theatre folk were both irresponsible and dissolute.

Madame Di Murska, at that time the great Patti's only rival, was the most famous prima donna by far to have set foot in Australia. She was a warm-hearted woman, and still beautiful, although in her middle forties, but scornful of convention. She was in the habit of appearing on the streets with a huge Newfoundland dog on a leash while her personal maid tripped behind, carrying an Angora cat on a satin cushion. The Hungarian Nightingale gave a large number of recitals in Melbourne, but it is improbable that the girl from Richmond, who was to outshine Di Murska in a few years, was present at any of them; her father would have refused to let his daughter so much as look on this scarlet, if musically talented, creature.

Madame Di Murska's earnings for many years were high, but money ran through her fingers, and when her voice failed some years after her Australian visit she was stranded in New York. In January 1889, while Nellie Mitchell, having become Nellie Melba, was just emerging as the great prima donna of the day, Ilma Di Murska, aged sixty-two, died in Munich. She was penniless, a dreadful warning to any diva who might be tempted to waste her substance in frivolous living. Nellie Mitchell needed no such warning to encourage her to practise thrift. She was too much her father's daughter for that.

4

Until she was twenty Nellie Mitchell had no experience of death in her family. Then in October 1881 her mother, who was forty-eight, died after a long illness; three months later the youngest child, Vere, aged four and a half, died suddenly.

A shadow lay heavy over Doonside, and David Mitchell felt he must escape for a few months. Always one who liked to combine business with any relaxation he permitted himself, he contracted to build a sugar mill in North Queensland, at a township called Marian, twelve miles inland from the seaport of Mackay. His two eldest children, Nellie and Annie, had helped him to bear the weight first of Isabella's death and then of Vere's, and he told them to pack their trunks and go with him. Even though it meant suspending her singing lessons with Signor Cecchi, Nellie did not demur; only a stick-in-the-mud would have rejected the chance to see the sub-tropical North, which at that time was exotic territory to Australians living in the temperate South, and with her father and Annie she boarded the steamer for Mackay, a journey of some 1,400 miles.

At that time Mackay was a frontier town inhabited by slightly more than 2,000 people; the population of the surrounding district was nearly five thousand. Even optimists did not foresee that within eighty-odd years these figures would multiply eight times. A bold and enterprising young Scotsman, John Mackay, had led an expedition to the region in 1860 and penetrated primitive and previously unexplored country. Two years or so later the first white settlers arrived, with their livestock and stores and high hopes, and ran up their shanties in what were then mosquito-ridden swamps and ti-tree scrublands. They were more discerning than the civilized stay-at-homes who thought them mad for believing they could ever conquer that wilderness, for the surrounding country was to become one of the richest sugar-growing districts in Queensland, with cane farms burgeoning and sugar mills proliferating in the valley of the Pioneer River, which empties into the Pacific Ocean at Mackay.

The development of Mackay and the neighbouring country was well under way and gathering strength when the three Mitchells disembarked there. David Mitchell at once busied himself recruiting men and getting them to work building the mill at Marian; his daughters who, with their citified frocks and hats brought an air of chic to Mackay, were quickly caught up in the social life, such as it was, of the growing town. They were invited into the homes of all the leading townsfolk, and Mackay soon discovered that Nellie Mitchell was an accomplished pianist and also sang quite charmingly. It was generally agreed by the vocal connoisseurs of Mackay that as a singer she was no match for a local girl named Julia Wheeler. Miss Wheeler, who was four or five years younger, and probably too vocally precocious for her own good, had only to appear on a local platform to command rapt silence. Mackay people believed that if she wished to make a career, in Australia or abroad, her success was assured. The two girls were friends and often appeared together in local concerts. Nellie played Julia's accompaniments and usually also sang herself as a supporting performer. Her interest in singing was as strong as ever, and on 15 September 1882 she wrote a letter to Signor Cecchi in Melbourne, in which she said:

'I suppose you will be astonished to hear from me, but I want to tell you that although I am nearly two thousand miles from Melbourne I am not forgetting my practising, for I manage to get a little every day. I am going to sing at two concerts, one on Monday and the other on Saturday. I hope I shall be successful.

'Will you please send me six or seven nice English songs up, as the people here do not understand Italian. I daresay you will be able to find some pretty ones; send them as soon as possible.

'I shall not be home for two or three months yet. I intend taking a long holiday, as I am enjoying myself so well. I go out either riding, driving or yachting every day. . . .'

Cecchi evidently replied quickly, because exactly a month later

Nellie wrote him another letter. In this she thanked him for his letter and the songs he had sent, then went on:

'I had great success at the two concerts I sang at, so much so that all the ladies up here are jealous of me. I was encored twice for each song, and they hurrahed me and threw me no end of bouquets. Everyone asks me who my master is, and when I say Signor Cecchi, they all say, "When I go to Melbourne he shall be my master, too!" '

She ended the letter by telling Cecchi that she would be home in the January, but that was not to be; by then she was married, and a new—and in some ways a disastrous—phase of her life had begun.

5

BOTH the Mitchell girls were liked in Mackay, and Nellie, hand-somer and of more forceful personality than Annie, roused a deeper emotion than mere liking in young Charles Armstrong.

Charles Frederick Nesbitt Armstrong was manager of a sugar plantation for a mill at Marian. He was the sixth and youngest son and child of Sir Andrew Armstrong, the first baronet, of Gallen Priory, King's County, Ireland, who had died in 1863, and a brother of the then baronet, Sir Frederick Armstrong. He is usually described as an Irishman, but always insisted that, having been born in England in 1858, he was an Englishman by birth as well as sentiment.

The Armstrongs were originally Scottish. A family legend tells that they moved to Ireland in the seventeenth century, after a fire-eating ancestor, Johnny Armstrong, was taken prisoner in a border raid on England and hanged as an example to other troublemakers. Charles Armstrong also liked a fight. His friends called him Kangaroo Charlie; he was three years older than Nellie Mitchell, a handsome young man, fairly tall, lean and muscular, with a longish face, thrust-ing jaw and arresting blue eyes, who moved with a horseman's gait. They said in Mackay that the horse he could not ride had never been born. He could talk and act with contagious gaiety, except now and then when a black mood would take hold of him for no clear reason. Most of the unattached young women of Mackay sighed over him.

Armstrong, a young man with a taste for adventure, had found England too tame. When he was sixteen or seventeen he went to sea as apprentice in a sailing-ship, but came home after a year or two having had more than his fill of stormy seas, wet quarters and poor food. When he grew restless again his family arranged for him to go out to Queensland and become a jackaroo on a cattle station. He liked the bush life, and particularly liked working among horses. He learned his rough-riding there, in a hard school; he had some painful falls, but was always game to try again, and was soon acknowledged by veteran cattlemen to be a horseman with few equals and no superiors.

Then Charles Armstrong grew tired of jackarooing and set off to see more of Australia. He liked some things about the country but detested others, especially the snakes (of which he had an almost pathological horror) and the prevalent flies; these were curious quirks of fastidiousness for a man who could rough it with the hardest-bitten outback drovers, living on a diet of mutton, damper and black tea for weeks on end. He drifted about Queensland and New South Wales, taking jobs as they were offered, but never staying for long in one place. He preferred the bush, but was in Sydney for a time, and while there brushed up his boxing at Larry Foley's so-called boxing academy, which produced many of the best amateur as well as professional scrappers of the day. Foley, a street brawler turned professional fighter, was the bare-knuckle champion of his time, and is credited with having founded scientific boxing in Australia. He had some famous professional pupils, including Bob Fitzsimmons, Peter Jackson, Young Griffo and Frank Slavin, and a flock of distinguished amateur alumni; some of these amateurs might have beaten Armstrong in the ring, but he would have been a handful for any man near his own size.

The measure of his boxing skill was never proved (although, being a hot-tempered man, he had a number of fights in his Pioneer River days, and rarely needed more than a few punches to polish off an adversary), but his talent as a horseman is indisputable. When he went back to England, as a married man, Buffalo Bill's Wild West Show was appearing in London, with a standing challenge to any horseman to ride their prize buckjumper for fifty pounds. Nobody could sit the outlaw for more than a few seconds. One day Armstrong went along and said he would like to try. The Americans, supposing him to be a misguided Limey fop, led their buckjumper into the ring. Armstrong bridled and saddled the horse in a few seconds, then sprang into the saddle. His mount bucked like an equine fiend, but for all the effect the whirlings, twistings and pigrootings had, the man might have been a part of the horse. The battle was over in a few minutes; knowing himself beaten, the horse abandoned the fight, and Armstrong cantered him round the ring to the plaudits of the watchers, led by Buffalo Bill and his men. Then he dismounted and collected his fifty pounds.

Charles Armstrong had been in Australia about two years when Nellie Mitchell went to North Queensland. He had gone to Mackay with a droving party, overlanding a mob of horses from northern New South Wales, a trek of perhaps 800 miles, much of it through hard country. A seasoned bushman, Lewis Gerald Ross, led the party which included, as well as Armstrong, two other young Englishmen, Thomas Drinkwater Chataway and William Rooke Creswell. Chataway, who had been educated at Charterhouse, was later to become mayor of Mackay, and a member of the Australian Parliament as senator for Queensland. Creswell, some years older than Armstrong and Chataway, had come to Australia after relinquishing his commission in the Royal Navy when the death of his father left the family in less easy circumstances. He worked in the outback until 1885, then joined the fledgling Navy in Australia; in 1904 he became Director of the Commonwealth of Australia Naval Forces and ultimately First Naval Member of the Commonwealth Naval Board, a post he held until 1919, when he retired as a knighted rear-admiral. These were the kind of men Charles Armstrong liked and understood, men of action who could ride horses, fight with their bare fists if necessary, and hold their drink in any company, but men also of birth, breeding and education.

Armstrong's attraction for Nellie Mitchell is easy to understand; he was not only handsome, dashing and masculine but also a baronet's son, and she always had a liking for a title. Her attraction for him is equally understandable; she was strong with life and had everything to rouse a passionate man's senses. Her talent for music was not a great bond between them; Armstrong never showed much interest in the higher flights of music. He loved light opera and could whistle most of Gilbert and Sullivan, and had a taste also for the rollicking old music-hall songs. Friends remember him, when in cheerful mood, singing one item in which two lines of the refrain were

I'm the mad butcher! I'm the mad butcher!
Against me all poor people struggle in vain.

If he wooed his Nellie with this and like ditties it is not on record. Probably he did not, which is to be regretted; had he done so she might have taken fright, packed her bags and gone back to Doonside, and then both she and Charles Armstrong would have been spared some desperate heartache. As it was, they were married at St Ann's Presbyterian Church, Brisbane, by the Reverend Charles Ogg on 22 December 1882 when Nellie was twenty-one. The ceremony could hardly have been quieter; except for Armstrong, Nellie and Mr Ogg, the only other people present were David Mitchell, Annie Mitchell, and a young Brisbane barrister named Arthur Feez. David Mitchell, who had disapproved of Nellie's match with the likeable but penniless Armstrong, then resigned himself to it when he saw that his strong-minded daughter was set on it, gave the bride away. Feez was the best man, and if it had not been for him the wedding would probably have been cancelled at the last minute.

Feez was twenty-two, and had been called to the bar only the year before. But even at the very beginning of his career he showed qualities of calm deliberation which were to make him the leading barrister in Brisbane from about the time he took silk in 1908 until he removed himself and his practice to Sydney some fifteen years later. He was a close friend of Armstrong, and when the marriage was arranged agreed to act as best man. He did not like Nellie Mitchell when they met in Brisbane a day or two before the ceremony; perhaps he sensed that an attempt to harness together in marriage two dominating personalities, such as hers and Charles Armstrong's, would be doomed, or perhaps his dislike of her expressed some fundamental antagonism between them. He did not mention his feelings about Nellie to Charles Armstrong, however, and even hid them on the night before the wedding when the agitated bridegroom went to him with a disturbing story. Armstrong told Feez he had heard from a friend in Melbourne that Nellie had been deeply in love with a young man there before going to Mackay, and his informant suspected she was still in love with the other man. Armstrong, in his high-tempered way, said he intended calling the wedding off; he had no wish to marry a girl who did not love him. Feez, whether wisely or not, believed it was too late for Armstrong to withdraw—no honourable man could abandon his intended bride practically at the church door. And after all, Feez said, the story might be no more than idle gossip; Nellie was only twenty-one, and if some probably harmless flirtation meant that a girl was no longer eligible to marry, then precious few couples would go to the altar. His persuasion was effective. Late that night the two young men shook hands and parted, and next day Nellie Mitchell became Charles Armstrong's wife.

If Arthur Feez ever regretted the use he made of his dialectical powers on that night of 21 December 1882 he never admitted it, even to his own family. But the marriage, like a ship which discloses a list on launching, got away to a wobbly start.

6

THE Armstrongs went south for their honeymoon and spent three months or so in Melbourne, staying at Doonside. Nellie took more singing lessons from Signor Cecchi and brushed some of the Queensland rust from her voice, while Armstrong took the opportunity to look to some business in Melbourne and Sydney. He and his wife did not see Mackay again until late in April, four months after their marriage. On the way back, they passed through Brisbane, and Arthur Feez called on them. They seemed happy enough, and Feez hoped all would be well with them; he was attached to Armstrong, and also had to concede that, whatever the basis of his antipathy to her, Nellie was a personable young woman.

The marriage appears to have had no chance from the first. They were the wrong kind of people to be married to one another. Nellie was not cut out to be a submissive wife, content to stay at home and cook her husband's meals, clean his house, iron his shirts, darn his socks, and bear his children; on his side Kangaroo Charlie was not the kind of adoring and complaisant lover who could submerge his individuality in his wife's, even to save a ricketty marriage.

Nellie became unsettled in her mind when she went back to Melbourne on her honeymoon and, having temporarily resumed her studies with Cecchi, realized what she had thrown away when she married a man living in the wilds of Queensland. Her unsettlement was aggravated when on their way back to Queensland she and Charles Armstrong stayed for a week or so in Sydney. She sang at several private parties of music-lovers there and was lavishly, perhaps extravagantly, praised on all sides; her hearers hailed her, not with excessive originality, as 'the Australian Nightingale', and asked her to sing at a public concert of the Sydney Liedertafel, but she had to decline because there was a ship to catch. And so they arrived back in Mackay – 'two thousand miles away from dear old

Melbourne and all my dear friends there', as she lamented in a letter to Cecchi, with her customary indifference to such insignificant items as statute miles. Her heart and mind were fixed on Melbourne and what was going on there; she was hungry for news, and in this and other letters pressed Cecchi for word of the progress her sister Annie was making in her singing studies with him. (Annie developed into an average amateur singer, but had neither the voice nor the wish to be more.)

In Queensland Nellie was miserable. The wet season was still over the North, and even the house at Marian in which she and Armstrong were to live was not ready; they had to wait some weeks before moving into it, and when they did take possession Nellie felt the sub-tropical wilderness closing clammy arms about her. It was far, terribly far, from the world she had always known. Ships which came in two or three times a week were Mackay's only regular means of communication then with Brisbane, Sydney and Melbourne, and no railway was to be built for many years. Yet Mackay was a bustling metropolis compared with Marian. Nellie's heart must have sunk when she arrived there as Armstrong's wife and realized that this was her home. The wooden house with its galvanized-iron roof was a hotbox when the sun beat down on it, and a place of dank vapours in the wet season. For one period of six weeks the rain pelted down, day and night, without stopping. The Pioneer River became a rolling leaden torrent, and the very air was heavy with water. As Nellie was to tell the story more than forty years later, in her ghost-written autobiography, *Melodies and Memories*:

'My piano was mildewed; my clothes were damp; the furniture fell to pieces; spiders, ticks, and other obnoxious insects penetrated into the house—to say nothing of snakes, which had a habit of appearing under one's bed at the most inopportune moments.'

She was a woman of prodigious energy, insatiable curiosity, and relentless ambition, and at Marian none of these qualities could find an outlet; as the weeks became months her sense of frustration grew. This was not just an expression of the perverseness of the high-spirited city girl who refused to accept a different brand of life. A North Queensland historian, G. C. Bolton, has written, 'Women were rather in the background in that plantation society, with its energetic, boisterous, masculine pastimes', and that is a fair state-ment. For Charles Armstrong life was more agreeable; he was by temperament a man of action, and the nature of his work constantly challenged his muscles and his mind. To him life was an unbroken

horse, which had to be mastered and made to obey his will. One
trouble was that his wife's will was as strong as his, and collisions
between them were inevitable.

Nellie had some happy weeks soon after they returned from their
honeymoon when a small but competent touring opera company,
led by Annis Montague and Charles Turner, put on a short season
in Mackay. It played to full houses every night, and Nellie Armstrong was one of the most ardent patrons. She and Charles met
the principals of the company, and took some of them driving to see
the sugar plantations. She enjoyed that interlude, but she felt that
life was stale and flat when the company packed its scenery and cos-
tumes and moved on, and Mackay settled back into the old dreary rut.

She made some good friends in the Mackay–Marian district,
notably John Ewen Davidson and his wife, Amy. Davidson, a pioneer
sugar-miller, was a Scot; his wife was a Sydney girl with some music
talent, and this provided a point of contact with Nellie Armstrong.
Nellie kept up her singing practice, and from time to time sang at a
small private party, and now and then at a public concert in Mackay,
often with Mrs Davidson as her accompanist. As a singer she had
many admirers, but nobody seemed to guess at the magnitude of the
name she was to make before ten years had passed. She sang with
particular success several of the charming, if musically modest,
drawing-room ballads of the Italian-born composer, Paolo Tosti. (In
spite of an undying legend in Mackay, perhaps the most famous – and
the most tearful – of all Tosti's songs, *Good-bye!*, which she was to
sing thousands of times in the next forty-five years, was not among
them. Unhappily for the legend, *Good-bye!* was not published until
1885, more than a year after she left Mackay never to return.) She
could not foresee then that Tosti himself, cynical, gay, irrepressible
and warm-hearted, with his limitless fund of risqué stories, would
within a few years be one of her close friends, and much less that he
would say, for everyone to hear, that she was the only singer in the
world who sang his *Mattinata* properly.

All through the first year of her marriage her eyes kept turning
south to Melbourne. It was also at that time that her thoughts of a
music career began to take solid shape. She mentioned the idea to her
husband, but at first he brusquely dismissed it; he could not see himself tagging around the Australian colonies or across the world tied
to the apron-strings of a wife whose singing earned the money to pay
the bills and let her rule the marriage roost. Yet, whatever her dis-
satisfaction with her life in general, she seemed happier when she

wrote to Signor Cecchi in July. The better weather had lifted her spirits; the mornings and the evenings were cold and the middle of the days was warm, which made her think of springtime in Melbourne. She told Cecchi in that letter that her voice was 'better than ever, although I am afraid I do not practise as I ought', but did not confide in him that she was pregnant. Her son was born on 16 October, and she and her husband named him George. He was the only child she was ever to bear.

A few weeks later she wrote Cecchi another letter. It is a pity she did not date it, because it records her decision to become a professional singer. This was the decision which, although she was not looking so far or so high at that time, put her on the road to her début at the Théâtre Royal de la Monnaie, in Brussels, and thence to Covent Garden, the Paris Opéra, La Scala, the Metropolitan Opera House and world fame. Her letter, with a number of words underscored for emphasis, was written late in 1883, and is the outpouring of an almost desperate woman, who was at odds with her day-to-day environment and yearned to escape at any price. After a few introductory lines of small-talk, she wrote:

'Now to business. My husband is quite agreeable for me to adopt *music* as a profession. I do not mind telling you that times are very bad here, and we are as *poor* as it is possible for anyone to be. We have both come to the conclusion that it is no use letting my voice go to waste up here, for the pianos here are all so bad it is impossible to sing in tune to them. Not only that, the heat is so intense that I feel my voice is getting weaker every day. So you will understand that I am anxious to leave Queensland as soon as possible. *I must make some money.* Could you not form a small company and let us go touring through the Colonies, for of course I should like to study for the Opera, but would have to be earning money at the same time. My husband will accompany me, and my baby will be quite big enough to leave in Melbourne with my sisters. Madame Emblad* would join us, I am sure. Do you think we could make money? I shall wait anxiously for a letter from you, for I am very unhappy, here where there is no music, no nothing. We spoke of August next year; let it be much earlier than that if you can possibly arrange it, for I believe I shall be *dead* by then. I shall be advised by what you say in this. I hope what I say will be agreeable to you. I hope you will answer this letter as soon as you receive it, so as to let me know

---

* A misspelling of Elmblad – Alice Elmblad, a Melbourne-born pianist, had returned to Australia with her husband, a Swedish singer, whom she married while studying abroad.

what ought to be done. Remember, whenever you are ready for me I can come at once, for there is nothing to detain me now that Mr Armstrong is agreeable. I want you to keep this quite a secret from my sisters and friends. Do not mention it to anyone until everything is settled. . . .'

The tone of this letter, and in particular the statement that 'we are as *poor* as it is possible for anyone to be', leave no doubt of one thing; this is that David Mitchell had not helped Nellie and her husband with money, even though she was his favourite child. That was characteristic of the man; having disapproved of the marriage, he refused to be the indulgent father and smooth the way for her when the venture turned out badly. Not that David Mitchell disliked Armstrong; on the contrary, he liked many things about the young man, but had seen that as husband and wife Nellie and Charles were unsuited. She herself doubtless knew it by then; her letter to Cecchi was written, not from Marian, but from the house of friends named Rawson at Mirani, another small sugar settlement, some miles higher up the Pioneer River. Nellie was staying there with her infant son after a series of quarrels with Armstrong, which had culminated in his consenting to let her take up a singing career. They had not separated in any definitive sense, but had agreed to spend a few weeks apart while their frazzled nerves and wounded egos were mending.

In Melbourne Cecchi read Nellie's letter and was alarmed. A letter from him would take a week or more to reach Mackay, and that, the kindly Cecchi told himself, was too long if he read the signs right. So he wired her to come as soon as she could. His telegram could not have said more plainly that he believed in her and knew she would succeed, and that was all she wanted. She showed the wire to her husband, and he read it, shrugging his resignation. They agreed that he should stay behind to work and keep the family pot boiling until the direction of his wife's future was settled; then he would go to her. So the marriage was not at that time dead, although it had suffered some severe wounds.

All the arrangements having been made, Nellie packed up, said farewell to her friends and sang her last songs for them. Then with her little son she caught the ship for Melbourne, via Brisbane and Sydney, on 19 January 1884. She never went back.

7

I N Melbourne Nellie Armstrong felt like a woman released from prison. She and her baby went to live at Doonside, and her father was glad to have her home even if he by no means approved of her wish to become a professional singer. He compressed his bearded lips when he thought of it, and in private shook his head over it. But whatever his feelings about her professional ambitions he was always proud of her gifts, although he never praised her to her face. Later in life she told with a kind of dismayed relish the story of how, in her full bloom as a prima donna, she sang in Scots Church, Melbourne, while on a tour of Australia. Her father was in the congregation, and at midday dinner she asked him if he had liked her singing. For answer he grunted, 'I dinna like your hat.' Yet behind his unresponsive façade he gloried in her success.

She flung herself into her studies. She would be up at six in the morning, practising scales whether other members of the household liked it or not. She was never a victim of that kind of fey optimism which drives some aspiring singers to disaster in the teeth of all sound advice, and even then had a clear understanding of the difficulties she must overcome to satisfy her ambition. Twenty-five years later she was to say this in an article in the Sydney magazine *Lone Hand*:

'The girl or youth–but more especially the girl–whose accomplishments expand to their utmost attractiveness under the genial influence of the home circle, is too often the one who is least fitted for the struggles, the labours, the sacrifices of a professional career, especially when entered on in a foreign land. The very qualities which are her strength in the world of her sympathetic friends become her weakness in the too often blighting atmosphere of cold, or designing, or indifferent strangers. It is not easy to imagine a sadder lot than that of the young musical aspirants whose once ardent hopes are wrecked in an alien land.'

The possibility that such a disaster would ever befall Nellie Armstrong did not exist; she knew her own capabilities better than anyone else did, and she also knew too much about people to be deceived by flatterers. While it is true that, particularly as she grew older, she listened to flatterers because she liked to have her surface vanity titillated, they never fooled her; their words were merely one of the prizes of the success she had won, and she took these baubles along with the rest. At times she even deflated a flatterer, especially if he laid it on too thick. In the days of her greatest fame, before World War I, the Australian artist, George Lambert, a fine portrait painter and a man of limitless vanity, who wore a ginger beard which he flaunted at the world like an arrogant banner, swept off his hat on meeting her and, bowing from the waist, made a courtly obeisance – a regal salute from greatness to greatness. She scrutinized him for a moment, then snapped, 'That will do from you, Ginger!' Even Lambert was struck dumb.

But in 1884 the time when she would command the adulation, whether genuine or simulated, of celebrities like Lambert, as well as bigger ones, was far off; or seemed so. She believed she could make a name as a singer, but she had a long way to climb and knew it. Cecchi never stopped encouraging her. She was able to sing well when she came back from Queensland, but she had many fine points to learn and he schooled her relentlessly.

Having promised in effect to launch her on a professional career, in the telegram he sent which brought her home, he did not fail her. As a preliminary he arranged for her to make an unpaid début at a benefit concert put on by the Melbourne Liedertafel to help Carl Gottlieb Elsasser, a Hungarian composer and conductor living in Melbourne. On the night of Saturday 17 May 1884, just four months after she had boarded the southbound steamer at Mackay, she walked on to the platform at the Elsasser concert in the Melbourne town hall, wearing a gown of golden satin. She had never sung better, and she was in high spirits as her father's coachman drove her back to Doonside, with the flowers her family and other well-wishers had sent packed all about her. A man had sent a large heart made of white flowers; on the way home she deciphered his card of good wishes in the light of a street-lamp striking into the carriage, and sat back roaring with laughter. At Doonside she got out of the carriage with the floral heart in her hands and said to the coachman, who had been with the Mitchells for years, 'Here, Dan, you can have this to wear to Mass. I hate the man who sent it. He used to call me Nellie Longdrawers, and now he sends me a damn' heart of white flowers as if I was a corpse.' And she hung the heart around Dan's neck and strode into the house in all the glory of her gold satin gown, chuckling to herself.

The Elsasser concert was important to her not only because it launched her career, but also because on that night she met a flautist, a tallish young man with fair hair and prominent blue-green eyes in an olive-skinned face. He had a strong nose and a full-lipped up-curling mouth, and the thing about him that struck everybody on meeting him for the first time was his calm. His name was John Lemmone, and he ranks alongside David Mitchell as the most in-fluential man in Nellie Armstrong's life. Many years later she said of him to her friend Una Bourne, the Australian pianist, 'He's the finest, whitest man I've ever known. I'd trust him with my life.' Those were big words for Nellie. Lemmone, on his side, liked and admired her no less; he called her 'Mrs Napoleon', because she 'always did things in a big way'. Nobody ever suggested that Lemmone was her lover, and this even at a time when gossips in general and Australian gossips in particular were eager to name her as the mistress of any man whom she so much as nodded to in public.

While the Duke of Orleans, the Bourbon Pretender to the Throne of France, was Melba's lover beyond all reasonable doubt, there is no evidence that she was a rashly incontinent woman, much less a promiscuous one. Any man or woman having normal sexual desires will find it impossible to believe that a woman so physically and psychologically vital as Melba, and so attractive to men, lived a celibate life from the time that her marriage, after creaking toward disaster for years, came to final smash about the time she made her grand opera début at Brussels in 1887. But whatever emotional diversions she permitted herself were managed with discretion, which lapsed only once; that was in her association with the Duke of Orleans, and her experience then, when she narrowly escaped social extinction, taught her a hard lesson. Although she liked men's society and made no secret of it, she was not among those who count the world well lost for love. In assessing her emotional life it is necessary to remember that she was never a voluptuary. If her pas-sions were strong, and they probably were, she kept them under no less strong control. Had she been less rigidly self-controlled she might have been an even greater singer than she was; but she might equally well have lost the very quality which made her singing unique.

The link between her and Lemmone, formed when they appeared together at the Elsasser benefit and he played a flute obbligato for her, was an example of how indestructible a platonic friendship can sometimes be. It lasted, as Lemmone recalled in old age, 'until the final curtain on 23 February 1931 when I was at the great diva's bedside at St Vincent's Hospital, Sydney, when she died'. In the forty-seven years of their association, Lemmone managed opera companies and concert tours for her, and toured with her as a flautist in Europe, the United States of America, Canada and Australia. He did not imagine when they first appeared together that their lives were to be so interwoven. From the start, however, he liked Nellie Armstrong's directness, bluntness and force of character; he also realized that, potentially at any rate, she was a great singer. Lemmone himself had force of character, but he preferred to get his way by diplomacy rather than direct action, perhaps because he was more considerate of other people's feelings. Nellie admired that quality in him, while knowing she could never possess it, and he on his side admired her down-to-earth ruggedness.

They had one thing in common which helped them to understand each other; both came of parents who had battled hard for a living, even though David Mitchell had made money where Lemmone's father had stayed poor. Lemmone was born in the Victorian gold town of Ballarat on 22 June 1861, a month after Nellie Mitchell was born in Melbourne. His father, a Greek named Lamoni, had gone to Ballarat seeking gold; he found a little, but not enough to brag about, but he did acquire a new name, when his fellow diggers transformed Lamoni into Lemon. This was the name the son bore through boyhood and elongated into Lemmone when he decided to make a career in music and realized that a musician who wished to succeed in those days enhanced his chances if he bore a name with an Italian ring.

In Lemmone's young days Ballarat was not a good town for an aspiring musician, but the boy had native talent and tenacity of purpose. Having taught himself to play the tin whistle, he saw a second-hand flute in a pawnbroker's window one day on his way to school. Young Lemmone borrowed his mother's pudding basin and went prospecting in a small waterway, the Yarrowee Creek. He panned gold worth sixteen-and-sixpence and bought his flute with a few shillings to spare. Many years afterwards Melba and he gave a concert in a Ballarat hall built over the Yarrowee Creek. Standing on the platform he whispered to her, 'Here's the place where I found my first flute.'

Lemmone built a distinguished career by his own abilities, both as a flautist and an impresario. As a flautist he made several tours with Patti and other lesser celebrities, and played as soloist with many of the great English, American and Canadian symphony orchestras, and as an impresario brought to Australia many fine artists, notably Paderewski. But it was his association with Nellie Armstrong that he remembered with most satisfaction. She went to

England many years before he did and was famous when he, with little more than an Australian reputation, arrived in London. As he told the story many years later:

'Melba was staying at the Savoy. What a dramatic change was here. When she left there was not much encouragement given to her, but her voice and her mind had won for her a unique place, and she was installed, a great lady, in a private suite at London's finest hotel. With what trembling I sent in my name to her. Would she have forgotten? Who was I that she should remember? I came into her room. She sprang up.

' "How is Mrs Palmer?"* How is this one? How is that one? Till my head buzzed she kept firing questions at me. Her tongue never stopped. Then, as now, Australia was more to Melba than the rest of the world put together. When at last her desire was satisfied, and she had learnt all of Australian history I could tell her, she came to my affairs. "Let me hear you play," she demanded. I played.

' "Oh, I must make them hear you," she cried warmly. Daniel Mayer was then the great man whose voice was all powerful in music. To him she sent me with a letter of introduction. . . . I played a long piece, the most showy I had. When I finished he was on his feet, and sending messages to half a dozen people—to Mancinelli† of Covent Garden among others. They came on the run, for Daniel Mayer only had to whisper to be obeyed. I was launched, but it was Melba who put me on the slips.'

Lemmone is not known ever to have said an unkind word about Melba, yet he was no sycophant, like some of those who clustered about her, especially as she grew older. To pretend that Melba was loved, or even liked, by all who knew her would be ludicrous; some of those who knew her detested her very name, and even many of those who liked her were able to see a multitude of flaws in her character. A few of her friends, however, found no fault in her, and Lemmone was one—their friendship, he once wrote, was 'never spoiled by a word that either can regret'. He was too perceptive to be unaware of her vanity, her capriciousness, her inconsiderateness, at times her childishness, but he accepted these oddities as one accepts frailties in a beloved sister. Although he was, by the calendar, a month younger than Melba, their relationship for most of their lives

---

* Rosina Palmer, a leading Melbourne soprano in the second half of the last century, and later a successful teacher. Although born in 1844, seventeen years before Melba, Mrs Palmer outlived her by a year.
† Luigi Mancinelli was for many years the leading conductor of the Italian repertoire at Covent Garden.

was that of the understanding older brother and the trusting younger sister, rather than of contemporaries having no blood ties.

Many people found her tight-fisted, even stingy; to others she was immensely generous, and Lemmone was one. On a winter's day in Melbourne, after a rehearsal, he left the theatre ahead of Melba and got into her waiting Rolls-Royce until she came, drawing the fur rug about him. When she appeared he remarked, 'My word, there's much to be said for a car on a day like this, isn't there?'

'Do you mean that?' Melba asked. '. . . Very well, from this moment this car is yours, and there must be no arguments. You are trapped!'

Lemmone protested, but she argued him down, and he drove the gift Rolls-Royce for many years afterwards.

Her affection for Lemmone never abated. He was seriously ill in Sydney in 1919, when Melba gave a farewell recital before taking a ship to America. At the end of the concert she walked to the front of the platform and said, 'My dear old John is sick. I'd love to give him a proof of how we love him. How if we give him a special concert? I'd love to, but I can't do it without you. We can just do it, for my boat doesn't sail for five days.' Her Sydney admirers—and his—responded by packing the hall. Next day she called on Lemmone in his hospital room. Too ill to read the newspapers, or even to see many visitors, he knew nothing of the benefit concert, and when she handed him a silver loving-cup filled with plums he was perplexed, wondering if this was one of Nellie's rather juvenile jokes. On a piece of paper fixed to the cup she had written, 'Put in your thumb and pull out a plum and see what your friends have sent you'. He picked out an envelope. It held a cheque for £2,113 18s. 0d.

8

SIGNOR CECCHI must have been a good showman as well as a good singing teacher. As he had foreseen, Nellie Armstrong's success at the Elsasser benefit brought her a series of paid engagements, and these led on to others, mostly in Melbourne but occasionally at one of the larger Victorian inland cities and now and then in another state. In her first year she earned about £750. For a time

Lyster's nephew, George Musgrove, who had become a concert manager, had her on his payroll at five pounds a concert; that was reasonable payment by Australian standards then for a soprano having nothing but a local reputation, and more especially for one bearing the utilitarian name of Nellie Armstrong. Less than twenty years later, she returned to Australia under his management and collected £21,000 for a total of nine recitals in Melbourne and Sydney, one of which yielded £2,350.

While she preferred to earn money when she sang, she appeared now and then at that time without payment, to widen her experience and for the satisfaction of winning the plaudits of an audience. Sorrento, a beach resort fifty-odd miles from Melbourne, was a favourite holiday place with David Mitchell and his family and when she heard the cemetery needed a new fence she organized a concert to raise money. She recruited the performers, hired a hall, and with her own hands pasted up the playbills. The concert was held in the hall of the Sorrento Mechanics Institute on the evening of Saturday, 24 January 1885. The programme, which was nothing if not varied, included vocal solos and duets, pianoforte solos, and a comic song, *Waltzing round the water butt*, given by a certain Mr Flood. One of Nellie Armstrong's solos was a ballad, *The angel at the window*. She possibly chose it as a delicate tribute to the departed souls whose last resting-place needed a new fence.

The Sorrento concert was an unqualified success, but her early Australian career was by no means one triumph after another. To the Australian public and critics she was just another young soprano who sang well at times and less well at other times. Some of her friends, with Cecchi in the van, believed she would make a great name abroad, but every promising young singer in a small city is surrounded by admirers whose unbounded confidence is more often proved to be wrong than right. Nobody of recognized musical weight publicly proclaimed at that time that her voice was unique—that here, in the person of Nellie Armstrong, of Richmond, stood Patti's successor.

One man who should have known better wrote her off as a singer of small merit, if any. This was Professor Joshua Ives, a Lancashire-born Cambridge Mus.Bac., who resigned a lecturer's post at the Glasgow Athenaeum to take the first Australian chair of music, at the University of Adelaide. Ives reached Adelaide in 1885, and soon afterwards went to Melbourne to recruit four soloists for an Adelaide performance of Handel's *Messiah*. He was particularly asked to consider a young soprano, Nellie Armstrong, word of whose singing ability had reached Adelaide. He heard her and, not liking the way she sang, crossed her name off his list and engaged another soprano. In after years Ives enjoyed telling the story of how he rejected the future Melba, rolling it out in his thick Lancashire accent and grimacing with comic ruefulness. It must be said that perhaps Ives's judgement had something to justify it, for Melba, like many another great singer, was less than a great oratorio singer. She was engaged as a soloist for the Sydney Philharmonic Society for its Christmas performance of *The Messiah* in 1885, and the critics were not captivated; the burden of their comment was that 'she was obviously unacquainted with the traditions and methods of oratorio'. She attempted *The Messiah* only once again; that was when she was paid a dizzy fee for a performance in an English cathedral city. The Australian music critic, Thorold Waters, reported that 'she emerged from the numbing ordeal with a gesture, a grimace, and a certain epithet that meant everything.' Waters did not specify the epithet, but those who knew Melba were able to supply it.

David Mitchell, if bedevilled by his eldest daughter's comings and goings, by her dedication to the career on which she had embarked, and by her determination to press on in face of the lukewarm response her singing often roused, did not try to deter her. She had the reputation in the family of being able to coax her father into doing anything she wished, and his willingness to accept her separation from her husband—at that time the breach admittedly did not seem irreparable—while she pursued this seeming chimera of singing fame suggests that her brothers and sisters were right about that.

He did not protest even when she joined the choir of one of Melbourne's leading Roman Catholic churches, St Francis's, in the last weeks of 1885. She had been brought up a Presbyterian, and her acceptance of an invitation to become treble soloist at St Francis's did not denote any change of religious heart on her part; she did it because the engagement carried a useful weekly fee. At that stage—perhaps at any stage in her life—Nellie would have sung for anyone who offered her adequate payment; she was a professional, and that was that. Her father understood her action and respected it; as he sold his building skill, and his lime, bricks, wine, bacon, cheese and the other things he produced, so she sold her talent as a singer. It was honest trading, honestly done. The old man pretended, however, to deplore Nellie's apparent defection. At that time a girl named Margaret Lillis, aged seventeen or eighteen, was in service at

Doonside. She was a Catholic, and every Sunday David Mitchell would drive her and Nellie to St Francis's in the family carriage, then go on with other members of his family to Scots Church, perhaps half a mile away. More often than not he bade the two farewell with a shake of the head and a half-joking, half-serious remark such as, 'Shame on you, Nellie! You ought to be singing at your own kirk'.

At that time Doonside was always ringing with music. If Nellie was not singing, then Annie or Belle was; and Nellie still liked playing the piano, and played it often, even though efficiency as a pianist had become for her no more than a background to her singing. She knew that singing was the talent which would carry her to the heights. Doonside was a happy house, for the servants as well as the Mitchell family. Margaret Lillis liked David Mitchell, whom she found to be unfailingly generous, even though his daughters were nervous of him when they had run up unauthorized dressmakers' and milliners' bills. At such times one or another of them would whisper to Margaret, 'Maggie, has Pa got the accounts this morning?' If she said yes they would keep out of his way until he had recovered from the shock. Although he made a show of indignation over his daughters' extravagance, he was largely play-acting; behind his frowns and scolding words lay an unadmitted pride in the girls' determination to turn themselves out as young women of fashion.

He was a kindly man. Soon after Margaret Lillis went to work for him he found out that she was an orphan, with three younger sisters. He told her she was to bring them to Doonside whenever she wished. 'This is their home,' he said, and when she took him at his word and had her sisters to visit her there he always welcomed them. Although he was an ardent Presbyterian she found no bigotry in him. Whenever the Little Sisters of the Poor called, soliciting donations, he would find a sovereign in his pocket and tell her to give it to the nuns with his best wishes for their work.

Of the Mitchell girls, Margaret liked Nellie best. At times Nellie would relax, especially when she was sitting quietly to have her hair done by Margaret, and talk of her hopes of a career, of her likes and dislikes, of her thoughts about life. She spoke of her disappointment with her marriage, and her words left Margaret with the impression that among the things the Armstrongs had violently disagreed on was the upbringing of their son; even though George was an infant Charles had wished to see him given a tough grounding, while his mother had wished to indulge him, perhaps to coddle him a little.

9

HER eyes were fixed on Europe, and she did not intend to accept anything less. She did not quite know how she was to get to Europe until one day her father told her she had better make arrangements to leave with him soon. He had been chosen to go to London as Victoria's Commissioner to the Indian and Colonial Exhibition, which was to open in London in May 1886, and had decided to take Nellie and her husband and their little boy, as well as two other of his daughters, Annie and Belle. He booked first-class passages for them in the RMS *Bengal*, leaving for London on 11 March, and Nellie wrote to Armstrong in Queensland telling him to join her in Melbourne before the sailing date.

For weeks beforehand Doonside twittered with excitement. Nellie had only two months' notice, but this gave time for her supporters to organize farewell concerts for her in Melbourne and Sydney. The concert in Sydney, where she was known merely as a promising young Melbourne singer, added only a few pounds to her savings, and even the Melbourne concert, in the town hall, netted her but a paltry £67 4s. 8d. She must have wondered then if she was not foolish in hoping to conquer a large world in which she was unknown when the small world which knew her well was so apathetic.

The meagre audience at the Melbourne farewell caught a glimpse of the imperious Melba whom the world was soon to know—the Melba impatient of any restraints upon her singing or herself. She was wearing a ball gown of black velvet, with a black velvet band about her throat, and when she started to sing the *Traviata* aria, *Ah fors' è lui*, the band apparently constricted her throat. She reached up and, with a fierce gesture, ripped the band off and flung it on to the platform at her feet, while her voice soared out over the auditorium. Standing at the back of the platform and watching her, Signor Cecchi smiled and nodded; this, he seemed to say, was the voice and the spirit which would make the world stop and listen.

Cecchi shared Nellie's satisfaction in the excellence of her performance that night, and her disappointment in the sparseness of the audience; yet within two or three days an episode occurred which cast a permanent shadow over their relationship. It is a pity that Cecchi left no record of his version of the affair; Melba's version, in

Melodies and Memories, has always been accepted at face-value, although other facts make nonsense of it. As she told it, Cecchi demanded eighty guineas from her on account of fees she owed him for lessons, and threatened to seize her trunks if she did not pay his bill before sailing. She went on:

'Had it not been for a dear old uncle and a friend, I might never have gone to England; but at last I raised the eighty guineas and stuffing them into my purse, I went to Cecchi and threw the money, purse and all, on his table.

' "Here," I said, "is the money you say I owe you. We had been friends for so many years that I thought you knew me better than you evidently do; for surely you must have known that if I made a success I would repay you tenfold."

'He shrugged his shoulders and put the money in his pocket.

' "That is not all," I said. "If I ever do have a success, I shall never mention your name as having been a teacher of mine. I shall never refer to you in any way whatever. So good-bye, Signor Cecchi, and may this gain bring you happiness."

'I never did mention his name, in spite of the fact that when I had made my success I was constantly being asked who had first taught me the elements of singing. And I honestly believe that Signor Cecchi died of apoplexy when talking of me and my ingratitude. But I realize that he was not a good teacher, for all that he taught me I had to unlearn when I was privileged to study under Madame Mathilde Marchesi.'

Even if one overlooks the operatic ring of the language with which, so Melba said, she lashed Cecchi, her story of the matter is still unacceptable and her refusal to mention his name in after years did not bring him to his grave with apoplexy or anything else; he died in Melbourne, on 4 March 1897, of a heart seizure, but he was not thinking of Melba at the time, much less talking of her. On that day he had been a witness in a court action and, having been a heart sufferer for several years, became distressed while in the witness-box and remained so for some time afterwards. In the words of a newspaper report of his death, 'Signor Cecchi had sat down to dinner with the household, his dishes being on the table before him, when, in the middle of a sentence referring to the lawsuit, he suddenly stopped, drew a deep sigh, and died sitting in his chair.'

Nellie did not break with Cecchi when she left Melbourne to conquer Europe. A letter in her handwriting still exists, written from Birley House, Belgrave, Leicester, England, and dated 27 June 1886, at least four months after the meeting with Cecchi which she described in *Melodies and Memories*. The tone and content of this letter, which is printed here in full, speak for themselves:

My dear Signor Cecchi,

It is already more than two months since we arrived in London. I have commenced writing to you two or three times, but I have never been able to finish them. I am charmed with London, and I think it is a beautiful city. I have heard all the great singers, viz.: Patti, who is divine, Albani, Nilsson (I do not like), Madame Patey, Trebelli, Mr Lloyd, Santley, Foli. I have been to hear Sims Reeves four times, but he has never sung once. Is it not disappointing? He was to have sung at Patti's concert on Wednesday, but of course did not appear, so Nicolini sang instead. I have also heard Rubenstein,* Halle, and de Pachmann. The latter is a wonderful pianist. Sarasate and Carrodus are wonderful violinists. It is really wonderful the beautiful music one can hear in London.

You will be pleased to hear that I have already sung twice in London, and had the greatest success, splendid critiques, and everyone predicts a great future for me. Herr Ganz, the man who wrote *Sing, sweet bird*, has taken a wonderful fancy to me, and declares my voice is more like Patti's than any voice he has ever heard. Vert, the concert agent, is working hard for me, so I am sure to get on. Antoinette Sterling† was singing at one concert where I sang, and she was in a fearful rage because I got a bigger reception than she did. The first concert I sang at I had the biggest orchestra in London to sing to. I sang, *Ah fors' è lui* and *Sing, sweet bird*. Ganz conducted both.

You will be sorry to hear that my Father has been very ill in Scotland. He is not at all well yet. The other day I jumped out of a train in motion (it was the wrong train) and landed on my head. I was knocked quite senseless, and felt very ill for two or three days afterwards. I have also had bad toothache, so I have been in the wars altogether.

I am very pleased to hear you have had success with another pupil. Will you give her my congratulations? I suppose it is the young lady I heard before I left. My husband has gone into the Army,‡ so as

* Presumably a misspelling of Rubinstein.
† An American-born contralto long settled in London and most popular there, especially as a ballad singer.
‡ A widely accepted story that Charles Armstrong was a British regular officer who reached captain's rank is untrue. He was commissioned lieutenant in a militia unit, the 3rd Battalion, The Prince of Wales's Leinster Regiment (Royal Canadians), on 29 May 1886, and resigned his commission on 3 September 1887.

his regiment will be stationed in Ireland for the next month I am going over there next Tuesday. I shall stay with my brother-in-law. Little 'Jackie'* has grown so big and fat, and talks so well. I hope you will write sometimes to me. My address will be c.o. Lady Armstrong, Seconfield House, Littlehampton, Sussex. Give Miss Dawson my best love and tell her I expect a long letter from her. I shall write to her as soon as possible. And now I shall cease. With love to all enquiring friends,

Believe me,

Your old pupil,

NELLIE ARMSTRONG.

This letter hardly suggests that it was written by a resentful pupil who, having been dunned for debt and raised the money to meet the demand, had delivered herself of a few scornful words and turned her back on the bloodsucker for ever. The most plausible explanation of the *Melodies and Memories* version of her break with Cecchi is that when Melba became a prima donna she preferred to be known as a pupil, not of the great Mathilde Marchesi and the obscure colonial teacher Pietro Cecchi, but of the great Mathilde Marchesi alone. Her assertion that Cecchi was not a good teacher, and that she had to unlearn 'all that he had taught me', will be examined later. It was preposterous.

10

THREE thousand people gathered at Port Melbourne to wave farewell when the *Bengal* pulled out on 11 March 1886, and the pier was, in the words of one journalist, 'an endless mass of parasols and pocket handkerchiefs'. Only a few of them knew and fewer still cared that Nellie Armstrong was on board.

Charles and Nellie Armstrong and their little son, with David Mitchell and his daughters, Annie and Belle, formed a solid little family group among the 142 passengers, most of whom were bound for London. The passengers were a mixed company, and Nellie Armstrong, who always had an eye for quality, must have been

* Her son, George, then two years and eight months old.

comforted to see, walking the deck with his wife, Bishop James Moorhouse, the Sheffield-born prelate who had come to Melbourne nine years before. As Bishop of Melbourne, he had made a deep mark on the spiritual and public life of the young city by his vigorous prosecution of progressive and unorthodox views, and was now returning to his native England to become Bishop of Manchester. It was doubtless at Bishop Moorhouse's insistence that Nellie accepted an invitation to lead the choir which was formed by the passengers even before the *Bengal* cleared Port Phillip heads. In any event there could hardly have been any rival.

Did she guess perhaps as the *Bengal* steamed down Port Phillip that sixteen years were to elapse before she would again see these shores and the city which was slipping away into the haze astern? Certainly, even allowing for all her self-confident determination, she could never have foreseen that her homecoming would be like the return of an empress—that she would be hailed by the roaring voices of tens of thousands of her fellow Australians where only the screams of swooping gulls bade her farewell.

NOONTIDE

1886–1903

1

DAVID MITCHELL had a furnished house waiting for him in London. It was at 89 Sloane Street, and he and the others were all glad to arrive there, after the grubby train journey from Tilbury. The *Bengal* docked on 1 May, in grey and rather threatening weather, and Nellie Armstrong felt dejected by her first sight of England. Her melancholy did not last long, however. She was not, she reminded herself, arriving to storm Europe as a friendless young woman with slender resources; as well as a wealthy father, she had her husband (even if the sea-trip had brought them no closer together), and her husband's people, who were waiting to make the acquaintance of Charles's Australian wife.

Charles and Nellie were met by news that his mother was seriously ill at the Armstrong home in Littlehampton, Sussex, and hurried down there to see her. Nellie and Lady Armstrong liked one another on that first meeting and their mutual liking never wavered. In fact, Nellie liked and was liked by all the Armstrongs, and kept up her friendship with the family all through the years, even when her estrangement from Charles was a matter of public gossip and after the marriage ended in divorce; his family did not take sides against him, but whatever their regrets for the wreck that his marriage made of his life they continued to accept his wife on warm, even affectionate, terms.

To Nellie London was a miracle and a revelation. On the hoardings and in the newspapers she read names which dazzled her. Most of the great singers of the day seemed to be in London for the opening of the concert season and the Covent Garden summer season, and she wanted to hear them all. One of the first was the famous Swedish soprano, Christine Nilsson, who, so Nellie wrote to a friend in Melbourne 'sang *I Dreamt I Dwelt* just like a schoolgirl'; Nellie, always with a realistic appreciation of her own ability, said, 'I think I can do better than that'. She heard the Canadian prima donna, Emma Albani, and was impressed, but said, 'I think I can do as well as that.' She had to wait a week or two for a recital

by Patti, and this was singing such as she had not only never heard
before but had hardly dreamed was possible; afterwards she said,
with a humility which was to become one of her less marked characteristics as she went from success to success, 'I shall try to do as well
as that.'

She started out to present her letters of introduction. The recipients were not helpful. Aspiring prima donnas from the colonies,
as well as America, came literally by the dozen at the beginning
of every season, clamouring for a hearing, but only one in a thousand had talent above the average, and many of them were worse
than mediocre. And this young woman? What was her name?
Mrs Armstrong, eh! She would be better advised to go back to
Melbourne or whatever barbarous place she came from, settle down
there with her husband, and raise a family. Arthur Sullivan said
if she studied for another year he might be able to give her a small
part in *The Mikado*. John Brinsmead and Alberto Randegger were
pleasant but negative, Sir Hubert Parry was too busy to see her,
Carl Rosa made an appointment and did not keep it. Wilhelm
Ganz was an exception. He exclaimed over the beauty of her voice,
and put her into a charity concert, which was held on a foggy June
afternoon in the obscure Princes Hall, in Piccadilly, before a handful
of sad-looking people, who rewarded her with a patter of mournful
handclaps, then went home and forgot her. As Melba tells it in
Melodies and Memories that concert was her London nadir. Then,
she says, she remembered she had one more letter of introduction;
this was addressed to Madame Mathilde Marchesi in Paris. So she
went to her father and asked him to give her this one last chance.

'If Marchesi does not like me, I promise you faithfully that I
shall return to Australia and try to be happy,' she assured him.

'Very well,' he replied. 'But this must be the last time.'

It is an engaging story, but like Melba's account of her break
with Cecchi it is not true. She did not write to Madame Marchesi
after the concert in June, but early in May, in the first days after
her arrival in London, and Marchesi wrote back inviting her to
go for an audition two months later. On 13 May, from her father's
house in Sloane Street, she wrote a letter to Rudolf Himmer, a
German-born tenor living in Melbourne, who had sung at her
farewell concert in the Melbourne town hall. In this she said,
'I am going over to Marchesi in about two months when I shall
tell you faithfully all she says of my voice.' So the conversation
which she reported with David Mitchell, if it took place at all,

did not take place in the context in which she remembered it. But then so much that Nellie recalled in later years was, like the recollections of old soldiers, remembered 'with advantages'. She liked to re-shape, to re-order, and then to embroider the facts of life. This was doubtless an expression of her histrionic instinct. Perhaps a singer could not devote much of her life to singing Italian opera unless she were able to see life itself in Italian operatic terms. Nellie seems to have been a victim—or perhaps a beneficiary—of this usually harmless form of make-believe, though only when it suited her.

2

THE heat of midsummer was heavy on the air of Paris when Nellie Armstrong and little George arrived there. They had travelled from London comfortably enough, but second-class; David Mitchell had paid a sum of money into his daughter's bank account to enable her to live for a year or so in Paris without having to worry about where the next meal would come from, but she would need to be frugal. She did not mind that; although Nellie could spend like an empress, as well as act like one in other ways, her Scottish blood always ran strong, and she could live austerely if she had to.

She and young George settled into a pension where the tariff was low and the cooking was said to be good, and one morning at ten o'clock she went along by appointment to Madame Marchesi's house, in the Rue Jouffroy. She took with her the letter of introduction she had brought from Melbourne; this was written by a Melbourne friend of the Mitchells, Madame Wiedermann-Pinschof, the wife of the consul for Austria-Hungary at Melbourne, Carl Ludwig Pinschof. Madame Wiedermann-Pinschof was a former pupil of Marchesi, and before marriage had been a successful opera singer in Europe, under her maiden name of Elise Wiedermann. Madame Marchesi admired her voice and her musical judgement, and would hear any young singer she recommended; but hopeful young singers who came well introduced to the Ecole Marchesi, begging to be accepted as pupils, outnumbered by perhaps ten to one those Marchesi could accept, for she was at least as celebrated a singing teacher as any of her day.

Although an inch or two shorter than Nellie and therefore not tall, Mathilde Marchesi was, on a first meeting at any rate, rather forbidding. Her eyes were searching, and her mouth was firm with a longish upper lip; her grey hair was drawn tightly back from her forehead and fastened in a bun on the back of her head. She seemed overbearing, and nervous aspirants shown into her presence were often disconcerted, even tremulous, as they stood before her. Nellie Armstrong was later to depict herself as having been terrified of Madame Marchesi on that first meeting at the Rue Jouffroy, but this was perhaps an example of her talent for retouching the picture when she looked back to it years later; if she now and then betrayed an uncharacteristic terror of other-worldly things she never appears to have been at all nervous of any flesh-and-blood presence.

For those who could be awed, however, the sixty-five-year-old Marchesi was an awesome woman. She was born in Germany of wealthy parents and, having a good mezzo-soprano voice, adopted singing as a profession when her father lost his money. After studying in Vienna she went to Paris and studied with Manuel Garcia. From Paris she went to London and, having established herself as a concert singer with a Europe-wide reputation, married the Italian baritone, Salvatore Marchesi. While still in her early prime as a singer, she forsook the concert platform for teaching, and in 1881 settled in Paris. When Nellie Armstrong arrived there the Ecole Marchesi was as highly regarded as any singing academy in the world. Scores of Marchesi's pupils had gone out to win fame in Europe and America, and at that very time western Europe was beginning to ring with the name of a young French woman who was to become one of the most famous sopranos of the day, Emma Calvé.

Nellie was shown into the classroom, which was furnished in rather heavy style, with a magnificent chandelier poised overhead. The room had a low dais, with a grand piano standing against one wall, and portraits of the reigning stars of the opera, some of them pupils of Madame Marchesi and all of them her friends, looking down from the walls. The story of the first time Nellie Armstrong sang to Marchesi must be one of the most familiar in the whole range of biography and autobiography. The original version appeared in *Melodies and Memories*, and since then it has been retold some hundreds of times in books and in newspaper and magazine articles. Even allowing for Melba's propensity for gilding the factual lily, her account of how Marchesi, having heard her sing *Ah fors' è lui*, hurried from the room to tell her husband, 'Salvatore, I have found a star!' is doubtless substantially·true. Marchesi knew that a singer of immense possibilities had come to her that day. She was to write ten years later that Melba 'is today without a rival on the lyric stage. As a vocalist, she more resembles a bird than a human creature, and it is impossible to conceive anything more musical or more flexible than her marvellous voice, which is always as clear as a silver bell. I am only repeating what the critics of every country, in Europe and America, have written, when I say that unquestionably, as regards taste, style, and vocalization, this pupil of mine is superior to any living singer.'

A voice alone does not make a great singer. In Melba's own words, in an article written when she was at the height of her powers, 'I cannot too forcibly insist that the mere possession of a lovely voice is only the basis of the vocal art. Nature occasionally startles one by the prodigality of her gifts, but no student has any right to expect to sing by inspiration, any more than an athlete may expect to win a race because he is naturally fleet of foot'. In short, the voice is only the starting-point; a combination of other, and less tangible, assets is necessary if the voice is to encompass with subtlety and precision the full range of emotions and moods in the music of the great composers. It is arguable that Melba lacked the ability to express in song the profoundest depths of feeling; this is a matter on which good judges who heard her at her zenith were apt to fall into angry dispute. Nevertheless she had nearly every one of the qualities which go to the making of a great singer, including an uncommonly large allowance of intellectual stamina. She devoted herself with almost ferocious concentration to the study of every branch of knowledge required by a singer. She had a gift for languages and was fairly proficient in French when she first arrived in Europe; after a few months in Paris she spoke it fluently and in a few months more almost like a Parisian. She also mastered Italian within a year or two, and could manage well enough, though less happily, in German.

Not long before Marchesi died, in 1913, an Australian journalist, Katharine Susannah Prichard, who was to achieve international notice as a novelist and short-story writer, called at the Ecole Marchesi. Mrs Prichard later described her meeting with Madame Marchesi:

'Her fine old face, ravaged by grief, did not smile. Silvery-white hair was piled in a trim coronet above it. Her eyes were an eagle's, bright and searching.

' "What language shall I speak?" she demanded.

' "English, please, Madame," I murmured.

' "You do not speak French?"

' "A little, Madame, but—"

' "Oh, you Australians, you are so stupid," she exclaimed. "Me, I speak twelve languages—perfectly. But Nellie Melba, she was not stupid. Do you understand. It was her brain that made Melba's voice."

' . . . We talked about Melba, Melba's voice, her studies and triumphs.

' "Other girls came to me with as good a voice as Nellie," Marchesi said, "but they had not the brains to learn, to use it so well. They did not put the whole life, and will, into their singing. Maggie Sterling*—she was another Australian girl with a beautiful voice, but too virtuous. . . ." '

Madame Marchesi did not elaborate on what she meant by 'too virtuous'. The omission is to be regretted. It might have been illuminating. Perhaps she was thinking among other things of her favourite pupil Nellie Melba's love affair with the Duke of Orleans.

3

ONE of Nellie Armstrong's gifts was her power of concentration. When she wished to reach some goal she could exclude all else and drive straight ahead, looking neither to one side nor the other, and giving little heed to the rights, or at any rate the comfort and convenience, of people close to her. She was sad when her father and her two sisters brought their European visit to a close before the winter set in, and took ship back to Australia; she always had a strong family sense, and her love of her father was deep and lasting, but she dried her tears once the ship carrying David Mitchell,

---

* A contralto, born at Geelong, Victoria, who early this century appeared as a recitalist in London and the English provinces. She was little heard of after she married and settled in London.

Annie and Belle disappeared over the horizon. She had her life to get on with, and her studies to fill her days and nights; extraneous things could not be allowed to intrude.

Her son, growing fast and demanding attention, was a problem, but not a major problem; she was efficient, almost frighteningly efficient at times, in organizing her life and economizing her time, and her child's claims on her could not make her swerve from her path. Not that she neglected him; the services of nursemaids were to be had for next to nothing in Paris then, and Nellie was able to engage an agreeable girl, even with her slender means. So, although she herself could rarely take young George to play in the pleasant green parks, she always had someone to do it for her. At times this outlay meant she had to make sacrifices, eating simpler meals and darning a worn dress to make it last longer, but she never jibbed; this was part of the price of success. Had not Madame Marchesi promised to 'make something extraordinary' of her if she would study hard for a year?

Charles Armstrong was trying to make a go of farming in Sussex, and two or three times, in her first year in Paris, he crossed the Channel to visit her. But the gulf between them grew steadily wider. He was a man of quick, even violent, temper, and Nellie, although she had better control of herself, was stubborn, and resentful of anyone's attempt to curb her, and perhaps of a mere husband's most of all. (They had always been quick to quarrel. Melba told a friend many years later that in Queensland, not long before George was born, Charles threw a heavy clock at her. It is a likely story; his anger was easily roused, and she could be an infuriating woman.) He had old-fashioned ideas about the duties of wives, and saw no reason to gentle her along or humour her in what he looked upon as her ambitious follies. Nor did he, with his insistence that he was an Englishman and that Englishmen were the salt not only of the earth but of the universe, care to see his son being brought up in a French environment. So when the Armstrongs met there were usually quarrels.

These were the blemishes on her life; the life itself, even when money ran so low that she could not find the few sous it cost to ride to and from the Ecole Marchesi in the horse-drawn omnibus, was for her a delight. She was so absorbed in what she was doing in that summer of 1887 that she was hardly aware that, across the Channel, England was *en fête* in celebration of Queen Victoria's fifty years on the throne.

Under Marchesi's guidance her singing technique improved; her voice had never before touched these heights. Marchesi's knowledge of the human voice, and what it could and could not do, was greater than Pietro Cecchi's, and she had a wizardry in imparting her knowledge which only great teachers possess. And yet for most practical purposes it was Cecchi, not Marchesi, who taught Melba to sing. Marchesi gave the lovely sexless voice its final polish; she coached Nellie in grand opera; she opened doors which would have stayed shut against the pupil of an unknown and insignificant Italian tenor teaching singing in Melbourne. But the Melba who made her grand opera début in Brussels, on the night of 13 October 1887, was as a trained singer the creation more of Pietro Cecchi than of Mathilde Marchesi.

The myth that Marchesi taught Nellie Melba to sing has been nurtured for more than seventy-five years. Writers of authority, who have been echoed by writers of no authority, have parrotted the story until it has acquired a seeming validity. Yet it is absurd on the face of it, and also on the unwitting authority of the two people who did most to create it: Nellie and Mathilde Marchesi. The simple facts are these:

Nellie Armstrong studied with Cecchi for between six and seven years overall; she had her first lesson from him in 1879 and her last in 1886, but her studies were only occasional from the time she went to Queensland with her father in the middle of 1882 until she returned to live at Doonside at the beginning of 1884. She was accepted as a pupil by Marchesi in the summer of 1886, and about fourteen months later, after a series of quasi-public appearances before small, but discriminating, Paris audiences, she made her début in Brussels as Gilda in *Rigoletto*. So if she learnt her singing from Marchesi alone, her feat was an astonishing one. Marchesi herself wrote:

'The majority of my successful pupils studied for three years, only very few remaining but two. What pupil is allowed to study for three years in these days,* when everybody is impatient to get money and fame? In one year, often in only a few months, all this has to be attained, without even having gone through the most elementary preliminaries. . . . Instrumentalists, without exception, give themselves over to many years of study. Then why should this be denied to singers? The former buy their instruments ready-made, the latter have to form and develop theirs. And is not the voice the most tender, the most fragile, of all instruments? We may

* Marchesi was writing about 1897 or 1898.

safely attribute the decline of the vocal art to these unfortunate causes, and blame especially those teachers who, partly through ignorance, partly through egotism, do not point out to their pupils the importance of their mission. Oh, holy art of singing, how sad a fate hath befallen thee!'

Melba gave her views in a magazine article published in the USA in 1907:

'The piano or violin student will devote ten years to the technic of his instrument, while the vocalist or the teacher too often regards research at an end after studying a year or two, or even a few months only.

'Just here, however, I should like to make it plain that the student who cannot give a promising account of herself after eighteen months' thorough study is, to my mind, never likely to do really great things. I do not mean for a moment that she should then be a full-fledged singer, but that she should be able to give clear indications as to future possibilities.'

It is a pity that poor Pietro Cecchi's grave in the Melbourne General Cemetery has no headstone because those words should be engraved on it. They testify that his name should be listed rather above Mathilde Marchesi's when Nellie Melba's teacher is being acclaimed.

4

NELLIE ARMSTRONG made some powerful friends while studying at the Ecole Marchesi. Most of these were men and among them were such music giants of the time as Charles Gounod, Ambroise Thomas, Léo Delibes, and Jules Massenet; all these men helped her in her climb to success. She also made at least one implacable enemy in the person of Blanche Marchesi, Mathilde's daughter. Blanche's detestation was to injure Melba, as will be told later; and, though it caused no lasting hurt to her career, the ill-effects were painful while they lasted. The reason of Blanche Marchesi's undying enmity is plain; she hated Nellie for her genius as a singer. For Blanche was also a soprano, and a fine artist, but lacked the divine fire without which a singer never touches the stars; Nellie was born with this very quality, and Blanche, feeling herself to be the victim of a dirty trick by fate, saw her mother's favourite pupil as the evil spirit who had come to wreck her hopes.

Nobody could have had a more propitious musical start than Blanche Marchesi. Her mother was possibly the world's greatest singing teacher, and her father also was a distinguished singer and an able teacher. One of three daughters, she first studied the violin, but from 1881 concentrated on singing, and was her mother's assistant at the Ecole Marchesi when Nellie Armstrong went there as a pupil. Blanche was two years younger than the Australian, but she had lived all her life in the rarified intellectual atmosphere of one or another of the great European cities and rather looked down on the young woman from Melbourne as a crude colonial. The discovery that such a woman had the very qualities as a singer which she, Blanche, had been denied must have been like a worm gnawing at her heart.

For musical scholarship at every level Blanche Marchesi, a handsome woman of compelling presence, was well ahead not only of the student Nellie Armstrong but also of the great prima donna Nellie Melba. Although Melba was far from being a woman with a voice and no knowledge of music, as her enemies tried to pretend, she had less knowledge than Blanche Marchesi of the pure science of singing. Few musicians of high standing ever knew Melba so well as Sir Landon Ronald, the English conductor and composer. Ronald, who used his two given names for professional purposes, was a son of the English singer, Henry Russell, a prolific composer of popular songs, including *A life on the ocean wave*. He was nineteen and struggling for a foothold when Melba first met him; she took him up, and he was her accompanist for fourteen years and made many professional tours with her. While he both liked and admired her, Ronald, a man of intellectual integrity and clear vision, was able to write:

'She was in no sense a great musician, and although in the early days I often begged her to sing some of the great classic songs of Schubert, Brahms and others, it was only towards the end of her life that she turned to singing some modern French songs and in an interview blamed the British public for liking *Good-bye!* and other songs which she had sung to them for years and made enormously popular.

'Considering the colossal success she had as a concert singer, it may seem odd for me to say that I am absolutely convinced that she was nothing but an operatic singer.'

Blanche Marchesi stood higher as a musician, and always sang with faultless taste, yet greatness eluded her.

One thing Nellie and Blanche had in common was vocal durability. Some critics believe Melba lingered rather too long on the scene of her triumphs, and waited until the lights had begun to sputter, even though they had not quite gone out. This is not altogether unjust, but she was still singing well when nearing the middle sixties and acceptably even some years later. It was not good luck that enabled her to sing well in old age, but the skill with which she always used her voice. Blanche Marchesi was no less remarkable an advertisement for the value of Mathilde Marchesi's method. She celebrated her seventy-fifth birthday, in 1938, by giving a two-hour recital at the Wigmore Hall, London; at the end she was still singing without showing the smallest sign of vocal strain.

It must be said for Blanche Marchesi that she distinguished between Melba the woman, whom she detested, and Melba the singer, whom she admired without stint. She openly said that her favourite singers were Melba, Emma Nevada, Jean de Reszke, Tamagno, and Maurel. But her personal dislike of Melba never abated. One of her pupils before World War I was an Australian girl, Mabel Emmerton, who later married Norman Brookes, the lawn tennis champion. One day when the future Dame Mabel Brookes went to Blanche's Maida Vale studio for a lesson Melba's name cropped up. Blanche said with deadly emphasis, 'She's the worst woman I ever knew. She came between me and my family.' She elaborated that point in an interview published in the London *Sunday Referee* in 1936. As reported by Constance Vaughan, she said: 'Melba's jealousy ruined many lives. Mine was among them. She was my mother's favourite pupil, and even she, most dear to me, Melba turned against me. . . . It is no exaggeration to say that Melba, who ruled the Edwardian musical and social world with a will of iron, kept me out of Covent Garden, the Scala, and the Metropolitan. No exaggeration, because she kept so many "stars" out of these holy of holies.' Melba was more rugged in any comments she ever made on Blanche. When an Australian journalist in London told her that an Australian concert tour by Blanche was being mooted she scoffed, 'Why, the woman couldn't fill the parish hall in Bunyip'. Bunyip, a Victorian agricultural township, had a population at that time of fewer than 700 men, women and children.

In *Melodies and Memories* Melba describes at length her debt to

Mathilde Marchesi but ignores Blanche's existence; she possibly shied away from it because any mention of it would have reopened the painful chapter of her life (also ignored in *Melodies and Memories*) revolving about her association with the Duke of Orleans. Blanche Marchesi also wrote an autobiography. In this Melba is mentioned several times, and, astonishingly, only in favourable, even flattering terms. Whether the original draft of the book held other and less friendly references to Melba is open to conjecture. At all events what Blanche wrote of Melba, as published, was so generous as to prompt the question whether there was not an element of ambivalence in her feelings. Among other things she told of the ingratitude of one of her mother's most celebrated pupils, Emma Eames, the American soprano, who after being launched upon her brilliantly successful career 'went her way, never turning her head back, never remembering her student years nor her master, and erasing from her memory everything that had been the making of her career.' She continued:

'Not so Melba. . . . Melba's friendship for my mother was one of her great joys; it made up for the forgetful hearts of many others. Needless to say that the success of Melba created much jealousy among students of the school, for unfortunately pupils often believe that success depends entirely on the teacher's managing powers, and that some are pushed and some neglected. The truth is that those who follow their work with steadfast seriousness must surely get ahead of those who work in an indifferent fashion, and whose ambitions are limited.'

Blanche Marchesi, whether willingly or reluctantly, thus acknowledged two of Melba's salient qualities—her capacity for loyalty to anyone to whom she believed herself to be indebted, and her willingness to work. Melba herself said that Madame Marchesi was 'more than a mother' to her, adding, 'And I loved her'. When the ruler of the Ecole Marchesi was long past her best, and had even become a menace to some voices, Melba continued to send pupils to her, proclaiming her to be the greatest living teacher, the only teacher of true creative genius. This was misguided loyalty; it could have had bad results for young singers who trustingly, at Melba's imperious behest, put themselves into the aged Mathilde's hands.

5

THE tension between Nellie and Blanche did not hinder the student's progress. Nellie had better things to do than worry about the animosity of someone who, as she saw it, was merely envious of the career she was going to make.

Madame Marchesi's enthusiasm for her work never faltered. She criticized her, severely at times, but only to drive her to overcome faults – to put from her the last remnant of student ways and use her voice with a sophistication matching its natural splendour. Marchesi, never satisfied, drove her hard, but never too hard, because Nellie Armstrong was endowed with the same perfectionism as her teacher, the same inflexible will to succeed as her father.

The beauty of Mrs Armstrong's voice began to be mentioned in Paris music circles after she sang at two or three of the soirées which Madame Marchesi put on from time to time at the Rue Jouffroy, before select invited audiences. Invitations to sing at musicales in other Paris houses reached her, and now and then Madame Marchesi let her accept one of these, if she seemed likely as a result to meet people who would help her. At that time the thought that cultured men and women wished to hear her sing was reward enough for Nellie; a few years later she would rebuff society hostesses who asked her to their parties as a guest, then tried to manœuvre her into giving an unpaid recital. But in Paris she was content merely to be in artistic demand, and almost ingenuous about it. One night a woman, living at the same pension, who had been reading late and had her light still burning, heard a tap on her door. Nellie Armstrong, wearing a simple white frock, was standing there with tears on her face. 'I had to tell someone,' she said, and poured out the story of how that night she had made a triumphant appearance at a musicale in a great house; when she had sung an aged French general had pushed forward to embrace and kiss her, telling her, 'You are already one of the great ones of the world!' Such tributes were commonplace in her life within a few years; she expected them and would have been indignant had they been withheld. But at that time she responded to anything of the kind like a young girl to the first declaration of love.

Nellie met many influential people at such functions, and liked none of them better than Charles Gounod, the sometime student of theology who had forsaken his ecclesiastical ambitions to become one of the most celebrated, if not one of the greatest, musical composers of the nineteenth century. Gounod was a memorable character as well as a sensitive aesthete, and Nellie never forgot her meetings with him—the twenty-five-year-old student, and the famous composer only a year off seventy—when she visited him at his house in the Boulevard Malesherbes. After World War I, thirty years later, an American friend, Dorothie Holland, was staying with Melba at her Paris apartment. Few traces of the student of 1887 remained; she had become Dame Nellie, and had an apartment in the Avenue Henri Martin staffed with expert servants, and moved about Paris in a chauffeur-driven Rolls-Royce. But, having scored her greatest triumphs and sung most of her songs (if not quite all of them), she was nearing sixty and no more immune from the pangs of nostalgia than any other ageing man or woman, nor less able to resist the temptation to look behind her than Lot's wife. One of the excursions on which she took Mrs Holland was to the Boulevard Malesherbes, and there she pointed out the white villa, behind its high wall, where she had visited Gounod, always a picturesque figure in velvet skullcap, velvet smoking jacket and flowing bow tie.

The appeal to Nellie Armstrong of Gounod's music, as well as of Gounod himself, is easy to understand. He enjoyed a bubble reputation as a genius while he lived, but was re-appraised after his death in 1893; the consensus today is that, as a composer, he was melodious but shallow, pretty and just a shade vulgar. Nellie Armstrong the student could hardly be expected to detect these shortcomings in his operas; more experienced and better educated judges of music throughout Europe were hailing him as a master, on the level of Beethoven and Mozart, and who was she to question their findings? But perhaps it is some indication of the height of her musical ceiling that thirty or forty years later she still found Gounod's operas enchanting, and sang Marguerite with no less zest than she had sung the role in her youth.

It was not however her taste alone that governed her choice of a repertoire. Although at one time she aspired to sing the heavy soprano roles of grand opera she discovered that nature had not meant her to do so. Her lovely voice, which some hearers likened to Dresden china, was not made to sing the music of Brünnhilde, say, nor even of Tosca or Aida. Whatever her inclinations, she was condemned to sing the lighter operas of Verdi, Puccini, Donizetti,

Gounod and their like, and she knew she could not break free from that artistic prison without destroying herself—or at all events without destroying her voice, which was most of herself. She was to defy this limitation once, in New York in 1896, and all but wreck her voice and her career, and that lesson lasted her for the rest of her life. Like it or not, she had to resign herself to being a Mimi, a Gilda, a Violetta or a Marguerite. She was a practical woman above all; she understood the difference between dreams and reality, and she knew the penalties for kicking against the pricks. So, after all, her acceptance of Gounod and the others, at whom some lofty connoisseurs sniff even if the public *en masse* loves them, was perhaps less a matter of poor taste than of good sense.

6

THE greatest days of the Théâtre Royale de la Monnaie, Brussels, were from 1875 to 1889. Melba made her operatic début there in 1887, when a Monnaie reputation still had a high value, and in that she was lucky. She shed her blunt Anglo-Saxon name of Armstrong some months before going to Brussels. Marchesi believed she would be handicapping herself in trying to make a reputation in grand opera as Nellie Armstrong, so they decided to give her the name, suitably modified, of her native city, Melbourne. It was a good choice.

Melba had two or three weeks in Brussels beforehand, and then, on Thursday 13 October, made her début in *Rigoletto*; she was twenty-six. Mathilde Marchesi, with her husband Salvatore beside her, was in a box at the Monnaie that night, and for her also it must have been a great night. Marchesi wrote later: 'The very next day and afterwards it was nothing but a chorus of praise everywhere; the entire press of Brussels declaring the young artiste to be a star of the first magnitude'.

Melba nearly did not sing at the Monnaie on that night or any other night. Some months earlier she had signed a contract with an impresario named Maurice Strakosch, a Czech by birth, who had earlier in his life earned a living as a pianist. Strakosch, a man of ruthless charm, had a wide experience of prima donnas: Patti was his sister-in-law, and for many years he managed her business affairs, having launched her in London in 1861. He was a good judge of a singer's commercial possibilities; he was also a cunning manipulator, adept in every move of the game. One day he heard Nellie Armstrong singing at the Ecole Marchesi and within a few minutes persuaded her to sign a contract, binding her to him for ten years, at a starting salary of a thousand francs (then about £40) a month, which was to double each year as her value increased. Some weeks later the Monnaie offered her three thousand francs a month with other inducements, for which she was to sing in ten operas a month. Melba said Marchesi told her to accept the Monnaie offer, saying, 'Strakosch is a great friend of mine. He will perfectly understand. I will arrange everything.' Strakosch did not understand, but told Melba he intended holding her to their contract, and soon after she arrived in Brussels for rehearsals a process-server presented her with an injunction forbidding her to appear at the Monnaie. As Melba described the episode she was an innocent young woman who, in her ignorance of business practice, placed herself in a dangerous situation. This picture somehow does not square with the gifts for business which Melba later revealed. F. W. Gaisberg, for many years recording manager of His Master's Voice, wrote much later of her recording contract: 'She was an astute business woman. Final negotiations for her contract had to be carried on through secretaries and solicitors. When the documents were at last completed they were of imposing length.' That tribute to her sharpness would be endorsed by anyone who ever had business dealings with Melba, so perhaps she was less ingenuous with Strakosch than she later pretended. At any rate the gods were on her side. Four nights before her début Strakosch considerately dropped dead, thus nullifying their contract and clearing her way to the stage of the Monnaie.

For her, *Rigoletto* was the beginning of a brilliantly successful season in which she sang Gilda several times and appeared also in *Traviata* and *Lucia di Lammermoor*; her singing of the Mad Scene in *Lucia* was then, and was to remain, a superb performance.

She had taken little George to live with her in Brussels. She could do nothing else; he was too young to be left in Paris with the only kind of help she could afford to hire at that time, so to Brussels he went—a small boy accustomed to his mother's comings and goings, who accommodated himself well enough to the need to live such a life. He turned four just three days after her début, and his birthday was suitably celebrated. Then, while Melba was adding to her singing laurels, Charles Armstrong decided to go to Brussels and see her; perhaps he was hoping to effect a reconciliation. He arrived without telling his wife he was coming, and went along to her apartment in the Rue du Bac. His visit was the subject of cruel misrepresentation by Percy Colson, in a biography of Melba published in 1932, whose version was seized on by later writers and given a seeming authority by repetition. Colson wrote:

'Melba's undesirable husband was still very much alive, and having, of course, heard that she was likely to become a star in the musical firmament, he came to Europe, and suddenly made his appearance in Brussels one afternoon when she was taking tea with a well-known painter, Monsieur Wauters.* There was a terrible scene; the little boy was frightened out of his life, and poor Melba was at her wits' end to know what to do, as Armstrong told her he would make life impossible for her. He even threatened to make a disturbance at the opera that evening when she was singing. She was naturally afraid to appear, and very sensibly went to the directors of the opera and explained the situation to them, begging them to interfere in some way. They fortunately succeeded in persuading Armstrong to leave Brussels. It is not known how and where he lived after this until the final denouement, but Melba and her child were henceforth able to live unmolested. She probably made him an allowance on the condition that he left her in peace.'

The factual basis for this farrago of misinformation, bad guesses, and cocktail-party gossip is slender. Charles Armstrong had a stormy meeting with his wife in Brussels, but Colson's depiction of him as something between a blackmailing hoodlum and a weedy pimp is at variance with everything known of his character. He was a proud and resolute man, and the notion that he could have been bought off in such circumstances, whether by his wife's money or somebody else's, is not so much offensive as ludicrous. Being naturally pugnacious, he may well have threatened to punch the head of any man friend of his wife who happened to be at hand, and equally well have put the threat into effect, but he was not one to sell out his rights as a husband for money; that would have been as foreign to his nature as to sit doing embroidery.

He did not stay in Brussels for long, and when he left he must have known that his marriage, except as a hollow legal bond, was

---

* Emile Wauters, born in Brussels in 1846, was known especially for his portraits and historical scenes. He painted a portrait of Melba at the time of her début, which now hangs in the Musée Charlier, Brussels. Wauters settled in Paris in 1890, and died there in 1933.

finished. He did not belong in Nellie's world of singing and footlights and operatic glory, nor could he have accommodated himself
to it even had she wanted him to. The marriage begun in Brisbane
five years earlier was to last, on paper, for another thirteen years,
but as an effective union it had reached its end.

7

Nothing about the start of Melba's career as a grand opera
singer in London suggested that a few years later she would
be the ruler of the Royal Opera House, Covent Garden. On the
contrary, even the possibility that she would be asked to come back
for a second season seemed remote. Her reception was not only some
degrees less than rapturous, but hardly more than apathetic.

The house was about half-full for her début in *Lucia di Lammermoor* on 24 May 1888, and although she later recalled the meagre
audience as having been 'wildly enthusiastic' impartial witnesses
who were present on that night remembered the hearers as merely
polite until she sang the Mad Scene, when they showed some
interest. The critic Herman Klein, in an appreciation written after
her death recalled that he went to hear her 'with a perfectly open
mind on the subject of her abilities, and . . . found myself a good
deal disappointed, at any rate during the first two acts of Donizetti's opera.' Most of the other London critics seemed, like Klein,
to resist any temptation to be carried away, although Francis
Hueffer, in *The Times*, cautiously predicted: 'That Madame Melba
will in the end be successful there is little reason to doubt. . . .' If
her showing had flaws it is not surprising; she went on in *Lucia*
after only one 'hasty and slovenly' orchestra rehearsal.

Melba, with the praises of the Brussels critics and the plaudits
of the Brussels people still ringing in her ears, found London a
discouraging city in that summer of 1888; thinking back to her cool
reception two years earlier by Arthur Sullivan, Randegger, Parry
and the others, she probably wondered if she would ever succeed
in touching London's steely heart, let alone in capturing it. She was
too intelligent to delude herself into believing that she was an
established operatic success merely because Brussels said so; she

knew she must go on and conquer other and greater opera houses, and above all Covent Garden, which so far seemed willing to listen to her but without betraying any semblance of ecstasy. It did not comfort her to remember that other singers had gone to Covent Garden with high Continental reputations, and been rejected by the London public. One of these failures was no less an artist than Josephine de Reszke, sister of Jean and Edouard de Reszke. So hostile was Josephine's reception by the London critics and public in 1881 that, after two performances in *Aida*, she asked to be released and went back to the Continent where she continued her career with undiminished success. The story of Josephine's failure, however, was calculated to depress rather than console Melba just at that time.

Standing at the window of her London lodgings and looking out at the grey-fronted houses, each exactly like the one next to it, Melba knew the sharp stabbing of disappointment. She had believed that her Covent Garden début would put the seal on her reputation: all it had done was to make her realize that nobody in London cared much whether she stayed or went. She was not short of ready money; her Covent Garden fees were paying her way, her father was still making her a small allowance, and she had saved a few thousand francs in Brussels. But another winter when she might earn little lay only a few months ahead, and she had to conserve her resources. It was all rather worrying.

She had wanted to make her Covent Garden début as Gilda, which she considered at that time to be her best part, but Augustus Harris, the director, had told her that Madame Albani, a long-established favourite, had first claim on *Rigoletto*. Melba was disappointed, but had to hide her vexation and make the best of it. It is ironical that within a few years talented but unknown young coloratura sopranos were to come to London, hoping for a chance to show their splendours, only to find that Melba, having gained a standing at Covent Garden which no singer possibly ever had there before and certainly none has had since, had first claim on the choice and showy roles they sang best, and would not readily stand aside for anyone.

As well as Albani, the soprano roster in 1888 included Zélie de Lussan, Lillian Nordica, and Minnie Hauk, while the two de Reszkes, Jean and Edouard, and Jean Lassalle were among the men. So if the new Australian soprano who came with a mere Brussels reputation found herself singing to poor houses it was hardly

71

surprising; however talented she and her friends might suppose her
to be, she was merely filling in between the nights when the great
stars sang and every seat was occupied. She sang Gilda once,
later in the season (by consent of Albani, who was a generous
woman and probably did not fear Melba's rivalry—in those days
at any rate), but the house was again half-empty and her reception
was in keeping.

A woman less confident of her own abilities would probably
have despaired, but Melba was never one to crumple up because
she suffered a reverse or even a sequence of reverses. One reason
of her lack of success in her first Covent Garden season was unknown
to her, or to more than a few people at the time; this was that she
had been engaged against Augustus Harris's judgement, and was
therefore a member of the company on sufferance. While Harris,
a man of charm, purpose, and intelligence, was the major directing
force of grand opera at Covent Garden when Melba arrived there
and continued to be until his death in 1896, he was not altogether
a law unto himself. He could make his seasons pay their way, and
perhaps earn a little profit, only with the support of the well-born
and the wealthy. The most influential of all his patrons was Gladys
Countess de Grey, whose husband Earl de Grey (later the Marquess
of Ripon) was a member of the committee which encouraged Harris
to stage grand opera at Covent Garden and ensured, by their example
and persuasion, that the costs of each season were covered by advance
subscriptions. Lady de Grey, a beautiful woman, who was six feet
tall and had a personality to match her height, was a competent
judge of singing and singers, and after hearing Melba in Brussels
in 1887 pressed Harris to engage her for Covent Garden. Having
given her a contract with some secret reluctance, Harris did not
exert himself to publicize her in London, and so she made her
Covent Garden début with no fanfare worth mentioning. Herman
Klein wrote:

'Thus the critics had been led to expect nothing phenomenal
when she made her début . . . a few of us had heard her at a concert
which she had given at Princes' Hall under her own name of Mrs
Mitchell-Armstrong in the previous year;* the impression she then
made had been decidedly amateurish and mediocre. The euphonious
name of "Melba" had as yet no magic in it.'

Klein's words say little for the London critics of the day, who

* This was the charity concert which Wilhelm Ganz arranged for her. It took place in
June, 1886, nearly two years before, and she sang as Mrs Armstrong.

apparently had to be told in advance that a new singer of unusual talent was to appear if they were to recognize the newcomer as such; an unheralded singer seemingly had little chance of being saluted, and so Melba was passed over as just another coloratura, neither particularly good nor particularly bad. Like most public performers she always pretended to care nothing for what critics said of her, yet she was an avid reader of the opinions on her singing published even by nonentities, in obscure newspapers where the music critic was likely to be also the court reporter, the agricultural correspondent, the assistant football writer and the religious editor. When she toured New Zealand in 1903 her singing at a recital in Christchurch on the night of 20 February was adversely criticized in the *Lyttleton Times*. The writer applauded her technical mastery, but regretted the 'soullessness' of her numbers, and was trenchant on the standard of some of the supporting artists. Melba went along in person next day to the *Lyttleton Times* office, swept in to see the editor, and demanded that the critic should be publicly thrashed. The critic evidently had either a showman's sense or a gift of mordant humour, and 'agreed to this on condition that she did the thrashing herself, that it should take place in a public hall, and that he would receive the whole of the takings. The case did not proceed.'

Melba does not appear to have urged in 1888 that any of the London critics should be publicly thrashed. She doubtless would have done so had she believed that anyone would heed her, but she knew she would be wasting her breath; at that time she was just another operatic aspirant whose ambitions seemed to outrun her abilities.

When she was famous some years later she was to be less submissive. A Covent Garden gala performance was abandoned at short notice, but a London women's magazine published an item about the event by its music critic; this had obviously been written and printed before the performance was cancelled, and the clairvoyant critic noted that Melba was not in 'her usual good voice'. Her almost pathological dislike of litigation swamped by her indignation, Melba sued the magazine and was awarded £100 damages.

She made three appearances at Covent Garden in 1888, growing steadily more disheartened. Then Harris offered her the secondary soprano role of Oscar, the Page, in *Un Ballo in Maschera*. Affronted, she packed her things and went back to Brussels, where everybody –the directors of the Monnaie, opera-lovers, even the hateful critics–wanted her.

When she asked Harris to release her he did not demur. He had

however modified the lukewarm opinion of her ability he had held
when Lady de Grey had jockeyed him into inviting her to Covent
Garden. Discussing her retreat from London, he said, 'In a little
time they will clamour for Melba above all others, and, by gad,
they'll have to pay for her. If any foreign artist had come to London
with the same qualifications as Melba, she would have been received
with unqualified enthusiasm.' Perhaps Harris's conscience was
troubling him when he said that, for he had not bestirred himself to
prepare London for Melba's coming. Perhaps he also felt it would
be diplomatic to soothe Lady de Grey's disappointment over the
premature return of her protégée to Brussels.

Lady de Grey was not a woman who took kindly to the frustration
of her schemes, and, being determined that Melba should succeed
in London, she refused to let the matter rest when the 1888 season
ended. She wrote to Melba, asking her to come back in 1889, and
saying, 'I know that things were badly arranged for you before,
but if you come back I promise you that it will be very different.'
Even months after leaving London, Melba was still smarting, but
she always had a sharp ear for opportunity's knock. She agreed to
give Covent Garden a second chance, but first she had to make her
Paris début as Ophelia in *Hamlet*. She scored both a critical and
popular success at the Paris Opéra, and stayed on to appear in
Rigoletto and *Lucia*. Then, riding the wave, she crossed to London,
and on 15 June 1889 appeared in *Roméo et Juliette*, which was being
sung in French for the first time at Covent Garden. The Roméo was
Jean de Reszke, whose brother Edouard was also in the cast as
Friar Laurent. The house was packed to the doors, and before the
performance was half-over Melba was walking the heights. Most
of the critics praised her. John Fuller-Maitland, in *The Times*, said,
'Melba's beautiful voice and excellent method are heard at their
very best.' The praise was not undiluted however. George Bernard
Shaw, a newspaper critic in those days, was among the dissentients;
he said, 'she was shrill and forward, the waltz ariette coming out
with great confidence and facility, which I think Madame Melba
mistook for art.'

Melba had an odd effect on critics; some of them began by disliking her singing but many of these sooner or later surrendered
to it. Shaw was one. Three years after making his acid comment
on her performance as Juliette, he heard her at Covent Garden in
Herman Bemberg's lightweight opera *Elaine*, and wrote: 'This
year . . . I find Madame Melba transfigured, awakened, no longer

to be identified by the old descriptions – in sum, with her heart, which before acted only on her circulation, now acting on her singing and giving it a charm which it never had before.' (It is possibly relevant that the transfigured Melba of 1892 had in the meantime met the Duke of Orleans and become enmeshed in one of the most talked-of love affairs of the decade.) After another two years, Shaw was able to write of Melba in *Faust*: '. . . you never realize how wide a gap there is between the ordinary singer who simply avoids the fault of singing obviously out of tune and the singer who sings really and truly in tune, except when Melba is singing.'

Shaw was only one of the many discriminating hearers who found that when Melba was at her best she sang with a superhuman beauty.

8

THUS Nellie Melba began her career at Covent Garden. It was to last nearly forty years, until her formal Farewell in 1926. She was nearly as powerful at the end as at the beginning, but only a perfervid idolater would argue that for the last fifteen years or so her sway did not depend as much on business wizardry and driving personality as on vocal magic.

Although she owed her success to her own talents above all, she was lucky to arrive at Covent Garden when she did. Covent Garden had been a theatre since 1732, and one of the famous opera houses of Europe for more than seventy-five years, but its golden period began in 1888, the year of Melba's début, and continued until the outbreak of World War I in 1914. Except for the opening years of that period she was the chief prima donna and the unofficial but pretty well all-powerful ruler of the backstage world.

Opera at Covent Garden had been travelling a rough road in the years immediately before 1888; then Augustus Harris, after putting on a successful season of Italian opera at Drury Lane in 1887, moved into Covent Garden for a summer season, beginning on 14 May 1888. One of his admirers said Harris was impelled by 'the idea of giving grand opera a decent burial or resuscitating it'. He was a son of parents with wide theatrical experience, and was himself, at thirty-six, an actor, a writer for the stage, and a producer as well as an impresario of proven ability, which at times bordered on genius. With the backing of his committee he made Covent Garden the equal, if not the superior, of any opera house in the world.

English opera-lovers were to stagger under the news of Harris's sudden death on 22 June 1896, but the tradition and standards he had established at Covent Garden survived for many years. On his death a group of men formed themselves into the Grand Opera Syndicate to continue his work; the chairman was Harry V. Higgins, a socially prominent London solicitor and company director, and his board included Earl de Grey, Lord Esher, and Lord Wittenham. They were all apostles of Harris, and also able and cultured men with ideas of their own for the maintenance and betterment of Covent Garden as a great opera house. The Syndicate, with Neil Forsyth, Harris's former secretary, as secretary and business manager, remained the controlling force at Covent Garden until 1914. It reappeared after World War I, but never seemed to recover its old direction although it survived until 1924, when it relinquished the main lease of the theatre. It was not the least part of Melba's good luck that she came in at the beginning of the Harris-Syndicate era and was there to the end.

The Covent Garden period from 1891 to 1900 has been called the Golden Age of Opera, and that from 1901 to 1914 the Indian Summer of the Golden Age, and, as handy labels, these could hardly be bettered. The twenty-five years, or rather less, which came after Augustus Harris rescued grand opera in England from its slump, was the time of Covent Garden's greatest glory. To be seen at the opera then was essential for the socially ambitious. The spectacle on a Melba Night or a Caruso Night—tier upon tier of lavishly gowned women and dress-suited men, the whole house flashing with the play of light on jewels—was no less enchanting than any spectacle on the stage. Possibly nothing of the kind will ever be seen in the world again. It is no wonder that Melba, the building contractor's daughter from the Melbourne suburb of Richmond, revelled in her glory as the monarch of Covent Garden.

Her success in 1889 established her there, and within two or three years she was firmly seated on her own supreme pinnacle. Her position was to be challenged many times, but never successfully. She was temporarily overshadowed when Patti returned to Covent Garden in 1895, after ten years' absence, but never in real danger; and how much of the adulation heaped on the ageing Patti, who as an eighteen-year-old coloratura had made her Covent

Garden début five days before Melba was born, was generated by nostalgia and how much by the quality of her still beautiful but declining voice, is a matter of opinion. The question whether or not Melba at her zenith was equal to Patti at her zenith is unanswerable, for they were eighteen years apart in age. Henry Russell, an English singing-master and impresario, and an older brother of Sir Landon Ronald, once debated the point with Don Prospero Cellini, whose knowledge of singing, Russell said, 'was greater than that of any man of his time'.

'Do you really think Patti had a greater voice than Melba?' Russell asked.

'Perhaps not,' Don Prospero replied. 'But she was a far better artist and a more intelligent singer.'

'As far as I can judge, Melba has a more perfect trill, more purity of tone and a better attack than Patti,' Russell replied, according to himself, and went on: 'I think you are severe. Public taste in singing is often a matter of locality. No doubt Melba's popularity is greater in England than in any other country. But there have been some great Italian singers who were failures away from Italy.'

Don Prospero and Russell left it at that.

The fifty-two-year-old Patti of 1895 was at any rate no long-term rival to Melba at Covent Garden, and the Australian went back to sing there every year until 1909, always as the reigning coloratura, and one of the very greatest exponents of *bel canto*. She missed the 1909 season, because she was travelling to and touring in Australia and New Zealand most of that year. When she went back to London in 1910 Covent Garden welcomed her as warmly as ever; and when, on 22 May 1913, she celebrated the twenty-fifth anniversary of her Covent Garden début by appearing in a gala performance of *Bohème*, her position was as unassailable as it had ever been.

Melba sang in most of the great opera houses of the world, and before all the crowned heads of Europe, but Covent Garden always remained the focus of her career. She was successful in many other cities; in fact, her most dazzling triumphs were probably scored, not in London but in New York, at Oscar Hammerstein's Manhattan Opera House in 1906–7. She gloried in these successes, but it was always to Covent Garden that she went back as if going home; she was never a sentimentalist at the expense of her pocket, but in this case sentiment and material profit marched, happily, hand in hand.

Her feeling was easy to understand, for after that aloof beginning

Covent Garden took her to its heart and never let her go. Probably a few other singers equal or nearly equal in calibre to Melba sang at Covent Garden, and two or three of them went back there season after season, but to none did the spirit of the place surrender as it did to her. She had her own dressing-room, and while she was on the regular Covent Garden roster nobody but she ever used it, whether she was in England or on the other side of the world. She kept the key, and when she went back, after an absence of six months, nine months, a year, or even longer, everything was in its place, exactly as she had left it. The door bore her name in bold letters, MELBA, followed by the words SILENCE! SILENCE!, and everyone at Covent Garden knew enough to tiptoe past that door when Melba was inside.

Her fee always had to be above any other singer's; even Caruso, at the height of his immense popularity in London, had to take £1 a performance less than Melba – £399 against her £400. The source of her power was not only the miraculous quality of her singing, nor yet alone the charm of her personality (although this was strong when she chose to exert it), but the combination of these two things with an array of other well-marked characteristics including her gift for making influential friends. Her first sponsor, Lady de Grey, not only admired her as a singer but also liked her as a woman, and Melba liked Lady de Grey no less; perhaps, although one was an aristocrat and the other came of hard-working stock, they found a meeting-point in their determination to take hold of life and wring from it what they wanted.

Lady de Grey's sway over affairs at Covent Garden in the 1890s and in the early years of this century was nearly unlimited. Neither Augustus Harris nor his successor, Neil Forsyth, who inherited all Harris's responsibilities as business manager at Covent Garden but by no means all his power, could afford to displease her; nor, once she accepted the Australian prima donna as a friend and a member of her circle, could they afford to displease Melba. Neither Harris nor Forsyth would have wished to offend Melba anyway, for from 1889 onwards she was a star whose name London opera-goers spoke in tones of adulation. No prima donna ever seriously threatened her supremacy until 1907, when Luisa Tetrazzini came to Covent Garden and the names of only two men singers, first Jean de Reszke, and later Enrico Caruso, held the magic of Melba's for the public at large.

The chances are however that Melba could never have achieved what she did without Lady de Grey as an ally. 'Dear Gladys' not only saw to it that Melba, on her return to Covent Garden in 1889, was launched in a manner befitting a great star, but also that she was admitted to the best houses in England, not through the tradesmen's entrance as a professional entertainer, but through the front door as a social equal. Lady de Grey was among the dozen or so most influential figures in English Society at that time, but even she could not have given a place in the social sun to some young woman who, while singing superbly, yet lacked poise, dignity and an adequate education. She would not have tried to do so. Nellie Melba had all the qualities required for social success; she never was the wild colonial girl that some backstage gossip-mongers tried to paint her, and even if some of those who met her disliked a hint of the domineering in her manner they could not accuse her of being socially inept. Every action of her public life was carried off in the grand manner, and when she travelled the world was aware that this was Melba passing by. In the early years of this century the famous New York–Chicago railroad train, the Twentieth Century Limited, carried many passengers with a taste for Arabian Nights luxury and the means to satisfy it, and Melba was to the fore among them. Writing of the year 1902, in his history of the train, Lucius Beebe said: 'Melba acted the part of the star performer both on stage and off and travelled in a cloud of hothouse flowers, couriers, personal attendants and the gastronomic prejudices of the well placed and determined of the world. One of her favourite dishes, plover's eggs *en croute* with fresh caviar, she was unable to get in New York, but *The Century* lived up to her standards. Before she boarded the train, her personal staff remade her bed and toilet appointments with the diva's own specially scented bed linen and towels, and the adjacent drawing room which she used as a sitting room was decorated with Melba's own sofa pillows, silver candlesticks and a few gold framed and autographed likenesses of crowned heads for company to Chicago where she was to sing *La Bohème*. It was all approximately as Bohemian as life in Buckingham Palace.'

She was not only accepted by Society, but played the part as if born to it—indeed, had she played her stage parts half so well she might have escaped the scathing criticisms her histrionic shortcomings often brought down on her. Melba at all times wanted full value for money spent, and scrutinized such items as household accounts with a searching eye, but she could, and did, spend with a lavish hand when spending was justified. She could afford to buy what she wanted. She never confided the details of her financial affairs to anyone, not even her father, and most published estimates of her earnings were mere guesses, but on her death in 1931 she left an estate valued for probate at £181,515, and would have left much more if the value of her investments had not been eroded by World War I. For many years opera appearances and concerts earned her not less than £1,000 a week, and in some years her earnings were considerably higher; her share of the profits of an Australian opera season in 1911 was £46,000, at a time when taxation was negligible, and for many years her gramophone records earned her about £18,000 a year.

She was an astute business woman in her own right, and also had the benefit for many years of Alfred de Rothschild's advice. One of the three English Rothschild brothers, Alfred, although a fop, a hypochondriac, and something of a poseur, was a brilliant financier who could afford such personal diversions as a symphony orchestra of his own, which he conducted with a baton of gleaming ivory banded with diamonds. Among the subjects of his connoisseurship were prima donnas. Patti was his favourite for many years, and he advised her on her investments. Then Melba succeeded Patti, both as the darling of Covent Garden and as the object of Alfred de Rothschild's strictly asexual passion. It was a profitable friendship; with the aid of his financial sagacity, not to mention his financial inside knowledge, her income from investments soon matched, or outstripped, her earnings from singing.

For her first fourteen years in Europe Melba made her home in Paris, and in her early seasons at Covent Garden lived while in London at the Savoy Hotel. Then she fell into the habit of renting a house in or near London for the period of the Covent Garden season, and a house in some socially fashionable part of the country for a few months each year. Soon after the turn of the century she bought a house in Great Cumberland Place, and spent many thousands of pounds in remodelling it in the style of the Palace of Versailles, which had captured her imagination in her student days in Paris. The work took two years, and was mostly done by skilled plasterers, cabinet-makers, glass-workers, and other craftsmen imported from Paris, because, Melba said, English workmen could not do what she wanted. When the house in Great Cumberland Place was finished it was a show-place in which she could entertain illustrious friends without feeling the smallest qualm of inferiority. It remained her London home for over twenty years.

Melba never cheapened her professional standing by singing for her supper; she would sing to guests in her own house, or at a party given by some intimate friend such as Lady de Grey or Mrs Hwfa Williams or Alfred de Rothschild, but never at some party to which the host or hostess had invited her, thinking it would be nice to have a song or two from dear Nellie Melba. She knew the value of the notes that came from her throat, and her commercial instinct would not let her give them away for nothing except to suit her own pleasure. Ivor Newton, the accompanist, who often worked with Melba, tells of an episode in an English country house. After dinner the hostess whispered to him, 'Do you think we could get Melba to sing?' Newton hesitantly said, 'Well, that possibly depends on who asks her.' Another guest, Lord Hewart, then Lord Chief Justice, agreed to try to persuade her. He sat with Melba and chatted, taking a circuitous route to the point. Newton, watching, saw Melba's mouth grow firm and her eyes become steely, and presently Lord Hewart left her and came back, shaking his head. 'I have been unsuccessful,' he said, crestfallen. 'I think I can put that down as my greatest failure.'

Melba revelled in being on first-name terms, as she was, with the aristocratic and titled, but she knew she had a genius which set her apart from and somewhat above all but the very greatest of them. A duchess, genuinely curious, once asked her if she would rather be a duchess or Melba. 'Melba!' she replied. 'There are lots of duchesses but there's only one Melba.'

She was in the habit of saying, 'I'm a damned snob!', and most of those who knew her well endorse that finding. But her snobbishness had something childlike about it; she never hid her pleasure in knowing and being known by peers and their ladies, by kings and queens. She delighted in dropping august names, such as those of Lady Warwick, the Duchess of Devonshire, the Duchess of Sutherland, Lady Cynthia Graham, Lady Helen Vincent, and in telling the story of how the Princess of Wales (later Queen Alexandra), having admired 'my poor little pearls, which were not worth more than a few hundred pounds, said softly, "What lovely pearls!" I felt like saying to her, "You darling." '

She could condone the worst kind of vulgarities so long as the perpetrators were socially irreproachable, and even find justification for an act of gross rudeness if the rank of the offender were high enough. A story she often told concerned a supper party in the 1890s, at which the then Prince of Wales was a guest. All the time that

Melba and an American baritone, Eugene Oudin, were singing a duet from *Roméo et Juliette*, the Prince sat on a sofa talking. Both singers were disconcerted, but Melba forgave all when she was told that the future king had been discussing affairs of state. His lack of interest in music was notorious, but it was too much to expect Melba to admit, even to herself, that he was talking simply because he was warm with wine and brandy and bored at having to listen to what was, to him, the caterwauling of a pair of fugitives from Covent Garden.

9

WHEN necessary Melba had the patience and inexhaustible capacity for forbearance of the successful courtier. She exercised those qualities to the full to win the throne at Covent Garden, and then to stay on it, but they were not the only qualities of mind and spirit she used.

First there was her greatness as a singer. Most of those who heard her in her noontide remembered ever afterwards the sexless purity of her voice; she sang, they said, not like a woman but like a choirboy. Jean de Reszke, the greatest tenor of his day (who always remained the greatest tenor for Melba), said she had 'a voice of gold, the most beautiful of our time'; Sarah Bernhardt thought it a 'voice of pure crystal'. To many of those who heard her she was the perfect singer, beyond criticism or reproach, but to some few an essential quality was missing. Ernest Newman, the great English critic, once described her singing as 'uninterestingly perfect and perfectly uninteresting'. James Agate, on hearing her in *Traviata*, wrote that she was 'faultily faultless'. Neville Cardus said, 'Never once did her singing move me in any imaginative way; it was flawless vocalism pure and simple; but never in my experience did it enter into the deeper world of music.' Those experts who found such deficiencies in Melba were outnumbered by the others, equally expert, who believed her to be among the greatest singers of her time. George Bernard Shaw's views, which have been noted, were shared by many discriminating critics, such as Alfred Kalisch, for example. Kalisch, an English barrister, abandoned the law when in his early thirties, to devote himself to music criticism and to the writing of librettos; he is particularly remembered for his translations into English of *Salome*, *Elektra*, *Der Rosenkavalier*, and *Ariadne auf Naxos*. Kalisch found Melba to be 'one of those perplexing people to whom the ordinary standards of criticism do not apply'. He wrote: 'She is at once the greatest of living artists and no artist at all. As an exponent of vocal art she stands on a pinnacle by herself. She is further removed from all possible rivals than Joachim is among violinists, or Paderewski among pianists. Her only equal in this one thing is Jean de Reszke, and even he is not quite so perfect; even his consummate art is not so entirely free from all trace of effort and premeditation as hers.'

She had the unusual experience of being approved by instrumentalists, who usually sniff at opera singers. A long line of instrumentalists—Joachim, Paderewski, Anton Rubinstein, Kubelik, Grainger, to name a few—admired her; they generally agreed that she had the same discipline in her singing that a violinist, a pianist, a harpist or any fine instrumentalist has in his playing. Grainger said: 'I'm not particularly fond of opera singers as a rule, but I must say I have never heard anything to compare with the beauty of Melba's voice, in any branch of singing. The top notes of course were very ringing and telling, as they are with a good many fine sopranos. But the curious thing with Melba was that her lower notes and middle notes were equally telling. They had a quality all of their own; and even when she was singing with a big orchestra, she was never wiped out. She had a tremendous carrying power and a tremendous beauty of tone and very great refinement of workmanship in everything she did.' Joseph Szigeti, the Hungarian violinist, who toured with Melba as an assisting artist (and evidently had no particular liking for her as a woman), wrote nearly forty years later that 'the girlish freshness of that voice and the indolent languorous grace with which she sang some things remain unforgettable to me to this day'. Szigeti went on: 'Recently, when arranging for publication of some short pieces for violin, I decided to include Lalo's Aubade from *Le Roi d'Ys* in the series, probably to give substance to my memory of her singing this song. A small thing, to be sure, but her own; and ineffably beautiful this small thing must have been to have retained its hold on me through all these years.'

Opinions for and against Melba as a singer could be multiplied almost without end, but repetition would serve no purpose, except to emphasize that discerning listeners to music do not necessarily all hear sounds in the same way, any more than discerning readers necessarily take the same meaning from the words printed on a page. Those who disliked her singing found it cold, aloof, passionless; to others it had the unearthly beauty of winter moonlight.

So her singing was the thing that put her on the throne at Covent Garden, but after the first few years her remorseless tenacity of purpose did more to keep her there. Her enemies damned her in her lifetime as a ruthless woman, and they have continued to do so since she died. And she was ruthless, with an eye constantly watching for the approach of someone aspiring to supplant her; she always fought them tooth and nail, and always won. If she had let herself be supplanted, gracefully surrendering her place to someone else, she would have been better liked while she lived and more quickly forgotten when she died. The world does not remember the amiable loser nearly so long or with so much respect as it remembers the man or woman with an appetite for success and a relentless and aggressive way of seizing and keeping it. Nellie Melba never hesitated to enforce her hold on the position she had won. She remembered how hard the climb had been, and she had no intention of letting all that effort go for nothing. She never committed the deadly sin of becoming complacent. She once told a friend, 'It's when you are the diva that you have to be nervous. When you are climbing up you just do your best. When you are the diva you have to be the best always.'

In grand opera, as in any other branch of the theatre, a man or woman gains a topmost place only by means of artistic excellence, but rarely, perhaps never, holds it by means of artistic excellence alone. As the years cause the individual's powers to decline, a willingness to crush challengers is indispensable. Melba, like Caesar, would brook no rivals. If she had done so she would not have held her supremacy for longer than her vocal powers were at their zenith; probably for no more than ten years, for she was twenty-eight when she established herself at Covent Garden – an age at which many a coloratura is already beginning to think about the future. Kings and queens in any field rarely abdicate until there is no help for it. Melba was like that. In her time she routed many challengers, and did it without a qualm, knowing that if any of them had prevailed against her she would have been destroyed.

She did not invent the conception of the prima donna supremacist; she was only one of a long line, although there has probably never been another who exerted her power with so much efficiency and with such deadly effect. One of her forerunners, the Swedish soprano Christine Nilsson, crushed rivals without displaying any prickings of conscience; and by all accounts Angelica Catalani, who sang in London with great success in the early years of the nineteenth century, and has been called 'probably the highest-paid prima donna in all operatic history', never showed much inclination to give aid and comfort to any young soprano who threatened her. Nearly all prima donnas at the peak of their careers will go to great lengths to safeguard themselves and perhaps Melba was no more merciless than most.

Her attitude to other sopranos mellowed somewhat as she grew older. In fact, she was almost too given to naming this one or that one as her successor—always, it seems, with the underlying implication that, while there could never be another Melba, this was the next best thing. A Polish soprano, Claire Dux, singing in *Die Zauberflöte* at Drury Lane, London, in a Beecham season in the spring of 1914 roused ecstatic enthusiasm. Beecham wrote later: 'For the next performance the whole of the front row of stalls was occupied by vocalists, among whom were Melba, Destinn, Caruso, and Chaliapin, all genuinely curious to see just what it was that Claire Dux did with a piece that all of them must have heard many times without suspecting its full possibilities. Naturally it was the opinion of Melba, a soprano of world fame, that was most eagerly awaited, and I was almost as gratified as Claire herself when the formidable Nellie hailed her in my presence with the words: "You are my successor".'

Melba never paid compliments to her professional juniors merely to see the light come into their eyes—rather the reverse; but in this case events did not confirm her expectations. After World War I Claire Dux appeared with success in Chicago, but then married a wealthy American and never fulfilled herself as a singer.

A flat kind of ending was by no means unusual when Melba prophesied fame for a young soprano. It almost seemed that, perhaps subconsciously, she reserved her highest praises for those who stood a half-head or more below her, and failed to see the merits of those who were nearer her own stature, even if not quite her peers.

10

For Melba the last decade of the century was a time of almost unbroken musical triumphs—almost, but not quite.

To list her triumphs at Covent Garden would be tedious, but the standard she set as Nedda in Leoncavallo's *Pagliacci* in 1893 deserves mention. Augustus Harris persuaded the rather shy Ruggiero Leoncavallo to go to London for the première of *Pagliacci*. With Melba as Nedda, Mario Ancona as Tonio, and Fernando de Lucia as Canio, the performance was a great success. Herman Klein, who said that Nedda's music was 'exquisitely sung' by Melba, noted: 'The walls of Covent Garden have often rung to thunderous salvoes of applause, but rarely in my experience to any so terrific as those which greeted the modest Leoncavallo when they dragged him on to the stage again and again at the end of the performance.' *Pagliacci* was sung nine times in 1893, with Melba as the Nedda at every performance.

Melba was commanded several times to sing at Windsor Castle before Queen Victoria and the Queen's guests. Music was esteemed then by English gentlefolk, and the Queen herself had set an example to her subjects by studying singing under the tutelage of the majestic Neapolitan bass, Luigi Lablache; even her most devoted subjects never suggested, however, that the royal voice was more than ordinary. Music enjoyed a high standing in other royal courts of Europe also, and Melba, as a tribute to her successes in Milan, Paris, Monte Carlo, and other centres, and in London above all, was bidden to St Petersburg by Czar Alexander III, to Stockholm by the King of Norway and Sweden, Oscar II, and to Berlin by the last of the Hohenzollerns, Wilhelm II. In America, too, she ranked high both with the critics and the public.

On the professional level her life moved smoothly, except for one incident. This was the product of her own folly—perhaps blind stupidity is not too strong a term—and the only victim of it was herself. It all but destroyed her voice, and if that had happened it would have meant, for Melba, professional and perhaps psychological death. What she did is possibly understandable in the circumstances of the time, yet still astonishing, for few singers knew as much as she did about the mechanics of voice production and the limitations of the human voice, or were harsher in correcting young aspiring singers who, whether wilfully or through ignorance, strained their voices.

For the music of the light and showy Italian operas Melba's voice was unsurpassed in her own day, and possibly never will be surpassed; as Mimi, as Gilda, as Violetta, as Lucia, and so on she was superb and, for most habitués of Covent Garden at any rate, unapproachable. But nature never intended her to sing Wagner, and only some kind of obsession would ever have let her attempt it. Unhappily for her own good, she had sung *Lohengrin* in London in 1890 with moderate success and without harming her voice; four years later, in New York, she had sung both *Lohengrin* and *Tann-häuser* with like results. While she was well suited by neither opera, she was able to manage the music competently enough, and this emboldened her. So at the Metropolitan Opera House, New York, on 30 December 1896, she attempted to sing, in German, the role of Brünnhilde in *Siegfried*. It was like asking a French rapier to do the work of a German battleaxe, and if Melba did not know that when the performance began – she probably did – then she knew it to her cost by the time the performance ended.

She was no stranger to the Metropolitan at that time, and, if the New York audiences were a little less rapturous about her than her Londoners, she still stood high with them. On her début as Lucia on 4 December 1893, Henry Krehbiel, the *New York Tribune* critic, put her down as 'the finest exemplar [of finished vocalization] heard on the local stage since Mme Sembrich made her American début ten years ago'. He found her voice 'charmingly fresh, and exquisitely beautiful', and her tone production 'more natural, and more spontaneous than that of the marvellous woman who so long upheld the standard of bel canto throughout the world [Patti]'. The patrons of the Metropolitan Opera House were rather slower to see her merits than were Krehbiel and some of the other critics, but she strengthened her reputation in 1894–5 and 1895–6, and when she came back for the 1896–7 season she was powerful enough to demand what she wanted and get it. One of the things she was misguided enough to want and unlucky enough to get was the role of Brünnhilde, with Jean de Reszke as Siegfried.

Melba sang – or tried to sing – Brünnhilde for a compelling human reason: she wished to do the fashionable thing. At that time Wagner was the rage with Anglo-Saxon audiences on both sides of the Atlantic, after a period of eclipse in which his operas had been convicted of every supposed sin from unmelodiousness to dramatic absurdity—as if dramatic absurdity ever handicapped any grand opera! When the tide turned in their favour every leading singer felt the temptation to show the public that he could sing Wagner if he chose. Most of those with voices too delicate for the demands of Wagner's music resisted the temptation, or were dissuaded from such follies by their friends. Melba succumbed to it and, her power at the Metropolitan being hardly less than at Covent Garden, nobody could convince her that she was embarking upon an act of madness. Jean de Reszke might have turned her back from Wagner; they were close friends from the first time they sang together at the Paris Opéra in 1889 and continued to be friends until his death in 1925, and with him, as with John Lemmone, her relationship was platonic. But when Melba sang Brünnhilde in New York it was reported that de Reszke not only did not try to dissuade her but even urged her on. He admitted having suggested she should sing in *Siegfried*, but said he had wanted her to sing not Brünnhilde but the secondary role of the Forest Bird. Melba herself never said what advice de Reszke gave her, and it does not matter. She should have needed nobody's guidance; she must have known that Brünnhilde's music was far beyond the scope of her voice. If she was unable to see it herself, her old teacher and life-long friend, Mathilde Marchesi, knew it, and had once bluntly told her not to be a fool when she had confessed to a longing to sing Wagner.

Her Brünnhilde was an artistic calamity. She got through it somehow, and next day the New York critics were kind but sorrowful, not so much in what they said as in what they left unsaid. Henry Krehbiel said in the *New York Tribune*: 'To the loveliness of her devotion and the loftiness of her ambition honest tribute must be paid. But the music of the part does not lie well in her voice, and if she continues to sing it, it is much to be feared that there will soon be an end to the charm which her voice disclosed when employed in its legitimate sphere. The world can ill afford to lose a Melba, even if it should gain a Brünnhilde. But it will not gain a Brünnhilde.'

Staying only long enough to announce that she would never try to sing Wagner again, and to confess, 'I have been a fool', she cancelled her American engagements and went back to Europe, nursing her damaged vocal cords. In London she put herself in the hands of Sir Felix Semon, the German-born laryngologist. Semon forbade her to sing for some months, while time and the exercises he prescribed repaired the injury. When the cure was complete she gave him a signed photograph of herself inscribed, 'To Sir Felix Semon, my guardian-angel, from his sincere friend and grateful patient, Nellie Melba'. In his autobiography Semon remarked: 'The description of "guardian-angel" was merited, for I had actually saved her voice.'

Melba's voice suffered no obvious lasting damage from her flirtation with Wagner, but the strain she put on it possibly left a permanent weakness. Sir Milsom Rees, the London ear, nose and throat specialist, who was her adviser for many years, read a paper at the annual meeting of the British Medical Association at Belfast, in 1937, in which he said: 'Melba, when near the end of her career, would occasionally in the last act of *Faust* make an error in production, and twenty minutes later a little mucous vesicle might have been noticed at the edge of one of her vocal cords, disappearing in a few days after rest and treatment.' Whether or not this was a legacy from that night of 30 December 1896 at the Metropolitan Opera House, there was a legacy of another kind, and that was the lifelong agony of frustration Melba suffered over her inability to sing Wagner. William Murdoch, the Australian pianist, writing just after her death said: 'She knew her Wagner exceedingly well, and it seemed odd that this lovely voice and superb technique could not be used for the exposition of his great music. But such is nationality in music. Wagner wrote for the Germanic and Northern European physique. There have not been many Wagnerian women born outside these regions.'

Melba's sense of defeat over Wagner doubtless lay behind her possibly subconscious but indubitable dislike of nearly every soprano who could sing the great Wagnerian roles. She was fairly successful in hiding this antagonism when the other singers were not Australians. She even managed to speak in loving terms of Lillian Nordica, the American soprano, and one of the most famous Brünnhildes and Isoldes of her day; when Nordica died tragically in 1914, after an unhappy tour of Australia, Melba told a friend who saw her in London, 'They murdered her in Australia, and I shall tell them when I go back!' This outburst was laced with irony, for when Melba nominated herself to sing Brünnhilde in New York, Nordica had believed, not without reason, that she had been robbed of the role and was furious.

Any Australian soprano who made a name in Wagner, or even

seemed likely to, never inspired Melba's affection. Florence Austral was, in the 1920s, one of the most admired Wagnerian singers in the world, vocally, if not histrionically; her voice, soaring, powerful and luscious, found no difficulty in encompassing the music of Brünnhilde and Isolde. Austral, then twenty-eight, made her Covent Garden début in 1922, and continued to sing in London with success, as well as in the great Continental and American opera houses. Melba was still a powerful figure at Covent Garden then, but Austral did not meet her for a year or so. In a gala performance one night Melba sang in a scene from *Bohème* in the first half and Austral in a scene from *Aida* in the second half. Next morning Austral was talking with the stage manager when Melba came in.

'You know Madame Austral?' the stage manager said.

'Austral?' Melba asked, 'Who's Austral?'

'You sang with her last night,' said the stage manager.

'Oh,' Melba grunted, 'she was black then,' and, turning on her heel, walked away.

Melba saw Austral many times later, but never spoke to her. It seems odd, because Austral was, like Melba, born in the Melbourne suburb of Richmond and began her singing studies, in 1914, at the Albert Street Conservatorium of Music, in which Melba took a special interest. These circumstances evidently counted for less than the thought that Florence Austral was born to sing Wagner. Yet Melba managed to swallow that pill in the end. In a press interview in Australia in 1924 she said that Austral had 'one of the wonder voices of the world, especially in Wagner'. It was a just tribute, if belated.

11

IT is never easy for a man or woman in the public eye to live even a moderately private life, but Melba managed it better than most celebrities. At any rate she did so after weathering a storm early in the 1890s, when scandal threatened to injure her personal reputation, to alienate many of her friends, and to bolt England's most socially desirable doors against her.

Writing of the Victorian era Anthony Trollope said that 'it

behooves an English novelist to be pure'. If a novelist, then how much more an opera singer? The power of Melba's personality probably never had a better testimonial than her survival of the gossip engendered by her affair with Louis Philippe Robert, Duke of Orleans, the fourteenth bearer of that title and Pretender to the French throne.

Men came and went in Melba's life, but only two of them were of much consequence in her emotional scheme. One of these was Charles Armstrong, and the other the Duke of Orleans. In the end she and the duke parted, like any pair of blighted lovers in an opera libretto, and Melba put him out of her life because she had to, but she never put him out of her heart and mind. Many years later she was making a concert tour of English provincial cities. The manager of an hotel in which she was staying came to her, and asked if she would autograph the distinguished visitors' book.

'I wouldn't ask you in the ordinary way,' he said, 'but this is something very special.'

He laid the leather-bound book down, open, on the table in front of her. She took up the pen, then paused and called to her solo pianist, Una Bourne, 'Oh, Una, come here!' Miss Bourne went across, and Melba smoothed a hand lightly over a page of the book bearing the Duke of Orleans's signature, inscribed there some years before. She touched the page and said, almost to herself, 'Ah, dear Philippe!' Then she signed her name on the opposite page.

When they met in 1890 Melba was nearing thirty, almost eight years older than the Duke, but this difference did not trouble them. She was physically more desirable then than at any other time in her life; her figure was still slim, and her face had not acquired the almost combative expression which settled on it later. If not beautiful, she was handsome, and surrounded by admiring men. She was relentlessly pursuing success in the difficult and treacherous world of grand opera, however, and that mattered more to her than romantic entanglements. At any rate it mattered more until she met the Duke of Orleans.

As the eldest son of the Comte de Paris, and the Dauphin to adherents of the Bourbon cause, he carried an aura of aristocracy which appealed to her. For good measure he was the kind of young man any woman enjoys having at her side – handsome, lean, six feet two inches tall and highly educated, entertaining, a gay companion. Melba never hid her liking for the lustre he shed on her.

They met while the Duke was living in England. Some years

before, in 1886, the Republican Government of France had exiled the Comte de Paris and Philippe, for what were compelling reasons of state; these were that the French populace had let itself go in a tremendous burst of enthusiasm for the House of Bourbon on the marriage of the Comte de Paris's daughter to Dom Carlos of Portugal (who succeeded to the throne of his country as King Carlos I in 1889, and was assassinated in Lisbon in 1908 with his elder son, Louis, Duke of Braganza). The exiled Comte de Paris and the Duke of Orleans settled in England, and the Duke, having finished his education at the Royal Military College, Sandhurst, had a year in India serving with a British regiment. After further military studies in Switzerland he went to Paris, in defiance of the terms of his exile, and demanded the right to do three years' military service, at that time obligatory on every Frenchman. He was arrested, lodged in the Conciergerie, and tried and sentenced to two years' imprisonment for having infringed the exile law, but the French government pardoned him after some months and released him from prison, then escorted him from the country.

He went back to England, and soon afterwards, in 1890, he and Nellie Melba met and fell in love. Looking back on their association after some seventy years, it seems possible that her love was the more lasting. Although the duke was ardent enough at the time—indiscreetly so perhaps—his passion was in the nature of a young man's infatuation for a mature woman; that it could ever have been the basis of a lasting marriage is doubtful. For a year or two Melba filled his horizon, but the possibility that he would marry her never existed; even if the objections to a marriage between the Bourbon heir apparent (who took his destiny with all seriousness) and an Australian commoner could have been removed, she was a married woman and the Duke was a Roman Catholic. His church would never have sanctioned such an alliance.

Melba went to Russia in February 1891, at the command of Czar Alexander III, and with Jean de Reszke and Edouard de Reszke gave a memorable performance of *Roméo et Juliette* at the Imperial Theatre, St Petersburg. Her singing was rapturously applauded by a tall and elegant young man sitting alone in a box; this was the Duke of Orleans, and since Russian court etiquette prescribed that nobody should applaud until the Czar did so the Duke's box was the target of a barrage of indignant stares. Alexander III was displeased and sent an emissary to tell this forward young man that St Petersburg, and Holy Russia, would be happy if he would take his leave.

Philippe had no wish to quit his beloved's side but since the Little Father made no secret of his intention to enforce the suggestion the Duke left.

He and Melba continued to be glimpsed, dining, driving and strolling together, in London, Paris, Brussels and elsewhere, and showing, for a married woman and a young nobleman, a rather indiscreet absorption in one another. Then they threw their hats right over the windmill, by travelling to Vienna together, and one night were recognized sitting *tête-à-tête* in a box at the opera. The next day this item of gossip was prominently published in the *Wiener Tageblatt.* Why not? The story that the Duke of Orleans and one of the greatest singers of the day were on sufficiently close terms to share a box at the opera was worth printer's ink any time in the gossip-loving Vienna of the Habsburgs. The inescapable implication that they were doubtless sharing greater intimacies gave the item first-class news value.

Vienna was already buzzing with the story before Melba saw it in print; she was too occupied to be reading newspapers. It was pointed out to her, probably more in malice than in friendship, by Blanche Marchesi, who also happened to be visiting Vienna, and must have secretly rejoiced in what she saw as the moral unmasking of 'the worst woman I ever knew'. For this was a disaster for Nellie Melba at a time when she was riding high. It could have ruined her, or perhaps it is only true to say it could have ruined a lesser singer; she was too great a singer to be totally wrecked by such a storm, but her career could have been badly hurt. The repercussions were alarming enough. Melba and the Duke cut short their visit to Vienna and went back to London by ostentatiously separate routes, but the gossip, once started, moved faster than they could travel. Charles Armstrong, never a patient man, had long chafed under his role of the husband in name only; to submit to being publicly proclaimed an uncomplaining cuckold was too much, and he instructed his solicitors to file a petition for divorce on the ground of his wife's adultery with the Duke of Orleans.

The Comte de Paris was furious when this burst of undesired limelight fell on the House of Bourbon. The Duke of Orleans did everything he could to evade service of the divorce papers and for a time succeeded, by keeping on the move about Europe, surrounded by attendants who formed a protective screen between him and any stranger resembling a process-server. Then one evening he arrived by train at Vienna, and according to a contemporary newspaper account 'was approached by a gentleman in evening dress, who, with many profound obeisances, handed some papers to the Prince as if he were presenting a petition or an humble address. The Duke glanced at the papers, and as soon as he became aware of their contents he angrily threw them on the ground, shouting something after the unknown individual who served them, and who hastily disappeared. The papers, which were scattered on the ground, were picked up by the Duke's attendants.' These were the divorce papers, and once they had been formally served Armstrong and his solicitors took all measures to press the action.

On the simple facts it seemed there could be only one outcome. Betting men in London clubs, where anything from the sex of an unborn royal baby to the result of a legal *cause célèbre* was apt to be the subject of wagers, offered good odds that the wronged husband would win hands down. It was not so simple. The Duke's legal advisers, reasoning that time was on their side, used every device to make the slow-grinding mills of the law grind slower than ever, and managed to delay a hearing for many months. Then suddenly the case was dropped. It has always been supposed that Armstrong yielded either to appeals or pressure from British diplomatic quarters, which were perturbed by the annoyance this protracted legal wrangle was giving to some influential sections of French opinion. At all events the case of Armstrong versus Armstrong, the Duke of Orleans co-respondent, dropped out of the English divorce lists in October 1892 and never reappeared in them.

It was the end for Melba and the Duke. He went off on a two-year safari in Africa; apparently his heart was mended when he returned, because soon afterwards, in 1896, he married the Archduchess Maria Dorothea, daughter of the Archduke Joseph, son of the last Palatine of Hungary; the marriage was childless, and the Duke died of pneumonia at Palermo on 28 March 1926. The Bourbon cause had lost ground in France over the years, and the news item in which the London *Times* reported his death ran to only twenty-two lines.

It was also the end for Charles Armstrong and Melba. He divorced her in Texas in 1900, charging that she had deserted him in 1894; this seems to have been a mere technicality to satisfy the letter of the law, since they were effectively parted some years before 1894, but Melba, who did not appear, formally denied the allegation through counsel. She was relieved when the marriage ended; all through the

1890s she was haunted by the fear that Armstrong would walk back into her life, and imperil her social and professional standing.

The world did not forget. The great French diseuse, Yvette, who had made her reputation in the *café-concert* world of Paris, was appearing in New York when Melba was singing in the 1895–6 season at the Metropolitan Opera House. Someone suggested to Melba that she should lunch with her sister celebrity from the other side of the tracks.

'With that chanteuse?' Melba scoffed. 'At the most, she might have been invited to come for dessert, for a fee, to sing one of her couplets.'

Yvette had a sharp tongue, too. 'I quite understand,' she replied with mock humility when Melba's words were reported to her. 'I am of humble birth, but Madame Melba of course belongs to the royal family of France.'

Remembering that the Australian was the former mistress of the French Pretender, New Yorkers hooted with joy.

Melba hit back hard. She, along with Plançon and Nordica, was billed to sing at the Metropolitan in a benefit concert for the French Hospital, in which Yvette was also listed to appear. Melba urged the organizers to drop Yvette from the programme. Yvette stood on the terms of her agreement and refused to be dropped. Melba then cancelled her own appearance and persuaded Plançon and Nordica to withdraw also. Yvette sang, but the occasion had lost much of its glitter.

When the divorce action, Armstrong versus Armstrong, petered out in the English courts Melba had to hide her wounds and go on with her life. She knew her personal reputation had suffered, but she was right in believing the damage was not irreparable, given time. It is true that Queen Victoria rebuked her by commanding a performance of *Faust* at Windsor Castle and naming, for the role of Marguerite, not Melba, the greatest Marguerite of the day, but Albani, a fine soprano and still a Covent Garden star at that time, but ageing then and even at her peak never Melba's equal. Melba accepted the royal snub and said nothing. There was nothing to say. The only thing she could do was wait for the storm to blow over. She knew it was just a matter of patience.

She was probably more worried about her father's displeasure than the Queen's, but David Mitchell accepted the storm and its aftermath as an accomplished fact, if not altogether a palatable one. He once told an old friend, 'My girl Nellie had a bad temper and

Charlie Armstrong had a bad temper. They lost their tempers on the same day.' That was an over-simplification, and David Mitchell was too acute not to know it, but if he ever spoke harsher words about Nellie's broken marriage they are not on record.

12

NELLIE MELBA probably never knew real loneliness until her romance with the Duke of Orleans ended; after that she was for some years often painfully alone. The heaviest blow of all was her discovery one day that her little son had been taken from her.

The boy had spent most of his early years in France, but his mother, and even more emphatically his father, wished him to grow up in an English environment. So, although they were estranged, they agreed that he should go as a boarder to a preparatory school at Littlehampton, in Sussex. He was entered there when he was ten or eleven, and arrived, a strange and shy little boy, looking more French than English, and even speaking English with a slight French accent. To the other boys he was an oddity; they dubbed him 'Froggie', and this made him more self-conscious and awkward than ever. George had been at school for some months when his father arrived one day, accompanied by an older brother, Montague, and told the boy he was taking him on a long journey; within an hour or two his clothing was packed and he and his father and uncle drove away. A few days later father and son took ship for America. Some time was to pass before Melba found out that George and his father were living on a farm in Texas. It was nearly ten years before George Armstrong, by that time a young man whose formal education had been neglected, although he had been transformed into nearly as fine a horseman as his father, was to be reunited with his mother and to see England again.

Although the demands for Melba's services as a singer were many times as great as she could meet, and although her social engagement book was always full, there was yet an emptiness at the heart of her life which mere activity could not dispel. She had many friends; most of these were the fair-weather friends who collect around any celebrity, hoping to catch a little reflected glory, but a few were men and women who liked to be with her because she was good company. Her taste in friends was cosmopolitan, and she was never chauvinistic in choosing them, but in the aftermath of her break with the Duke of Orleans she showed a liking for the company of Australians. She made particularly close friends at that time of two Australians living in London, the sculptor Bertram Mackennal, and the playwright Haddon Chambers. For some years these three were much together; she and Mackennal remained friends until she died in 1931, a few months before his death, but her friendship with Chambers burnt itself out quickly, because he was more devoted to her than she to him.

Melba first met Haddon Chambers in 1895, and was taken by his wit and zestful charm, by the mercurial liveliness of his mind, and by his striking, and astonishingly youthful, good looks. He was a year older than Melba, and so in the middle thirties then, but he looked ten years younger and was a physical as well as a conversational ornament to any party. Having been born in Australia of Irish parents, he settled in London in 1882, and within ten years made a substantial reputation as a writer of plays, which were popular in London, America and Australia. None of his plays had any lasting value, but they were pleasantly entertaining in their day; some of them, including *Captain Swift*, *The Idler*, *John o' Dreams*, *The Tyranny of Tears*, and *Passers-by*, were extremely successful and brought him a large income.

He was important in Melba's life chiefly because he helped to develop her stage personality. Just before their first meeting he was toying with the idea of turning one of his plays into a libretto for an opera and went one afternoon to discuss the project with Henry Russell, an old friend. The talk turned to Melba, and Chambers said, 'What a pity that she is so cold. Her voice is the most divine thing in the world, and if someone could only teach her to act she would be perfect.' Russell was expecting Melba for supper that evening, and asked Chambers to stay and meet her. He recalled later: 'Few people knew more about the stage at that time than Haddon, and Melba realized at once how much she could learn from her talented compatriot. The friendship grew and the diva undoubtedly benefited by the care that Haddon bestowed on every new role she learnt, teaching her gradually to be an intelligent actress. I remember Melba telling me how grateful she was for his assistance and how she considered her art had improved by her association with him.' This is a debt that Melba forgot when she worked on her autobiography some thirty years later; Haddon Chambers is nowhere mentioned, whether as an acting coach or a friend. She talks of the guidance in the fine points of acting and make-up which Sarah Bernhardt gave her, but poor Chambers, who contributed far more to her stagecraft, is overlooked. It is a little reminiscent of the obliteration of Pietro Cecchi as her singing teacher.

Melba was never a great actress—on the stage at least. Critics were apt to dismiss her attempts at acting as the fumblings of a determined but untalented novice, even though, ironically, on her Covent Garden début in 1888 most of the London critics ignored her singing and praised her acting! Percy Colson, who knew her well, admired her as a singer, and liked her in a wry kind of way, said she 'was never able to call up a look of tragedy more intense than that of a lady who has forgotten the name of the gentleman who is taking her out to supper and doesn't want to hurt his feelings.' Yet some of those who watched her career considered her to be, if not a gifted actress, at least competent by the standards of Italian grand opera. Phil Finkelstein, for many years on the executive staff of J. C. Williamson Limited, Australia, who was closely associated with the management of the 1924 and 1928 Melba-Williamson grand opera seasons in Australia, although a hard-bitten man of the theatre, said, 'Melba was primarily a singer, but she was also a very good actress.' Her dressing-room in Melbourne, in the 1924 season, was next to Finkelstein's room, and he recalled how, when *Otello* was the opera of the night, he would hear 'a tiny ghost of exquisite melody issuing from Melba's room', in the interval between the third and last acts. It was the Willow Song, and Melba habitually sang herself into the mood of the last act by crooning the aria to herself. 'I would listen to this thread of melody, and then I would hear the dressing-room door open and, looking out, would see, not Melba, but Desdemona's self, stately, sad, wronged, passing on her way to her doom.'

But it was as a singer that the people of her own time went to hear her, and as a singer that she lives. It was also as a singer that Giacomo Puccini selected her as the ideal Mimi for *La Bohème*. Melba went to Lucca, the town in which Puccini was born in 1858; there, among the hills of Tuscany, she spent six weeks studying Mimi's part under the supervision of Puccini, who worked with her for some hours nearly every day, annotating her score of the opera with his own hand.

Puccini was possibly influenced to choose Melba by the knowledge that *Bohème* was having a battle to establish itself in London and America. After making a shaky start in Italy, on its première at Turin in 1896 (incidentally, with the young Toscanini as conductor), it had begun to be accepted by Italian opera-goers, but neither in England nor America had it roused much enthusiasm. This is surprising now, when *Bohème* is perhaps the most popular of all Italian operas in English-speaking countries, but it was understandable at the time; both in England, where it was first played by the Carl Rosa Company at Manchester in 1897, and in New York, where it arrived in 1898, it was presented by hard-working but not particularly gifted casts, who were unable to sing Puccini's music well enough to make the feathery drama of the piece seem plausible.

Melba saw the possibilities; she liked and admired Puccini, but was too careful of her professional reputation ever to put months of study into a part unless she believed it would add something to her name. At all events she was convinced from the start of the merits of *Bohème*. After its English première in Manchester, the Carl Rosa Company brought *Bohème* to London and staged it twice in the course of a short minor season at Covent Garden in 1897, but with little success; after that the Covent Garden Syndicate did not want to put it on, because they believed it would fail, but Melba, using all her power bullied them into producing it on 1 July 1899. The love affair between Covent Garden audiences and *Bohème* began then and has never ended. The love affair between Melba and Mimi was nearly as lasting; she continued to sing it until her retirement. Nothing else in grand opera seems to have so pleased her as did Mimi's scintillating and tuneful music; it fitted her voice and temperament and spirit in the very way that Wagner's music did not. Not all Puccini's operas were made in heaven for Melba. She hankered to sing *Tosca* and nearly did so once, but was saved by a benevolent fate; the part was not for her. Nor was *Madama Butterfly*. Melba said Puccini wrote *Butterfly* for her, and she studied the part with him, but some element in it eluded her and she never sang it on the stage. Yet as Mimi she was unequalled.

Mary Garden, the Scottish soprano, who professed to like Melba but had little reason to, wrote, 'I never saw such a fat Mimi in my life. Melba didn't impersonate the role at all—she never did that— but, my God, how she sang it.' Mary Garden described the way Melba sang the high C, which comes at the end of the first act, as 'the strangest and weirdest thing I have experienced in my life', and went on: 'The note came floating over the auditorium of Covent Garden; it left Melba's throat, it left Melba's body, it left everything, and came over like a star and passed us in our box, and went out into the infinite. I have never heard anything like it in my life, not from any other singer, ever. It just rolled over the hall of Covent Garden. My God, how beautiful it was!

'Since then I always wait for that note when I hear the first act of *Bohème*, and they reach and reach for it, and then they scream it, and it's underneath and it's false, and it rolls down the stairs, and it never comes out from behind that door, never. That note of Melba's was just like a ball of light. It wasn't attached to anything at all—it was out of everything.'

On the other hand Elena Gerhardt, the German soprano, was not impressed. She said: 'I still remember how disappointed I was when I heard Melba for the first time, at Covent Garden, singing Mimi in *Bohème*. She did not move me for a moment, not even in the dying scene in the last act. Of course, hers was a lovely silvery voice, clear as crystal, but also as icy. And the same in *Traviata*. She had this incomparable thrill and fluency in her coloratura, but how common it sounded when she forced her lower notes up to F and even G from the chest register! I do not believe she would be so much admired now, although people still get drunk with enthusiasm when they hear an unusually beautiful voice, and are prepared to forgive any faults.'*

The rulers of the Metropolitan Opera House, New York, were no more enthusiastic than the Covent Garden Syndicate about *Bohème* until it proved itself. They did not want to stage it, but Melba kept at them until they gave in; she was a persistent woman. Although she was the Metropolitan's first Mimi, on 26 December 1900, *Bohème* was only tolerably successful. Henry Krehbiel, in the *New York Tribune*, damned it as 'foul in subject, and fulminant but futile in music'; he found that Puccini's attempts to express passion were superficial, and depended upon 'strident phrases pounded out by hitting each note a blow on the head as it escapes from the mouths of the singers or the accompanying instruments.' Krehbiel approved most of the singers, including Melba, but gave his verdict that *Bohème* was 'not her opera'. These findings must rank among the most resounding critical clangers of all time, for, although *Bohème* was dropped from the repertoire the next season, it was

* The findings of Mary Garden and Elena Gerhardt illustrate the way in which Melba's singing could rouse conflicting opinions in equally well-qualified judges.

A LIGHT DUET.
Mimi Melba having got the right key from Rodolfo Caruso.

© *Punch Ltd*

then restored, and had been heard 400 times at the Metropolitan by the end of the 1960–61 season.

Melba sang Mimi to the Rodolfo of scores of tenors, beginning with Fernando de Lucia at Covent Garden in 1899, and ending with a fellow Australian, Browning Mummery, at Melbourne in 1928. The greatest of all her Rodolfos was Enrico Caruso, the only singer of the time whose combination of vocal splendours matched hers. She and Caruso first sang together at Monte Carlo in 1902, and *Bohème* was their first opera. Caruso made his Covent Garden début later that year in *Rigoletto* with Melba as Gilda, and ten days later the two sang their first London *Bohème*. Rosenthal says 'His Rodolfo . . . did most perhaps to establish his fame in London, and he and Melba made the popular reputation of the Puccini opera in this country.'

She liked singing with Caruso, of whom she once said: 'The higher he sings the more easy it seems to him. In the third act of *Bohème* I always feel as if our two voices had merged into one.'

He was not however the greatest tenor of the age to her. She was visiting Australia when he died at Naples on 2 August 1921. The newspapers went to her, and she paid a warm tribute to him as a singer, but said that the greatest tenor was Jean de Reszke – the 'dear Jean' of her early years as a prima donna. Caruso's sense of fun, which had an exuberant peasant simplicity, did not amuse her much; for one thing he did not keep his jests off the stage, and Melba was too businesslike a singer to find pleasure in practical jokes which threatened the quality of her performance. Once in *Bohème* while singing *Che gelida manina* (Your tiny hand is frozen) to her, he pressed into her hand a hot sausage which he had had his dresser heat over a spirit lamp in the wings. Yelping with shock, Melba flipped the sausage into the air and it bounced across the stage. She gritted out a few choked words of anger, but Caruso's superb voice continued with the love-song. Then in a pause for breath he whispered, 'English lady, you like sausage?' Caruso also laughed too heartily once when her dignity – and taste-buds – were hurt. She habitually chewed chewing-gum, or for preference a piece of Australian wattle gum, on opera or concert nights to keep her mouth and throat moist. Making an entrance at Covent Garden, she took her gum from her mouth and put it on a little glass shelf, provided for the purpose in the wings. When she came off the stage she went to the shelf, picked up her piece of gum, as she thought, and put it in her mouth. She spat it out and two or three strong words with it. A stagehand had substituted a quid of tobacco for the gum. Melba demanded that all the stagehands should be sacked, but she was probably less furious with them than with Caruso, who thought the incident was the best joke of the Covent Garden season and went about backstage bellowing with laughter, his eyes shining with tears of joy. And Melba knew it was of no use her demanding his dismissal.

13

AT any given time in her adult life Melba had a number of close friends who were associated with her professional career; this was not merely a matter of cultivating people who could be professionally useful to her, but also of enjoying the society of men and women – preponderantly men – who understood her language and could talk it.

Apart from John Lemmone, she probably never had a closer platonic friendship with any man than with the French composer Herman Bemberg, who was born in Paris two years before she was born, and died in Switzerland in 1931, the year she died in Sydney. Bemberg was a typical young exquisite of the 1890s; his talent was minor but his manners were impeccable, and no woman of fashion could have asked to be squired in Paris or London by a more engagingly gilded youth. He was of enormous value to Melba's self-esteem in the years immediately after her break with the Duke of Orleans.

She knew Bemberg before she met the Duke, so their friendship was well established when that affair ended. She wrote later that if Bemberg 'had not been a rich man, he would have made an imperishable name for himself either as a composer or a clown.' This finding is too eulogistic. Bemberg composed some tuneful music, and a few of his ballads are still heard now and then. His four-act opera *Elaine*, which George Bernard Shaw found 'inanely pretty' was written for Melba. Shaw dismissed Bemberg as 'a music-weaver who, having served an apprenticeship to Gounod, and mastered his method of working, now sets up in business for himself. In *Elaine* we have the well-known Gounod fabric turned out in lengths like the best sort of imitation Persian carpet, the potential supply being practically unlimited.' It was only through Melba's influence that *Elaine* was ever performed at Covent Garden and the Metropolitan Opera House, New York, each time with casts which she headed.

Melba's musical taste always ran to prettiness rather than grandeur, and she sang Bemberg's songs with enthusiasm, but did not hesitate to tell him when he composed something she disliked or found unsingable. He wrote for her probably his most widely known ballad, *Nymphes et sylvains*. She looked at it for a few minutes, then told him, 'You don't know the limitations on what a soprano can do.' After she had expanded her criticism he altered the song to meet her objections.

Perhaps she considered *Elaine* to be a masterpiece of its kind, but a suspicion lingers that her admiration for Bemberg was inspired by what she saw as his genius for clowning first, and his genius for music only second. In *Melodies and Memories* she told at length of the practical jokes he played on her, and of those she played on him in retaliation; they were possibly funny in the doing, but they are conspicuously unfunny to read about, these elaborate capers in which Bemberg ordered tens of dozens of boxes of cakes to be sent to her Paris apartment until it overflowed with them and she retorted by coating the inside of his hat with black greasepaint, cutting his umbrella so it would fall to pieces when opened, and putting an egg in each of his overcoat pockets. Melba's idea of fun was never conspicuously subtle; her preference was always for the hurtling custard pie over the epigram. Anyone acquainted with this element in her nature could at times achieve astonishing results in business dealings with her. Long after the skylarking days with Bemberg were behind her, an Australian bank in which she had an account needed her signature on a certain document. For reasons of peasant caution which do not matter here, she kept refusing to sign, and her bank manager was desperate. He could have forced a lesser client's hand, but Melba, a privileged personage, could only be coaxed. She called one day and after other matters had been discussed the manager laid the unsigned document on the table before her and begged her to complete it.

'No,' she said.

'Then, Dame Nellie,' he told her, knowing that logical argument would achieve nothing, 'I shall sing to you!'

She gazed at him in mock horror for a moment, then exclaimed, 'Give me the bloody pen!' and scrawled her dashing signature across the document.

The very qualities of mind which made her enjoy Bemberg's schoolboyish idiocies meant that she was little impressed when she met the greatest wit of the day, Oscar Wilde (who dedicated his play, *A Woman of No Importance*, to Melba's friend, Lady de Grey). Melba told of her meeting with him later and of the 'brilliant fiery-coloured chain of words' which fell from 'his coarse lips'. She seems to have felt no impulse to establish a friendship with him, as she did with Haddon Chambers, Bemberg and a few others; nor did he, on his side, appear to be interested in her personality, although he said to her, 'Ah, Madame Melba, I am the Lord of Language, and you are the Queen of Song, and I suppose I shall have to write to you a sonnet.' Melba had another story of Wilde, however. As she told it, she was walking in Paris three years after he was sent to prison in 1895, when 'there lurched round the corner a tall shabby man, his collar turned up to his neck, a hunted look in his eyes'.

'Madame Melba,' he said, 'you don't know who I am? I'm Oscar Wilde, and I'm going to do a terrible thing. I'm going to ask you for money.'

Melba had about ten louis (20-franc pieces) in her purse, which she handed to him. He 'almost snatched it—muttered a word of thanks and was gone'. She never saw him again.

This story must be regarded as one of her more ambitious melodramatizations. Hesketh Pearson commented: 'All we need to say is that Wilde, whose attitude to women was chivalrous to a degree that would nowadays be considered affected, did not borrow money from them, and was scrupulously careful, after his downfall, never to speak to any of the famous women he had once known unless they made the first step. . . . It happens that at about the time when the Melba meeting was supposed to have taken place he met a man to whom he had once lent money; and when [Robert] Ross asked whether he had suggested repayment of the loan, he replied that he had not: "Gentlemanly feelings linger in the most improbable places. . . . If I could have the feelings appropriate to my position – or rather my lack of position – it would be better for me – but while natures alter, what is artificial is permanent always." '

A greater realist than Melba never walked, but at times she was capable of seeing life in the most absurd operatic terms—if it was good enough for Verdi or Puccini it was good enough for her! Whatever Wilde's shortcomings he was never a furtive beggar in a scene from grand opera. The costume would not have fitted him.

14

ALTHOUGH Melba evidently found Wilde's wit disconcerting, she liked the companionship of men and women who were successful in writing, painting, composing, or any other of the creative arts. As a schoolgirl she learned the rudiments of painting and then, and also later, before her marriage, did some watercolour landscapes of an orthodox kind; these were of reasonable amateur standard but revealed no special talent.

While concentrating all her personal energies on singing she continued to be interested in painting as a connoisseur, and her purchases showed a well-developed taste. Norman Lindsay, whom she visited several times at Springwood, in the Blue Mountains of New South Wales, in the last decade of her life, said, 'She always insisted on going to the studio and looking over my works there, and this was no mere courteous gesture, for she was genuinely interested in painting, and had an unquestionable good taste in selecting examples of it.' On a visit to Melbourne, Lindsay found Melba's Australian home, Coombe Cottage, at Coldstream, 'full of examples of the best Australian painters' work'. Her collection included pictures by Arthur Streeton, Hans Heysen, J. J. Hilder, Lionel Lindsay and Norman Lindsay himself, Elioth Gruner and many other esteemed Australian artists of the time.

However far she might be from Australia and however long she stayed away, Melba never lost her love of the Australian landscape. When the young Hans Heysen returned to Australia in 1903, after studying in Europe, and began to paint landscapes, and in particular the studies of gum trees which made his name, Melba was enchanted by his work. She bought many of his pictures and told her friends, 'This is the coming man.' Her partisanship had a strong influence in pushing Hans Heysen's prices up.

She did not confine her patronage of Australian art to buying pictures for her walls, but, as her means grew with her professional success, also dipped into her pocket, often deep, to give direct help to some young artist in whom she saw talent. She had to recognize talent for herself, of course; resourceful opportunists sometimes tried to lure her into helping them, but she was proof against such approaches. She travelled from Australia to England in 1908 in the RMS *Orontes*. One of the passengers was a man with large artistic ambitions and small abilities, and, knowing Melba's reputation as a patron of art and artists, he unpacked some of his canvases one day, and ostentatiously put them on show in the passenger lounge. The great moment arrived; Melba walked into the lounge and her eyes travelled from one uninspired painting to another.

'Good God!' she exclaimed, and went on and out of the lounge without breaking her stride.

Melba's Scottish blood always rebelled against the thought of wasting money. She was not cheeseparing once she decided to support some deserving cause or some deserving individual, but if she found reason to suppose that either the cause or the individual had ceased to be deserving she would close her purse with a definitive snap, and when she did that the purse stayed closed. A young

Australian artist, Ambrose Patterson, whose brother Tom was married to Melba's sister, Belle, found out to his cost that the diva's protégés must toe the line she drew or take the consequences. In 1901, aged twenty-four, he was in New York, working as a cartoonist on the *New York Herald*. Melba arrived on a concert tour accompanied by one of her sisters, Dora Mitchell, who arranged a meeting with young Patterson. Melba became interested in his work, and gave him a cheque for $200, telling him to go back to Paris, where he had studied earlier for a year or so until his money ran out, 'and be a gentleman and I'll see you through'. The understanding was that she would give him enough money to study in Paris for five years, and he joyfully packed his few belongings and went back to Paris to fulfil himself and justify Melba's faith in him.

All went well for about two years. Then Patterson fell in love with an English girl, whose parents were living in Belgium, and married her. He did not tell Melba, but word of the marriage reached her and she at once stopped his allowance, saying she had agreed to help him, not so he could marry, but so he could study painting. He and his wife, who had a baby daughter by this time, were soon deep in debt. They worried through in Europe for as long as they could, then took a ship for Australia, where relatives and friends helped them to find their feet. Later, with a family enlarged to two girls and a boy, they went to Honolulu, and some years afterwards the marriage broke up and ended in divorce.

Ambrose Patterson, who in 1903 had been elected Sociétaire of the Salon d'Automne, Paris, and had exhibited work in Paris, London and Brussels, and then in Australia, continued to paint and made a small but respected name as an artist in America and Europe, and a larger reputation in America as a teacher of painting; he was for some years Professor of Art in the University of Washington, Seattle, and retired in 1947. Some of his friends felt Melba was heartless in jettisoning him merely because he had married without consulting her, but as far as is known nobody ever dared to tell her so; nobody ever much liked telling her such things.

Her taste in painting was uncomplicated. She probably preferred landscapes to anything else and Australian landscapes above any others. A contributory reason for her abandonment of Ambrose Patterson was his adoption of a French painting style; she believed Australian artists should paint unmistakably Australian scenes in an unmistakably Australian way, as Hans Heysen did. At the same time she had an eye for quality in a painter, as she showed when she came to the help of Hugh Ramsay, who died in 1906 and sixty years later was still widely considered to be among the finest artists Australia had produced. Ramsay ranks as an Australian because, although he was born in Glasgow in 1878, his parents took him to live in Melbourne when he was a baby. Having done his early study there, he did not go to Europe for further study until 1900, with the foundations of his painting style already laid.

In Paris Ramsay studied at Colarossi's, and shared a studio with another Australian painter, James MacDonald. Their neighbour on one side was Ambrose Patterson, who one day took Melba to their studio. Liking Ramsay's work, she invited him to visit her in London, and promised to help him find a footing there. He went to London soon afterwards, and Melba welcomed him, introduced him to influential people, and commissioned him to paint her portrait. He was the very kind of young man of whom Melba approved. He lived for his work, and cared for nothing else; he was always up soon after dawn, putting in an hour or two at his easel before breakfast, and at night he would stay up late painting by the light of an oil lamp and at last tumble into bed, exhausted. Melba understood such industry. It was the kind of thing she had done herself.

Given two or three years, Ramsay would probably have made a big European reputation, but incessant work and sketchy meals damaged his health, and he went down with tuberculosis of the lungs. His doctor told him to get away to a warm climate. Why not Australia? There was one obstacle; Ramsay had no money. He went to Melba who at once wrote him a cheque for £100, to pay his fare and leave something in his pocket when he got home.

She found him in Melbourne when she arrived there in 1902, on her first visit to her homeland since she had gone away in 1886. His health was still troublesome, but he was doing a little painting and had added a few canvases to those he had brought home from abroad. Melba, who rented a large house in the fashionable Melbourne suburb of Toorak for the period of her Australian stay, looked at Ramsay's pictures and said, 'I know, we'll have an exhibition at my house.' She organized a three-day exhibition in the ballroom, and most of the pictures were sold, giving Ramsay a substantial sum and enabling him to live for at least a few months without worrying about food bills and rent.

Within a year of Melba's return to London he was able to write to her and report that he was painting as prolifically as ever, and probably better than he had ever painted before. But it was a mere interlude. Tuberculosis flared again, and he died in 1906. He was only twenty-nine, but left enough work behind him, including two or three portraits of Melba and other portraits commissioned by her, to give him a secure place among Australian artists of his own or any time.

But painters who accepted commissions from Melba did not always find her easy to please. It was ironical if human that she, who was quick to resent any attempt by a layman to tell her how she should sing an aria or a ballad, believed herself qualified to tell a painter how he should paint a picture. She commissioned Ramsay to paint a portrait of her father. When it was finished she examined it with critical eyes, then said: 'Oh, no. I don't like the way you've painted the hands. You've made them look very rough. That won't do at all.'

'Well,' said Ramsay, who had painted a faithful likeness as he saw it of David Mitchell's hard-working hands, 'that's the way they look to me, and I'm not going to alter them. I'll paint gloves on them if you like.'

Melba told him not to trouble, but she never liked the portrait and in 1924 presented it to the Castlemaine Art Gallery, one of Victoria's leading country galleries. The gallery rates it a good Ramsay but not one of his best. Connoisseurs have given the opinion that the ungloved hands are among its most striking points.

15

ALL through the 1890s Melba added to her triumphs, both in London and America, and also in the great opera houses of the Continent. As the nineteenth century ended and the twentieth century came in she was secure on her own mountain-top, even though her reputation never stood quite so high on the Continent, except possibly in Paris, Brussels and Monte Carlo, as in London and New York. So her life was full and triumphantly successful. When she travelled she was accompanied by a small but imposing entourage, like a minor potentate. And yet the need to know that she shone in her family's eyes as well as the world's was ever-present; although she was the one child of David Mitchell's who had won world renown she ceaselessly craved the approval of the others.

Always a vigorous and fluent letter-writer, she constantly wrote home to Australia, sending a stream of letters, mostly undated, which were penned in her strong and dashing handwriting, each with many words underlined for emphasis. To read her letters is like listening to the talk of a woman with positive views on everything and a lively interest in all events of public moment.

The South African War cast a shadow on her life, but not an intolerably dark one. The news in letters from Australia that her brother Ernest had volunteered to go to South Africa with an Australian contingent stirred conflicting emotions in her. On the one hand, she was proud that her youngest brother should have enlisted as a soldier; on the other, his action confirmed her suspicions that he was not dedicated to his vocal studies and had no real ambition to make a career as a singer. She could never work up much interest in the dilettante who was content to sing, play, paint or do anything else just to amuse himself and a few friends; she had no time to waste on any man or woman, no matter how talented, who was not driven by inner forces to achieve professional success.

As her own success grew so did her spirit of dictatorial maternalism toward her family, and she fell into the habit of telling her sisters how they should furnish their houses, bring up their children, and generally order their lives. At one time, when her enthusiasm for the British royal family was running high, she acquired a matching enthusiasm for the Established Church, and wrote to Australia advising her sisters to see that their children adopted the Church of England creed. Melba's own religious record was somewhat mixed. She was born a Presbyterian, and was taken as a child to worship at Scots Church, Melbourne, or at the Presbyterian Church in Lennox Street, Richmond; for some time in her teens she had an active association with the Richmond church, and as well as singing in the choir played the harmonium at the Sunday services. She was however confirmed in a Church of England at Mackay, in Queensland, and after that had her mercenary flirtation with Rome as a member of St Francis's choir, in Melbourne. She appears never to have been irrevocably committed to any denomination. When nearing sixty she told an Australian protégée, Stella Power, 'You know, Stella, if I were any religion I'd be a Catholic like you.' She told other friends she would have liked to be a Christian Scientist. In practice however she alternated impartially between the

Presbyterian and Anglican communions. She was buried from Scots Church, Melbourne, but only after the family had rejected a proposal from the then Anglican Archbishop of Melbourne, who urged that she should be buried from St Paul's Cathedral. Even in death, it seems, the patronage of Australia's most celebrated daughter was coveted by a great church.

On the whole Melba's sisters tended to listen to her advice, unless it conflicted too strongly with their own ideas. They saw her as a remarkable woman, inhabiting a social milieu far higher than any to be found in Australia and therefore the custodian of knowledge they could profitably heed. She was generous in the gifts she sent home, whether to her brothers and sisters or their children; but some of her school-age nephews and nieces wished she had chosen the items of clothing she presented to them with more knowledge of what the well-dressed Australian child of the time was wearing. These garments were always expensive, and doubtless highly suitable for the French or English child, but oftentimes quite inappropriate for an Australian, and some of the recipients suffered agonies of embarrassment when they were sent to school wearing Auntie Nellie's gifts. She sent a young nephew a hand-stitched blouse, made by one of the leading fashion-houses of Paris. The small boy was dressed in the blouse to go to a children's party. Knowing the ridicule awaiting him, he went outside, dipped his hands in mud and smeared the offending blouse until it was unwearable.

Melba's door in London, Paris, New York or wherever she chanced to be was always open to any members of her family; they were welcome to go to her whenever they chose and stay as long as they pleased. Her youngest sister, Dora, then in the twenties, joined her in America in 1901, and went back to England with her. They had not met since Melba left Australia in 1886, when Dora was twelve; meanwhile Dora had developed a strong personality of her own, and the two temperaments collided now and then with some violence. Sisterly regard survived these jolts, and they parted amicably enough, but a visit by Belle was more successful.

Belle and her husband, Tom Patterson, a Melbourne business man, were the parents of three boys and a girl when Melba wrote urging her to come to England, bringing with her the two younger children, Nellie and David. From the time Melba became a prima donna she always had an imperious way with her, and saw nothing odd in her proposal that Belle should leave her husband and two older boys for some months. The Pattersons had a deep affection for her, however, and decided that Belle, and Nellie and David, should make the trip. This they did, and spent some months in 1901 living with Melba at Quarrywood Cottage, a house on the Thames at Marlow in Buckinghamshire, which she leased for the summer.

Musical, financial and social lions constantly came and went at Quarrywood Cottage. Landon Ronald spent a Sunday there when the great violinist, Joseph Joachim, was a house-guest, and years later was still able to chuckle over his recollections of that day: 'The heavy, ponderous, learned Hungarian fiddler, used to being listened to with awe and bated breath; and the vivacious, chaffing, light-hearted prima-donna, throwing all seriousness to the wind and heartily disliking hero-worship in her own home. They were in very truth the two extremes meeting, and yet Joachim's fascination and admiration for Melba was very real and very sincere.'

After their summer on the Thames, Belle Patterson and her two children started back to Australia in the September. Melba missed them desperately, and this made her more determined than ever to go home to Australia and sing to her own people—perhaps, above all, to her own family, and in particular her father, now over seventy, who had not heard her sing since, having shed the name and obscurity of Nellie Armstrong, she had become a world celebrity. She had toyed before with suggestions that she should make a concert tour of Australia, but thoughts of the tedious journey had discouraged her, and it was only in 1901 that she opened serious negotiations.

At first the negotiations, carried on at the Australian end through Tom Patterson, did not prosper. Melba thought the Australian entrepreneur, J. C. Williamson, was too grasping, and he took a like view of her. She knew her value, and even when Patterson cabled her the details of an offer and ended his message with the words, 'Father and all earnestly desire you may accept', she was unmoved. Experience had taught her that she had something unique to sell and that if she waited she could get her price. She was right about that. Having spurned J. C. Williamson, she entered into a contract with the Australian concert manager, George Musgrove, toward the end of 1901. She engaged herself to arrive in Australia in September 1902 and give concerts in Melbourne, Sydney, Brisbane and Adelaide. The arrangement served both her sentimental yearnings and her commercial sense; she would see her family and sing to her fellow Australians, and at the same time earn some twenty thousand pounds for her trouble. It is little wonder that her letters home bubbled with excitement as the time for her to leave drew near.

The Covent Garden season of 1902 ended on 28 July, and three days later Melba caught the ship for New York. She sailed from Vancouver six weeks later, and trod Australian soil at Brisbane for the first time in sixteen years on the night of 17 September.

16

AUSTRALIA was excited by Nellie Melba's return. Theatrical ballyhoo was then a relatively undeveloped craft, but Melba did not need it when she went home in 1902; everything about her compelled the curiosity of her fellow countrymen. First, she was the foremost singer of her time and by far the greatest singer in Australia's history, who, having gone overseas unknown, came back wrapped in glory. Second, she had defied convention by casting off her husband to become the inamorata of a nobleman who would have been the king of France if dynastic rights were immutable. If not quite the story of the peasant girl who marries the prince, it was near enough.

Australia was no less changed to her eyes than she was to Australia's. She came back to a more politically and socially sophisticated country than the one she had left; Australia was no longer a collection of loosely-linked colonies, each running its own postal, customs, and even defence services, but a commonwealth with a national parliament which had been formally opened the year before. The six colonies were now states, each with its own legislature and its own jealously guarded rights. Australia had become a nation, on paper at any rate, even though the mystique of nationhood was not to be created until Australians fought in World War I and established traditions which fused into a whole the stones of the national edifice. The link with the British Crown remained as close as ever, through the medium of the governor-general and the six state governors; many Australians still spoke of England as 'Home' and automatically looked to Britain for leadership in foreign affairs and for protection in times of trouble. But the ground was being prepared for changes in these fields also, even if Melba was to be dead before Australia realized its destiny as a nation thinking more or less independent thoughts and taking more or less independent action.

Brisbane gave her a joyous welcome, although she was to stay only overnight, then catch the train south on the thousand-mile journey to Melbourne, where her father, her brothers and sisters, and Doonside waited. In those days big oversea ships could not go up the river to Brisbane and had to dock at Pinkenba, some miles downstream, and an official party went to Pinkenba to greet her. She accepted their flowers, listened to the speeches, and replied; but she was more interested in a small boy named Jimmy Mullens, who had nothing to do with the official party but had edged on board the ship with it, and then, seizing his chance, stepped forward and presented her with a sheaf of flowers. Melba, who was often brusque and curt with adults, was always kind to children, and Jimmy Mullens captivated her. He was an office-boy working for a Brisbane business man, Edward Rees. A man in Melbourne, who was an old friend of Melba, had wired Rees asking him to have flowers delivered at Pinkenba. Rees chose Jimmy Mullens to take the flowers to the ship, and Melba was charmed by the boy's appearance and manners. She made him ride back to Brisbane with her in her reserved railway carriage; she also took a note of his and his employer's addresses and sent them tickets for the concerts she gave in Brisbane a month or so later. She remembered them both for the rest of her life, and sent them complimentary tickets whenever she was singing in a city where either of them happened to be.

Melba had a long memory for good turns done to her as well as bad ones. When she gave what was advertised as her Sydney farewell to opera twenty-two years later, Jimmy Mullens and Edward Rees, who were both living in Sydney then, were in the audience as her guests. They enjoyed her performance as Mimi to the full, even though it turned out, after all the fussings, the tears and the headlines, not to be her final farewell to Sydney audiences. Four years later she gave another Sydney farewell, and that really was the last.

She started south from Brisbane next day by rail. It was a rather dirty journey, even though she travelled in the state railway coach which the Duke and Duchess of York had used on their visit to Australia the year before, but she was cheered, and also when time permitted orated to by local bigwigs, at every stop along the way. She was also in demand for newspaper interviews, and was most willing to give her opinions on the state of music in Europe, the prospects of young Australian singers hoping to make their names in grand opera abroad, the graciousness of the royal family, and the everlasting durability of the British Empire. The reporters listened politely when she mentioned these matters, but as soon as she paused one of them would try to steer the talk to her association with the Duke of Orleans. Australians had read only gossip about the affair, then equally unsatisfying reports of the legal skirmishing in the divorce suit which had come to nothing; they also knew, from brief reports in the Australian press, that Charles Armstrong had divorced her in Texas in 1900. But public curiosity was still running high when Melba came home in 1902.

The editors who hoped to persuade Melba to open her heart in public about one of the most intimate episodes of her life did not know the woman; she would as soon have told strangers the state of her bank account. She was however too wise in the ways of newspapers and newspapermen to treat questioners with queenly dudgeon; instead she coolly parried their questions about the Duke of Orleans. The Sydney *Star* (now the *Sun*) and the *Sydney Morning Herald* each sent a reporter to board the train at Newcastle, seventy-odd miles north of Sydney, to interview her. The reporters, Bill Targett, of the *Star*, and Gerald Marr-Thompson, of the *Herald*, agreed between themselves that Targett should see her first. A tall good-looking man of engaging personality, who had served in the South African War with an Australian contingent and seen some lively action, Targett was one of Australia's most determined interviewers. He was admitted to Melba's compartment and she, watching with appreciative eyes the Australian countryside roll past outside the window, pointed and said, 'Ah, a beautiful white cockatoo!'

'That's no good to me, Madame,' Targett replied, in his tearaway style. 'Tell me what sort of a cove the Duke of Orleans is.'

Melba was unaccustomed to this blunt type of journalistic assault, but she was not thrown. She answered Targett with a peal of laughter, shook a forefinger at him, and settled back comfortably to talk about anything he wished, excepting only the Duke of Orleans. Whenever he mentioned the Duke's name she looked him straight in the eye, gave him a tomboy grin, and talked of white cockatoos, kookaburras, the scent of the Australian bush, or something equally innocuous. He put up a hard fight but conceded defeat at last, and then Melba, bidding him stay, pushed the bell and told the steward to show in the *Herald* reporter. As Marr-Thompson came in for his interview Melba glanced out of the window and said,

'Ah, a beautiful white cockatoo!', accompanying the words with a broad wink at Targett.

Melba never talked publicly about the Duke of Orleans. She sometimes mentioned him to one intimate friend or another as the years went by and the memory of the break lost its sting, but she never said much.

17

IN Melbourne the Mitchells impatiently awaited Melba's coming. They knew all her oddities, her eccentricities and her failings, but they were proud of her achievements as a singer and fond of her as a woman. There was no need to tell them that she went her own way, and went it at her own gait, regardless of what they or anyone else thought; they knew she could not have climbed from nothing to a supreme place among opera singers if she had stopped to consider the wishes of even her nearest and dearest.

David Mitchell, now seventy-four, with white hair, white beard and white moustache, and one of Victoria's wealthiest men, was not only reconciled to what Nellie had done but perhaps prouder of it than any of the others. He was too stiff-necked ever to admit that his prejudice against the stage and all this play-acting nonsense was an expression of insufferable narrow-mindedness, but he was also too staunch a supporter of the doctrine that worldly success is the reward of personal merit and hard work to do anything but rejoice in his Nellie's triumphs. If he continued to grumble against her choice of a career he did it now with a smile in his eyes and a proud undertone in his voice.

It had taken him years to comprehend the magnitude of her success. To him the theatre was an insubstantial thing; unlike the bricks that he built with and the lime dug from his quarries, which had a solid permanence, the stage and stage people seemed to him to be in danger of vanishing if an adverse wind should blow. Some years before Melba first came back to Australia he determined to find out for himself if she was really making so wonderful a career as newspaper and word-of-mouth reports said. George Musgrove was just back from a visit to Europe, and old Mitchell put on his hat and stumped along to Musgrove's Melbourne office, and sent in his card. David Mitchell's name meant little to Musgrove, but he told his secretary to show the caller in, and they faced each other across his desk.

'It's about my daughter,' Mitchell said, wasting no time. 'Is she as famous as the papers make out?'

'First,' Musgrove replied, 'you might tell me who your daughter is.'

'She calls herself Nellie Melba,' the old man said.

Musgrove blinked. Then, 'All I can tell you,' he said, 'is that your daughter is one of the great ones of this world. She's the Queen of Song.' He related some of the salient details of Melba's career, and at the end David Mitchell stood up, thanked him, and went away content.

David Mitchell travelled by train to Albury, 191 miles north of Melbourne, on the border of Victoria and New South Wales, to meet his daughter. The effort was too much for him. The physical strain of the journey added to his excitement brought him down with a stroke, and when Melba arrived in Albury he was in bed, partly paralysed, with doctors and nurses in attendance. She went to his bedside, and he told her she must go on to Melbourne.

Her welcome in Melbourne was the most remarkable ever given to any homecoming Australian anywhere in Australia; it remains so to this day. The Australians of 1902 were still a fairly homespun people, living far from Europe and its great cities, and Melba, one of themselves, came back into their midst with the prestige of a woman who had conquered all those cities, had met the bearers of the great names sitting at the centre of world affairs, and had even commanded the love of a man who, his partisans said, should wear the crown of France. It was no wonder that her own city decked itself with bunting and that people turned out in their tens of thousands, jamming the approaches to the central railway station and the streets along which her open carriage bore her. Many of those who welcomed her must have remembered that she had gone away in 1886 with merely the reputation of a competent singer driven by possibly overweening ambitions, but nobody mentioned it. The day she came home in triumph was no time to recall such things.

A few days later she made a triumphal return to Lilydale. There the people acclaimed her like a reigning queen and the local news-paper, the *Lilydale Express*, was for the occasion printed in gold

on paper tinted pale blue. The highlight of the Lilydale celebration was a picnic at David Mitchell's Cave Hill estate; quarrying
operations were suspended for the day and privileged employees
were allowed to shake the boss's famous daughter by the
hand.

Melba's homecoming tour was an unqualified success, not only
because she was still at her zenith as a singer but also because, to
Australians, she represented national aspirations and their fulfilment.
As a nation, Australia was groping for recognition, hungry to be
taken seriously by older nations. As a people, Australians still remembered the rasping of the colonial halter about their necks and
were conscious of the supposed disgrace of their beginnings as a
place of exile for the off-scourings of England's overtaxed prisons.
They laboured under a sense of inferiority and here, in the
person of Nellie Melba, the local girl who had made good, was a
corrective.

She opened her tour in Melbourne on 27 September, and gave
five concerts in the town hall – the same hall in which she had sung
at the benefit concert for Herr Elsasser in 1884, and two years later
at her own farewell concert when she had ripped off her constricting
throat ribbon while singing *Ah fors' è lui*.

The whole tour went about as smoothly as anything of the kind
ever can go. George Musgrove's arrangements were irreproachable, apart from one flaw, and that was no fault of his. He was not
to know that she would conceive an unreasoning terror of a man he
had engaged as her accompanist, Benno Sherek, a Polish pianist
settled in Australia. Melba was not normally superstitious, but now
and then she surrendered to an unaccountable fear of occult forces,
and this was one of the times. For some reason the inoffensive
Sherek frightened her, and nobody could persuade her that she
was being rather silly about it. Sherek was a born showman, and
a skilled amateur conjuror and mind-reader, with a glib routine
he had perfected to amuse himself and his friends. He demonstrated
these talents to Melba at their first meeting, and she, seeing him
as a master of dark powers, ordered Musgrove to replace him with
another accompanist as soon as possible. Years later a friend mentioned Sherek, and Melba said, shuddering, 'That man reads your
mind. He's weird, weird!' It was an illogical eccentricity in a woman
who for the most part was bluntly practical. She always put her
faith in ability, not lucky charms, but she did cherish one talisman
all her professional life. This was a piece of amber, threaded on a

black moiré ribbon. She called it her 'lucky amber' and would give it a facetiously ritualistic rub before appearing in an opera or on the concert platform.

Melba's one sorrow at her first concert was that her father was still too ill to be there; but his Scottish toughness came to his aid and he was in a place of honour at her second concert when she sang his favourite song, *Comin' thro' the Rye*, especially for him. Her concerts in Sydney—where the unknown Nellie Armstrong's qualities as a singer had been perhaps rather better appreciated than in her home town—were even more successful than in Melbourne. Her share of the proceeds of one Sydney concert, £2,350, stood for many years as a world record for a fee paid to any singer for a single concert.

As her tour drew to its end in October, she must have congratulated herself that, back with her own people, she was among friends, and that here, under these kindly skies, everybody loved her and wished her well. She was wrong about that. One man was out to smear her with his own special kind of mud. His success in doing it was uncanny. The central point of his allegation—that Melba was a drunkard—pursued her all through her life. It even pursues her in death.

18

THE man who set out to destroy Melba—to destroy her in Australia at any rate—was named John Norton. Norton was an Englishman, born in London in 1858 or thereabouts, and grounded in journalism in Europe. As a young man he spent a while in Constantinople, working for an English-language newspaper. He left that city in some haste, after being caught in a harem, the master of which gave him the option of leaving by a mail-steamer then about to sail, or being trussed in a weighted sack and dropped into the Bosphorus. Norton chose the ship, and after a short stay in London went to Australia, arriving in Sydney in 1884. He was twenty-six, and within a few years got control of a Sydney weekly scandal-sheet, *Truth*, which presently expanded into other states and ultimately gained a nationwide circulation as the 'organ of radical democracy and Australian National Independence', to quote *Truth* on itself.

Norton was a strident bully, devoid of scruples, whose path to affluence was paved with lies, violence, blackmail, seduction, and empty whisky bottles. This megalomaniac guttersnipe made a profitable business of character assassination and just-within-the law pornography. Being undersized, he took Napoleon for his hero, and persuaded himself that he had inherited the Little Corporal's aura; he even called his Sydney mansion St Helena, and furnished it with hundreds of statues and pictures of Napoleon. He was four times a member of Parliament, and three times an alderman, and when he died in 1916 left an estate valued at £100,000. As recorded by Cyril Pearl:

'He had been publicly denounced many times as a thief, a black-mailer, a wife-beater and an obscene drunkard, without ever refuting the charges; and he had been accused of killing his oldest friend in a drunken quarrel.

'Norton was a Fascist when Mussolini was a schoolboy . . . he assumed the title of "the people's tribune" and by violent, skilful, and cynical demagogy, persuaded thousands of Australians that he was their champion.'

Norton apparently never met Melba. He did not meet most of the people he defamed, nor did he need to know anything about them. It is true that he often poured vitriol on his personal and political enemies, but at least half his victims were men and women whose only sin in his eyes was that they had become respected public figures. That was enough at any time to rouse Norton's paranoiac bile and set his pen raging across the paper, excoriating his subject of the moment in his alliterative style, which his half-educated readers pored over as if it were the finest flower of prose. He was a man seething with insensate hatreds. The vandal expresses his grudge against society by wrecking a public telephone booth or smashing street lamps; Norton did it by destroying the reputa-tions of successful people, or at any rate by trying to. The bigger they were in worldly stature the better he liked it. On Queen Vic-toria's seventy-third birthday he splashed in *Truth* a tribute-in-reverse to 'The dull and brainless woman whom the English call "the Queen".' At another time he published an article in which he described the then Prince of Wales, later King Edward VII, as 'a turf-swindling, card-sharping, wife-debauching, boozy rowdy, an unmitigated scoundrel and foul-living rascal.' George V, Norton wrote at another time, 'loves the liquor, likes it good and in quantity, "little and good but often" being the motto of the Guelphs, most of whom have been guzzlers if not always gross gorgers.'

He was obsessed with drunkenness, and if Norton's word was to be taken then about four-fifths of the public men of Australia in his day spent their lives in a state of alcoholic frenzy or stupefaction. Being himself an habitual drunkard, who was much of his time in and out of hospitals under treatment for alcoholism, he wrote on the subject with indisputable authority, and when he decided—for whatever reasons—to bring Nellie Melba to the dust an addiction to alcohol was the chief although by no means the only wickedness he charged her with.

The storm that Norton brewed for Melba broke in 1903, a few days after she left Australia to return to London for the Covent Garden summer season. His timing was cunning. First, Melba was on the high seas when it began. Second, she could not press an action for libel against him without returning from Europe, and thus accepting months of professional idleness while waiting for the case to be tried, with a loss of anything from £20,000 to £50,000 in earnings, depending on how long the court proceedings lasted.

Melba rounded off her first homecoming visit with a tour of Western Australia and New Zealand, and finished with a concert in Sydney in March. As part of this tour she intended giving a concert in Launceston, before going to Hobart to catch the steamer to New Zealand, but cancelled the engagement after a rough overnight trip across Bass Strait. Launceston people were disappointed and some were angry, and a story spread that Melba was 'too drunk to sing'. This was widely believed in Launceston at the time, and John Norton, who happened to be visiting Tasmania, wired a story to *Truth*, accusing Melba of bad faith and promising to reveal later 'the real reason' for her failure to sing. He was evidently even then cooking up in his own mind the terms of the attack he was later to make.

The evidence that she was ill, not drunk, is irrefutable. A member of her concert party was Elva Rogers, then a nineteen-year-old contralto, whom Melba engaged in Melbourne. More than sixty years later Miss Rogers (who as a young woman abandoned her singing career to marry, settle down in Melbourne, and become the mother of two sons) remembered the trip across Bass Strait. 'It was an awful trip,' she said. 'We were all sick. The captain said it was the worst crossing he had ever experienced. As soon as we were settled in the Hotel Brisbane, in Launceston, Melba called me and said, "Miss Rogers, I don't think I'll ever be able to sing again. My throat is bleeding after the dry retching. Come and listen! I can't even get high C." We went to the piano and she sang a few scales. Anyone, much less a singer, could have told that her vocal mechanism was in bad shape. The doctor ordered her to bed, and she stayed there until next day, when we took the train to Hobart. She was in bed in Launceston nursing her bleeding throat at the time she was supposed to be so drunk she could hardly walk.'

Even apart from the Launceston episode, the tour was trying. One member of the concert party was a young Melbourne tenor, Walter Kirby, who had a fine lyric voice but was psychologically unstable. Standing in the wings of a theatre one night while he sang, Melba said, 'Lovely voice! Pity he's such a fool.' Then, contemplating his bulbous figure and bulbous eyes, she snapped, 'He's like a pregnant frog!' When leaving Tasmania all but one of Melba's party managed to catch the ship at Hobart; Kirby missed it. The New Zealand tour opened in Dunedin, with a local tenor in the missing Kirby's place. Then the party moved on to Christchurch, and there Kirby appeared, wan, woebegone and scruffy. He arrived at the hall a few minutes before the concert and presented himself at the door of Melba's dressing-room.

'Kirby, you ass!' she said. 'What did you miss the boat for?'

His eyes watered and he exclaimed, 'Oh, Madame, the suspense and the agony I have been through!'

He had managed to catch up with the party by begging a passage in a fishing-boat which he had found in the Hobart docks, making ready to sail for New Zealand. For one of his sybaritic tastes, the journey across the Tasman had been a horrible ordeal. (Melba never knew that, beginning with that tour, Kirby cherished an undying hatred of her. Many years later after Melba's death he told Blanche Marchesi that Melba would not let him sing the songs in which he excelled or enchant his audiences by taking any high notes—he had to be merely a shadow in the background. He also told Blanche Marchesi a fantastic story which she apparently believed. This was that he went to Melba's grave, stamped his foot on the ground as though to command attention and cried, 'Well, Nellie, now you've got to listen to me! Even you can't stop me now!', then for three hours to a 'passive audience of one and to the heavens . . . sang his loveliest songs, his topmost notes, his trills, his melodies

. . . the songs she had forbidden him to sing.' At last he stopped and asked triumphantly, 'Well, Nellie, what do you think of that?' The story is interesting, if implausible, although it is doubtless what poor Kirby would have liked to do.)

Having been overtaken by Kirby in New Zealand, Melba – possibly influenced by the thought that no substitute tenor nearly so good was available – forgave him and let him finish the tour. They gave their last concert in Auckland, and Melba left New Zealand for Australia with a warm glow in her heart for her fellow men. In Sydney John Norton was waiting to douse it.

She gave her last concert of the tour in Sydney on 18 March, and left a few days later for Europe. On Sunday 28 March, *Truth* published an 'open letter' to Melba over Norton's name. Filling nearly four broadsheet columns, and headed 'Concerning Her Champagne Capers, Breaches of Public Faith, Outrages Against Good Manners, and Insults to Australian Citizens!', it opened thus:

'Madame – Marvellous Melba, Mellifluous Melba, Supreme Singer Crowned Cantatrice, and Monarch of Matchless Music though you be, your public and private conduct during your short six months sojourn in Australia makes it compulsory that you should be told the truth. Genius is mostly eccentric; the eccentricities of genius are generally pardoned – up to a certain point. You have great genius, which is only excelled by your eccentricity. The public have heard too little of the first, and a great deal too much of the last. The turpitude of a talented termagant can be forgiven ten times ten, but there is a limit of licence which cannot be condoned. You have so often transgressed that limit that the public has at last become tired of your truculent tricks and vicious vagaries. Public patience is exhausted; public opinion exasperated; and in that style of language to which you have shown that you are not a stranger, you have to be told, on behalf of an abused and outraged community, that "it's time you took a pull," or were "pulled up with a round turn". Your scandalous breaches of public faith, and private propriety are no longer to be borne without protest. That protest I now make; and if you resent it, I invite you vindicate yourself by civil or criminal process in a Court of Law.'

Having warmed up, Norton derided the explanation that her Launceston concert had been cancelled because she was physically prostrated by the rough trip across Bass Strait. There was, he leered, another reason for her failure to appear, and continued:

'You are in the heyday of your cultured, ripened powers, at the zenith of your fame; and occupying, of right, the position of proud pre-eminence formerly filled by the peerless Patti. Your powers are ripe; your reputation is made; all the world asks of you is the privilege of paying to hear you, and applauding you. What more could woman wish or desire? What woman with a heart or soul would rashly risk such rich gifts and golden opportunities as yours by wantoning in wine? The careers of great divas – some of whom have died drunk and destitute – who have caressed the cup and drowned their songs in strong drink, should cause you to look upon champagne with a shudder, and to shun it with a shiver so long as God shall give you leave to sing. Your voice will not last for ever; it should be cherished like chastity, and not submitted to the risk of ruin that banquets and drinking bouts entail. Divas as divine and delightful as yourself have been dethroned and damned by Drink before today. That you can escape their fate, if you follow in their footsteps, is not in the Providence of God, who gave you your great gift of song, in trust for the gratification of the highest instincts of your generation.'

Norton went on to accuse Melba of 'parsimonious and cantankerous conduct' to her assistant artists and members of her personal staff, while 'raking in the shekels by charging prices probably higher than she could ever obtain or average in London or on the Continent of Europe'. He demanded:

'Surely you have made enough money out of your offended and outraged countrymen and countrywomen, and given so little of your easily gotten superfluity to the deserving charities of your native land, to enable you to deal not only fairly but liberally with the few second-rate artistes who accompany you, and with two such responsible and deserving attendants as your private secretary and your personal companion. It is altogether too bad to add to the truculence of the termagant, the vagaries of the virago, and the proclivities of the poculent pocharde* those of a miserable miser, who, while revelling in wealth and swigging champagne, balances and buncoes dependants who have kept better faith with her than she has kept with the public who have paid her so liberally, and generously forgiven her so much.

'Madame, I've done with you for the meantime. Perhaps now that

---

* Norton's logic in bracketing the English word 'poculent', meaning 'drinkable', with the French word 'pochade', a slang term which might be translated as 'boozer', is not apparent. Perhaps it merely sharpened the general effect he was trying to make, while serving his passion for alliteration.

I've done with you you'll think it about time to begin with me. Be it so, but be sure you count the cost before commencing; and consider well who will gain most by a public investigation by way of cross-examination in the courts—you or your legal advisers. I tell you frankly that I court such a contest, and feel confident that if it is commenced that I shall come off more than conqueror. Maintenant il faut que je vous fasse mes adieux, en chantant to the classic air of *Dolly Gray*.

> 'Good-bye, Nellie, I must leave you!
> 'Give up swigging dry champagne;
> 'Else your friends will surely leave you
> 'In disgust and poignant pain'.

Norton continued to pursue Melba in print throughout 1903. He published articles about her (though not another open letter) on 1 August, 24 October, and 28 November, but these attacks were mild compared with his opening blast; he seemed to have exhausted his deadliest ammunition in that first thunderous barrage, and his later writings against Melba werē an anti-climax. His charge that she was a drunkard lived on, however; Australians forgot that John Norton, the most scurrilous and unscrupulous liar in the history of Australian journalism, was the source of these stories, but did not forget the stories themselves and they haunted her in Australia to the end of her life and beyond.

It was a painful thing with her. She knew that if she cancelled a professional appearance on any Australian tour somebody would greet the news with a knowing wink and a remark such as 'She's on the booze, you know!'; then other tongues would take up the story, and soon the word would spread that she had been seen carried into her hotel, dead drunk. The knowledge that this kind of gossip was always on the tip of scandalmongering tongues sometimes made her sing—in Australia, although not anywhere else—against her own and her doctors' judgement.

While touring Australian inland cities and country towns in 1909 she contracted a sore throat. Her concert that night was in a large town, and people had driven in from many miles around to hear her; some of them had stayed overnight. A local doctor examined her throat and said, 'I won't be responsible if you sing.' She said, 'I must keep faith,' and the concert went on. In the first part of the programme she sang the Mad Scene from *Lucia*, with

John Lemmone playing the flute obbligato. She was obviously having trouble, and at the interval the doctor told her she must ease the strain on her voice. She agreed to amend her later programme, replacing the coloratura items with less trying songs. Someone was sent out on to the platform to announce the change, and while the announcement was being made Lemmone unobtrusively stationed himself at the back of the hall to see how the audience were taking it. There was a buzz of talk, studded with such remarks as, 'She's drunk, of course', and 'I hear she's been hitting the bottle all day', and 'You've only got to look at her to see she can hardly stand'. Melba would have spared herself some physical distress if she had cancelled the concert. She achieved nothing by going through with it; the label John Norton had pinned on her would not come off.

When she was in Melbourne for six weeks in her Australian grand opera season of 1911, she stayed with friends, Edward and Kate Fanning, and their family, who lived at East St Kilda. Strangers repeatedly telephoned on days she was advertised to sing, asking if she would be sober enough to go on stage. The Fannings felt that, although some of these callers were prompted by a perverted sense of humour, many of them sincerely believed her to be a drunkard.

The human relish for seeing the mighty show their feet of clay is no less strong in Australians than in any other people, so many thousands of them were ready, even anxious, to believe that Melba spent half her time in an alcoholic daze. She had feet of clay, but she did not display them by getting drunk. If nothing else had stopped her from running to the bottle her passion for protecting her voice would have done so. She guarded her voice as she would have guarded a priceless diamond; and, even in the money sense, her voice was worth more to her than the finest diamond. A powerful male voice will quickly deteriorate if its owner drinks heavily, and a voice like Melba's, as clear and delicate as fine crystal, would have coarsened and lost its quality after a few years of drinking bouts. None of the pedlars of these yarns has ever explained how Melba habitually drank to excess and yet outlasted, as a singer, all her great contemporaries. Her voice was naturally less magical after she reached the fifties, and its splendour had been almost imperceptibly declining since her early forties, but even when she was past sixty she could still outsing many of the popular prima donnas of the day.

The Italian soprano Toti Dal Monte, who became famous as a coloratura between the world wars, made a resounding success in the 1924 Melba-Williamson opera season in Australia. Whether or not relations between Melba and Dal Monte were, as freely reported at the time, strained by the younger woman's success – she was thirty-one to Melba's sixty-three – she paid a generous tribute to Melba as a singer forty years later when she said: 'Although Melba was almost at the end of her career she was still capable of producing some notes of the unmistakable "lunar colour", which was always her prerogative.'

No scientific examination of Melba's singing mechanism ever detected signs of the type of damage heavy drinking would cause. Sir Milsom Rees, who died in 1952, aged eighty-six, was for many years laryngologist to King George V and Queen Mary and the Royal Household, and, perhaps more important, to the Royal Opera House, Covent Garden, and the Guildhall School of Music. Although a showman with a liking for the limelight, and described by one of his contemporaries as 'famous outside the medical profession and rather notorious within it', he was highly regarded as a laryngologist. Many leading politicians and legal men would go to him, in his rooms at Upper Wimpole Street, to have their throats sprayed before making important speeches, and most of the great singers of the time were among his patients; Melba had a standing arrangement with him to cleanse her nose and throat on the morning of a performance, whenever she was appearing in London. Rees had no reservations about the effect of alcohol on the vocal cords; he said it ruined the voice. He also believed that Melba was the greatest of all singers, and said her larynx and vocal cords were 'the most perfect he had ever seen', with Kirsten Flagstad's as the nearest approach. He placed Jean de Reszke first among men singers.

It is easier to find Australians acquainted with somebody who saw Melba rolling drunk than to find anyone who saw that interesting spectacle with his own eyes. And she had none of the dedicated drinker's possessiveness with liquor. Early in World War I she recruited a party of singers and entertainers and gave a series of concerts for patriotic funds, some in large Victorian country towns. At Healesville, in the Great Dividing Range, thirty-seven miles from Melbourne, the mayor presented her with a case of champagne; perhaps, having heard the stories, he thought it an appropriate gift. She accepted the champagne with suitable thanks, and at the first chance said to John Lemmone, 'I don't want the damn' stuff! Give it to the boys.' This meant her brothers, Charlie and Ernest; a Melbourne journalist named Franklin Petersen, who had

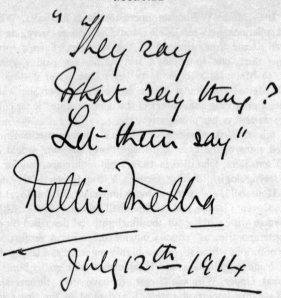

"They say
What say they?
Let them say"

Nellie Melba

July 12th 1914

gone to Healesville to report on the concert; Frederick Collier, a bass-baritone, who was later to make a sound reputation as an opera singer in England; and other camp followers. Melba had a special train to take the party back from Healesville, and the boys, whooping with delight, fell on the champagne as the train moved off. It was a gay journey, and Melba did not have so much as a sip of the gift champagne.

She was born with an internal toughness which let her shrug off most of the tales that sensationalists, scandalmongers, and faceless enemies invented to do her harm. She knew that for a prima donna not to be talked about at all is perhaps worse than for her to be talked about adversely. She once called on the then editor of the Melbourne *Argus*, Edward Cunningham, and said, 'Edward, I haven't seen any reference to my presence in Australia in the last week or two.'

'Oh,' said Cunningham, 'there's been a good deal in the *Argus*.'

'No, no,' she said, 'not enough! Not enough! I don't care what you say, for me or against me, but for heaven's sake say something *about* me.'

While it was not quite true that she did not care what newspapers and public gossip said of her, she was generally willing to take the rough with the smooth where publicity was concerned. She once told a Melbourne friend, Inez Hutchison, 'You won't be famous till people start saying the worst they can of you. Don't worry! It's a good sign!' Another time she wrote in an old friend's autograph book filling a large page nine inches wide and eleven inches deep: 'They say. What say they? Let them say.' That was a fair indication of her attitude.

Australians were fascinated by tales of her drinking exploits above all, but gossip about her supposed love-life also commanded an earnest hearing. From 1915 until her death in 1931 she was closely associated with the Albert Street Conservatorium of Music, in Melbourne, which was later renamed the Melba Memorial Conservatorium in her honour. The director throughout that period was an English-born conductor and composer, Fritz Bennicke Hart, who became Professor of Music in the University of Honolulu in 1937, and died at Honolulu in 1949. Although Hart and Melba were close friends, nobody who knew them well ever supposed that they were romantically attracted to each other, but apparently some eyes saw theirs as a sinful alliance. Soon after Melba's death a woman who had been a student at the conservatorium called on Hart's son, Basil, at that time a young Melbourne solicitor.

'Basil,' she said, 'I want you to answer me a question. Did Melba have an illegitimate son by your father?'

Basil Hart mastered his impulse to laugh. Then he said, 'Well, since Melba was in the middle fifties when she met my father I think it highly unlikely. But I'd have been very proud to have had such a stepbrother.'

He always suspected that his caller went away unconvinced, believing she had been fobbed-off with a legal sophistry.

Melba would have loved the story that she had borne a bastard to Fritz Hart or any other man. While she always behaved with impeccable decorum in the company of Lady de Grey and such great ones of Society, she liked to shock the consciously worthy and the earnestly bourgeois. Once while visiting Australia she heard that an artificial insemination society had been formed in Sydney. Her eyes shone and she said, 'How I'd love to have a baby! I'd love to walk down Collins Street while I was pregnant and shock all the old tabbies.'

But she was always sensitive to stories that she was a drunkard; perhaps what she most disliked was the implication that anyone should think her a contract-breaker, a bad business woman, who drank too much to be able to keep her professional engagements. In Sydney, in her 1911 opera season, she went down with laryngitis and could not appear for some nights. A newspaperman, Claude McKay, was her press-agent for the season, and one morning John Lemmone went to him with a note in Melba's handwriting. This ran:

'Isn't it disgusting? The people say I am drunk, What can be done about it.

Yours, heartbroken,
NELLIE MELBA.'

McKay, a wise and experienced man of the world, asked Lemmone to leave the note with him. Then, as he tells the story in his autobiography:

'That night I called on Heney, then editor of the *Sydney Morning Herald*. I showed him Melba's letter. He asked what could be done.

' "Print it facsimile," I said, "with a note that Melba has laryngitis, rebuking anyone who holds the uncharitable thoughts that many do."

'Heney hesitated. I told him I represented Melba, and assured him he had full authority to do as I requested. With all the indignation I felt, I remarked that it was a shameful way to malign our most famous Australian woman, and urged him to administer the reproof. After a while he agreed.

'Next morning John Lemmone came hot-foot to see me.

' "What have you done?" he moaned. "I've never been so upset in my life! Good God! What will Melba say? You'll have to come along with me and see her, and may God have mercy on your soul!"

'We drove out to Rose Bay and were shown to Melba's bedroom, where she was sitting up in bed, the *Herald* in front of her.

' "Who did this?" she demanded.

' "I did," I confessed.

' "Come here!" she commanded. "Lean over."

'This I did, expecting the worst. She threw her arms round me, kissing me on both cheeks.

' "I knew John wouldn't have the audacity to say anything," she said, laughing, "and I would never have thought of this myself."

'When Melba reappeared a few nights later the house stood up and cheered her for minutes. She always said that this was the reception that moved her most deeply of all.'

It cannot be denied that for many years a few irreproachably reliable citizens of the substantial Victorian country city of Ballarat were willing to swear that, on a certain night long ago, they stood with hundreds of others and heard themselves cursed by an obviously tipsy Nellie Melba. It came about thus:

After giving a concert in Ballarat Melba was followed back to her hotel by hundreds of members of her audience, so enthralled with her singing that they could not bear to let her go. They gathered in the street outside the hotel, calling 'We want Melba! We want Melba!', their number and the volume of their incantation growing as other Ballarat citizens joined them. Three Melbourne newspapermen were lodging in the hotel that night; they had gone to Ballarat to report a conference of the Australian Natives Association. The conference had ended that afternoon, and the three reporters, having telegraphed their stories, were spending the night in alcoholic relaxation. Since Melba did not show herself the crowd in the street continued chanting, and at last one of the reporters, glowing with whisky and high spirits, said, 'I'll give 'em something to yell about!' He drew on a dressing-gown of rich floral pattern and twined a towel about his head in imitation of a woman's toque. Then, urged on by his two colleagues, he flung open the french windows of his room and stepped out on to the balcony. He stood, swaying slightly, while the crowd roared a welcome, then raised an arm, enjoining silence. The street grew hushed, and the watchers below gazed raptly upward. Perhaps they expected the putative Melba to make a pretty speech. Perhaps some of them dared to hope she would sing a verse of *Home, sweet home*. At last the figure on the balcony spoke, in a voice high-pitched but oddly harsh, and the words, though slightly slurred, fell unmistakably on the ears of every listener:

'I wish all you buggers would go home and let me get some bloody sleep!'

The crowd dispersed muttering that the horrid stories were true after all! Nellie Melba drank!

19

MELBA must have had mixed feelings about her homeland after that first return visit. The enthusiasm of her audiences, not to mention the profits of the tour, was sweet, but she would have been more than human if she had not felt buffeted and wounded by John Norton's hoodlum iconoclasm.

If she had sued him for libel she would undoubtedly have won a judgement against him with substantial damages but no sum a court could have awarded her would have compensated her for going back to Australia, then staying for months to fight the case. She also knew that Norton would have defended himself by dragging into evidence every scrap of unsavoury gossip about her, both the true and the apocryphal; he would have rejoiced in the chance to have her cross-examined, on the pretext of testing her character and credibility, about the Duke of Orleans, Haddon Chambers, and other men whose names had been linked with hers, then head-lining her answers in *Truth*. Her counsel could have retaliated by questioning Norton about his alcoholic exploits, his career as a blackmailer and a seducer, and his brutality to his wife, but this was old stuff, familiar to every Australian. And since Norton had no reputation to lose he did not mind mud; on the contrary, he revelled in it.

Astonishingly few of the men and women whom he libelled ever did challenge him at law. For example, he published an article, over his own name, charging the Earl of Dudley, Governor-General of Australia from 1908 to 1911, with 'concupiscent capers', with 'playing pornic pranks with matrons and maids', and with 'libidinous lecheries and lascivious lapses'. The earl replied that he had heard these charges with 'the most profound amusement', and left it at that. He probably showed good sense in refusing to be drawn into a legal roughhouse with a psychopath like John Norton.

Melba arrived back in London toward the end of April, and in her own dressing-room at Covent Garden, making up as Mimi, surrounded by familiar faces and familiar scenes, John Norton seemed hardly more than a malignant figure in a nightmare. He receded even further when she sang at a command performance at Buckingham Palace on 6 July, in honour of President Emile Loubet of France. Within the intangible yet stout walls of privilege and power which protected her in London, Nellie Melba felt she was really home. Although she was to go back to Australia many times over the years, Covent Garden was perhaps the only true home she knew from the day she left Doonside in 1886 until her death. She tried later to create a home for herself in Australia, Coombe Cottage, at Coldstream near Lilydale, and even raised up there a clock-tower bearing the words for every passer-by to see, 'East, West, Hame's Best'. She filled Coombe Cottage with her choicest possessions and the relics of her greatest triumphs, yet somehow the place never quite possessed her, always her mind kept turning back to London and Covent Garden.

She was to lose Covent Garden at the end and spend her last years vainly trying to recover the old sense of rapture she had once known, but she did not foresee that time when she went back to London in 1903. How could she have foreseen it? She was still a young woman—or almost. The voice that God had given her was still as magical as ever—or almost. She was still in the noontide of her glory—or almost. The evening seemed immeasurably far away.

AFTERNOON

1903–1918

1

T HE years of Edward VII's reign were warm and mellow for England's handful of privileged people, a good time for English men and women of social position and wealth to be alive. They inherited a world of dignity and elegant manners. A system of taboos, which were unwritten but inflexible, still governed behaviour, but much of the stuffiness of Queen Victoria's time had been dispelled by the influence of her son's genial personality. The Edwardians took their pleasures at a leisurely pace because they felt they had no call to hurry.

A few of them knew the good life could not last. Perhaps the King was one. Although his political acumen was less sharp than some of his admiring biographers admit, he was interested in foreign affairs for much of his period as Prince of Wales, and this interest did not wane when he ascended the throne. Seeing that the concerns of Britain and the ambitions of a militarized Germany were incompatible, he was positively if discreetly anti-Prussian. While Prince of Wales he also learned to detest his nephew, Wilhelm II. Whether this antipathy was inspired by patriotism or by the Kaiser's gift of showmanship, and especially his liking for resplendent uniforms which enabled him to outshine his Uncle Edward on state occasions, is a matter of conjecture. At any rate it was strong.

Nellie Melba was not among those who saw the Edwardian era as a passing day of late summer. She wanted it to last because it offered her so much that she looked upon as her due, and so she believed it would last; this seemed to her to be logical as well as agreeable. For her the advantages were manifest. She was acclaimed, at Covent Garden anyway, as the greatest prima donna of the day, and honoured—and paid—accordingly. When in London she lived like a minor empress in her house in Great Cumberland Place, among the plaster cupids which symbolized something of the spirit of the time. When she went abroad she travelled in semi-regal state. Wherever she was someone was at hand to satisfy her whims and wishes. She liked these attentions; she was a demanding woman, and often inconsiderate of the convenience or comfort of others, but perhaps it is surprising that she was not more demanding. Every circumstance of her life once she was established at the top of her profession encouraged her to believe that her place was at the centre of the universe—that she belonged to a specially favoured group of mortals.

At Covent Garden she stood supreme; if she did not exactly make the laws she could break them with impunity. She rarely took liberties, but now and then a devil possessed her for a few moments. In a performance of *Bohème* in 1903 the Musetta was a young Austrian soprano, Fritzi Scheff. She was not a potential rival of Melba, but perhaps the audience's response to Fraulein Scheff's singing irritated the diva. At all events near the climax of Musetta's second-act aria an unmistakable voice came sailing out from the wings when Scheff was singing the high B, and finished the phrase with her. The second singer was of course Melba, and Percy Colson, who was in Melba's box that night with Herman Bemberg, reported that Scheff 'tried to scratch Melba's face, and then had hysterics'. Fraulein Scheff was unable to go on with the performance, and an announcement was made that she was indisposed, so that night *Bohème* ended with the unrehearsed duet between Mimi and Musetta. To compensate the audience for the loss of the last two acts Melba, ever self-possessed, sang the Mad Scene from *Lucia*.

That power and money brought Melba anything but fleeting happiness is to be doubted. She loved life and lived it vigorously and exuberantly, and her friends agree that it was impossible to be dull in her company. But many of them felt she was always reaching out for something, perhaps something humanly unattainable, which forever eluded her, retreating as she approached. Perhaps she did not know what she wanted. If she did know she never expressed it in specific terms. Nobody who knew Melba ever suggested she was a profound philosopher. She was too occupied with the tangible world—with things that her eyes could see, her ears could hear, and her fingers could touch—to have time to speculate on the higher meanings of life; in fact, she never showed any intellectual capacity for doing so. As she grew older her name appeared now and then on a newspaper or a magazine article in which one or another of the shallower reaches of philosophy was gently explored, but these writings never bore any stamp of her blunt pragmatic mind; the suspicion remains that, like many another famous public figure to whom publicity is a professional necessity, she was willing to put her name to any article written by some journalistic hack if it showed her in a reasonably amiable light.

An article published in the 1920s, as one of a widely syndicated newspaper series, invitingly entitled 'Where Is Happiness?', was of that order. These articles were presented as the work of 'famous happy people', and Melba's words, along with those of the other contributors to the series, were doubtless accepted by hundreds of thousands of readers as the findings of an authority on happiness.

'Where' (Melba asked in the article) 'is happiness? Why, it is to be found in the world all about us, in the stillness of a summer night, in the pride of a good thing done, in the flush of a summer dawn, the following of an ideal, the strong grip of a friend, the perfect heart of a rose, or the wild sweetness of a song. It is always very near, you may come upon it at the very next turn of the road. It is often within the reach of you if you but stretch out your hand. The secret of finding it? I cannot tell you. I know that fame alone does not bring it, and I know that it is within the reach of all, rich or poor, celebrated or unknown.'

The girl from Richmond who, by means of a superlative voice, a strong personality, uncommon business acumen, and remorseless ambition, had climbed to the top of the grand opera tree and stayed there must have smiled an inward smile as she considered those fruity sentiments. They revealed nothing of the mind of the real woman, nor did they throw any light on the nature of the thing missing from her life.

2

Some of her friends expected her to marry again after Charles Armstrong divorced her in 1900. She was still a handsome woman, even if her figure had begun to take on prima donna contours as she entered into her forties, and she did not lack suitors; some of these were men awake to the material advantages of marrying a celebrated singer who was moderately wealthy already and whose career had many years to run, but some were rich men of good social standing, and a few were titled as well, and highly eligible. Melba must have been tempted by some of the proposals of marriage she received, for to the end of her life she had in her nature a touch of the romantic; this never by any means fogged her ability to make hard-headed judgements, but occasionally it would assert itself and cause her to become almost dewy-eyed over the connubial delights which had eluded her. The disaster of her alliance with Charles Armstrong made her wary of risking marriage again, but almost to the end of her life she liked to toy with the idea. After being a guest at a wedding in America toward the end of World War I she told a friend, 'If ever I marry again I shall certainly have an American wedding. It is so pretty.'

Whatever her marriage to Armstrong lacked, it gave her the experience of motherhood; and in due time her son, George, was to become the father of a daughter, Pamela, born in 1918, who was the joy of Melba's declining years. As the son of a broken marriage, George Armstrong had a difficult youth. After his father took him to the United States of America in the 1890s, they were together for about ten years, running small ranches, first in Texas, then in Oregon, and the boy became a fine horseman and an expert in handling farm animals, even though his formal schooling was neglected. His mother worried about him on that score, and she was also determined to restore him to her side if possible, for as she grew older she became increasingly conscious of the emptiness of her personal life. The Texas court which had given Armstrong a divorce decree had also given him custody of his son, but this order could not bind them together for ever, so when George Armstrong was about twenty he returned to his mother in England. Father and son were never estranged and maintained a warm relationship until Charles Armstrong died in 1948, but their life together, except for occasional visits one to the other, was ended.

George Armstrong must have been rather confused in Melba's glittering world at first. He had been transplanted, all within a few weeks, from his father's ranch near Klamath Falls, Oregon, where none of the townspeople had known him as Melba's son, to an entirely strange environment. It was enough to test any young man's ability to make a radical psychological adjustment. This was the world he had to live in, because it was Melba's world, the world she had conquered for herself and in which she towered above everyone else, the world over which she ruled and intended to go on ruling. To her it went without saying that her son would accept her world; the idea that she might make certain modifications to create an environment more agreeable to him did not occur to her.

The truth is that Melba was a supreme egoist; what she achieved would have been unattainable to anyone who was not. Most of the actions of her life, whether personal or professional, reflected this quality. Gerald Moore, the accompanist, recalled that on her last tour of the USA and Canada she made a habit of testing the lighting effects in the halls along the way not before each concert began but while her assisting artists were performing. As he described it: '. . . during the first group of violoncello solos with which Beatrice Harrison opened, lights were raised and lowered, spots, foots, flashed on and off until the *diva* was satisfied with the result. That 'cellist and audiences were disturbed was of small moment: Dame Nellie was not personally inconvenienced.' Nobody but rather silly idolaters pretend that Melba would not be guilty of such a lack of consideration if it suited her; and yet she often went to some trouble to do kindnesses for people whose goodwill could be of even less moment to her than an assisting artist's. One was an aged post-mistress in a Victorian country township named Narbethong. Melba made a habit of visiting this old woman every now and then and singing two or three songs for her, while accompanying herself on the tinny upright piano which had several notes missing and usually needed tuning. She could also be observant of someone else's distress. Singing at a concert, she noticed an elderly woman in the front row drooping, as if on the point of fainting. She finished her song and, handing her own bottle of smelling-salts to her flautist John Lemmone, told him to take it down to the woman.

She was particularly responsive to children. On a tour of the USA some years before World War I she stayed in Baltimore at the home of an old friend, Ernest Hutcheson, at that time chief pianoforte instructor at the Peabody Conservatory; Hutcheson was also a native of Melbourne, where he had been acclaimed as a child prodigy. He was ten years younger than Melba, and they had appeared on the same programmes several times in the 1880s when she was singing as Nellie Armstrong. He went to Europe a year ahead of her, and after studying at Leipzig became a successful solo pianist and a teacher and composer, and then settled in America. But he and Melba always kept their friendship in repair. When she stayed with him in Baltimore he was married with two young sons. One of the boys, Harold, was ill in bed. He asked to see the famous singer, and Melba, dressed for her concert, climbed the stairs and presented herself. Round-eyed but not overawed, he asked her to trill for him. She smiled, raised her chin, opened her mouth, and sent a long trill, like a beam of silver light, flashing and dancing around the sick boy's room. Harold Hutcheson remembered the magic of it ever after.

Many men and women who were children when they knew Melba remember her for such acts of kindness. These memories of her help to counterbalance the more numerous tales of her aggressive selfishness which people on hearing her name tend to recall above all else—that is, above all else but her singing, which was the *raison d'être* of her life and the foundation of her immortality.

3

THE years immediately after Melba went back to Europe in 1903 were busy for her. Every year she was at Covent Garden for the three months or thereabouts of the summer season; this, whatever other seasons of grand opera went on at Covent Garden, was always the major season, musically and socially—the season denoted by the name 'Covent Garden' standing alone. She spent some months in England each year, taking her place in Society as an equal with Lady de Grey, the Duchess of Sutherland, Mrs George Keppel and their set, with regular concert appearances in London and recital tours of the English provinces, but also making yearly professional sorties to the USA and the Continent.

Nearly every Australian who arrived in Europe bent on making a career in music found his way to Melba. She was the one who had discovered the golden key, and young singers in particular believed their battle was won if they could but enlist her interest and support. This belief was based on a misunderstanding of the professional music world's indifference to any but conspicuous talent, but it persisted. In her early years in Europe Melba was too busy making and consolidating her reputation to have much time to devote to other aspirants to fame, but after her return from Australia in 1903 she was more accessible; any Australian who came satisfactorily introduced could count on an interview and some good advice, if nothing more.

She found time to receive even the egregious Walter Kirby, who had sung with her in Australia and New Zealand, and had distinguished himself by missing the New Zealand-bound steamer in Hobart. Having gone to Europe in 1903 to pursue his studies, Kirby went by appointment to see Melba in her suite at the Hotel Bristol in Paris. He told her he had been recommended to study with a Paris teacher named Jacques Bouhy, a Belgian-born baritone, who had earlier been famous as an opera singer, and had been the Escamillo in the world première of *Carmen* at the Opéra-Comique in Paris in 1875.

'Bouhy?' Melba said. 'I've never heard of him!' Having thus dismissed Bouhy, she gave the crestfallen Kirby a note to another singing teacher in London.

Melba not only knew Bouhy but knew him well; he had been one of the principals of the company in her first season at the Monnaie, in Brussels, and after they had sung together she asked him for an opinion of her voice. He told her it was a beautiful voice, but too fragile for heavy operatic roles, and advised her to concentrate on the lighter roles. At that time Melba had not realized her vocal limitations, or perhaps had not admitted them to herself, and Bouhy's advice left a residue of resentment in her mind. Most of her antipathy against him had its origin, however, in what she chose to see as his theft of a promising pupil from Mathilde Marchesi.

The pupil was the Australian soprano, Amy Castles, who was born in 1882 in the Melbourne suburb of Carlton, perhaps three or four miles distant from Melba's birthplace in Richmond. She came under notice in Australia when only about sixteen, and, after raising £2,000 for her studies abroad by giving a series of concerts in Melbourne, Sydney and other Australian cities, arrived in Paris in 1899. The only European singing teacher most Australians knew at that time was Mathilde Marchesi, who had put Melba into opera, and it was to the Ecole Marchesi that Amy Castles went – a wide-eyed seventeen-year-old from the Antipodes, hoping she would impress the great teacher. To her delight Marchesi accepted her as a pupil. The results were all but disastrous.

Marchesi did not agree with Amy Castles's Australian teacher, E. Allan Bindley, that her voice was a soprano; after a few weeks she was training the Australian girl as a mezzo-soprano, and after a few weeks more as a contralto. Eighteen months of Marchesi's training nearly sufficed to destroy Amy Castles's voice, but just in time her mother arrived in Paris and made her leave the Ecole Marchesi and put herself under Bouhy. From London Melba, who had previously taken little interest in Amy Castles, sent a message to her saying in effect, 'Unless you return to Marchesi at once you will never be heard of again.' This was a terrifying threat from the unofficial ruler of Covent Garden, but Amy Castles stayed with Bouhy. He restored her voice but took some years to do it, and, although she made a concert tour of Australia and also appeared as a concert artist in London, she was not ready for grand opera until 1907. She made her début in *Hamlet* in Cologne, and also sang there in two of Melba's own favourite operas, *Roméo et Juliette* and *Faust*. She was never called to Covent Garden, which astonished connoisseurs of the soprano voice who heard her at that time; the best of them believed her to be within measurable distance of Melba, if not quite Melba's equal. Landon Ronald, who was then closely in touch with Melba, admired Amy Castles as a singer, but once told her, 'You'll never get to Covent Garden, you know.' He did not elaborate, but she interpreted his words as meaning that Melba was incurably hostile toward her. In some departments of singing Amy Castles was possibly Melba's superior. The Australian critic, Thorold Waters, who said her voice 'combined the attributes of a dramatic and coloratura soprano', believed that the only tones resembling hers in quality 'were the gorgeous ones of Emmy Destinn, but even that dramatic soprano's exploits did not extend to coloratura flights'. Melba either never shared these opinions, or did not admit to sharing them.

Events did not bear out Melba's poor opinion of Amy Castles. She never did scale the ultimate heights, but this was not due to any shortcomings either of her voice or the way she used it. In 1913 the Imperial Opera House, Vienna, gave her a five-year contract to sing Mimi, Butterfly, Desdemona, Marguerite, Juliette, Tosca, and other roles. She was doing well when war in Europe became inevitable and she had to leave Austria, abandoning her contract, and as it turned out her career as an opera singer in Europe. A woman dedicated to success would have waited for the war to end, then picked up her career where it had been cut short. Amy Castles had more than enough talent to re-establish herself, but by the time the war ended she had lost interest. She was a timid woman, with none of the driving egoism which was a strong element in Melba's success, nor even much appetite for fame. She loved singing, and at her best sang magnificently, but she was as happy singing to the Castles family circle as to a great opera house blazing with diamond tiaras and snowy shirtfronts. Soon after the outbreak of war she went home to Australia to be with her ageing parents, and when peace came she would not leave them; she was able to make a good living in Australia as a concert and oratorio singer, and the idea of again storming Europe did not appeal to her.

Two of her sisters, Dolly and Eileen, and a brother, George, were also talented professional singers. None of them was in Amy's class, but Eileen, a soprano, went abroad and made a small name in opera, and sang secondary roles at Covent Garden. Eileen was also a student of Jacques Bouhy, but Melba did not appear to hold that against her. She was perhaps influenced by the thought that Eileen Castles was a lesser soprano than her older sister, and never could be any kind of rival.

For all her unhelpfulness to Amy Castles, Melba always seemed to be busy, from the time she went back to London in 1903 until she retired nearly twenty-five years later, guiding the feet of one or another promising young musician along the slippery professional paths. She was consistently helpful to young artists with the exception of sopranos having both voices and personalities of the highest quality. With her own reputation established and consolidated she had time to play the role of the supreme prima donna, off the stage as well as on it. A word from her was enough to assure a hearing in London for any young singer or instrumentalist. She was not infallible in separating the musical sheep from the goats, and many of those she sponsored were politely listened to, then allowed to sink back into obscurity. Melba never made a mistake in assessing the quality of a voice or the technical possibilities of an instrumentalist, but she often went wrong in estimating character, and that was why many of the young people for whom she predicted brilliant futures were forgotten within a few months of making a professional début. Now and then, however, one of them produced the stuff of lasting success.

One of her protégées at that time was an American soprano named Elizabeth Parkinson, from Kansas City, who for professional purposes used the name of Parkina. Although a throat weakness ended Parkina's career within a few years, she scored a success while her voice lasted and always acknowledged her debt to Melba. The point deserves to be made since Melba has been accused of destroying Parkina at Covent Garden by deliberately making her drunk. The story had no basis except in gossip, which always flourishes backstage. Parkina broke down in a performance of *Bohème* in 1904, when she was singing Musetta to Melba's Mimi, and had to be replaced by another singer, but the trouble was caused by a drug prescribed by a medical specialist for a throat ailment, not by champagne. Since she sang again as Musetta a few nights later, and returned to Covent Garden every year for some years, the story that Melba set out to wreck her career is patently absurd. Anyway Melba could have had her removed from the Covent Garden roster at that time merely by flicking her fingers.

Melba did not fear Parkina, who was not her equal and never could have been, but she was less benevolent toward some other sopranos. For instance, it was a different matter when Luisa Tetrazzini came to Covent Garden.

4

IN considering the Tetrazzini affair the background of Melba's life at Covent Garden is relevant and particularly a glance at the younger rivals she cut down. She had gained success by fighting, and she kept success by fighting. If she had lacked the will to fight and go on fighting she would have been overthrown by the time she was fifty, and probably long before that.

In the years between her 1902–3 visit to Australia and the outbreak of World War I (which put an end to grand opera at Covent Garden for five years) a season rarely passed without bringing rumblings from backstage of a collision between Melba and some other singer. It was for the most part sopranos whose Covent Garden careers withered under Melba's eye, but sopranos were not the only casualties. After the first bloom passed from her voice she never much cared to be thrown into direct competition with any fine young singer, whether a woman or a man. When Alessandro Bonci, the Italian tenor, then thirty, made his Covent Garden début in 1900, Melba showed her displeasure at the number of curtain calls he received as Rodolfo to her Mimi. Her unwillingness to let even male singers take too much of the limelight grew with the years. The first time that John McCormack, then rising twenty-four, appeared at Covent Garden in 1908 he started out to take a curtain call with her. She waved him back, saying, 'In this house nobody takes bows with Melba.'

That was an inauspicious beginning to an uneasy professional association, for Melba and McCormack never liked one another, even though she took him to Australia in 1911 as principal lyric tenor of the first of the three Melba-Williamson grand opera companies. She disliked his irreverent bearing and he disliked her autocratic air, and so they were rarely together in the same place for long without clashing. Melba had a passion for punctuality; she was never late for anybody else and expected nobody to be late for her. One day she arrived at the London studios of His Master's Voice to make a recording of the Quartet from *Rigoletto* with McCormack, the contralto Edna Thornton, and the baritone Mario Sammarco. Sammarco was on time, but Edna Thornton was a few minutes late and Melba greeted her tartly. When McCormack, relaxed and debonair, strolled in half an hour after the appointed time Melba flung a savage rebuke at him, and at once the air crackled with an exchange of eloquence which made the other singers and the bystanders gape. That kind of storm was always apt to break when Melba and McCormack were near one another.

Perhaps the most famous of all men singers to fall foul of Melba was Titta Ruffo, the baritone. A contemporary, Giuseppe de Luca, himself a fine operatic baritone, described Ruffo's voice as 'not a voice, but a miracle'; another contemporary found Ruffo's high notes to be 'resplendent in their liquid beauty, like enormous melted jewels'. Ruffo made his début at Covent Garden in 1903, when he was twenty-five, and early in the season was asked to take the name-part in *Rigoletto*, in place of Antonio Scotti who was ill. Melba, cast as Gilda, did not sing in the orchestra rehearsal but listened from a box. Ruffo's singing roused extraordinary enthusiasm; after one of his arias the whole orchestra spontaneously applauded, and at the finale the chorus and orchestra combined to give him a prolonged ovation. When he presented himself at the theatre next day he found he had been removed from the cast, and was told Melba had refused to sing with him 'because I was still too young to undertake such a part'. Ruffo left London that afternoon and never went back to Covent Garden, but poetic—or perhaps operatic—justice prevailed in the end. As he told the story in his autobiography he was singing some years later at the San Carlo Theatre, in Naples, and Melba, on her way home to Australia, came through as a visitor and heard him in *Hamlet*. Ruffo wrote:

'After the third act, De Sanna* came into my dressing-room to greet me and to tell me that Melba was in his box, applauding

* Robert De Sanna was Director of San Carlo Opera House, 1901–13.

frantically, and that she had asked me to sing with her in a performance of *Hamlet*, in which she would play Ophelia. Naturally De Sanna was enthusiastic. Then I, assuming the same coldness shown by the English Manager in his office in London, replied to De Sanna, "Tell Melba she is too old to sing with me." Melba, with a little mental effort, remembered the time when she did not sing *Rigoletto* with me because I was too young. I really do not like retaliation or pique. However, it seemed to me in this case that Melba's London blow was fittingly answered by Titta Ruffo's Parthenopian reply. Even De Sanna, who at first was amazed at my rudeness, agreed that I was right, and, at my request that he should quote my words exactly, faithfully delivered the message.'

Nobody can deny that in Melba's years at Covent Garden, as Blanche Marchesi once put it, 'some powerful invisible spirits were hard at work to eliminate artists who might have easily settled in the heart of the public'. It was astonishing how often an ousted soprano had been, like Melba herself, a pupil of Mathilde Marchesi. Even when age had sapped Marchesi's genius and she was liable to make mistakes, she was not a negligible teacher; she had a special understanding of the lyric soprano voice and what it can do, so that any young prima donna she sent out to sing in grand opera was a potential threat to Melba's supremacy. Whatever the reason, Melba showed little inclination to help any of Marchesi's star sopranos, at Covent Garden anyway; she preferred them to find their fame in Continental or American opera houses. Marchesi did not mind; she was a realist also and too well experienced in the ways of prima donnas to suppose that one of them, Melba or any other, would willingly lend a hand at her own dethronement. So the rivals came and the rivals went. To list them all would be tedious, but one or two may be named.

Selma Kurz, an Austrian, who made her début at Covent Garden in 1904, and later headed the soprano roster for some years at the Imperial Opera House, Vienna, was among the most brilliant. A product of the Ecole Marchesi, she was just thirty when London first heard her, and not only a fine singer, with a trill resembling Melba's, but also a beautiful woman, slender and graceful. Rosenthal says: 'She reappeared at Covent Garden the following summer, but she never became a permanent fixture there, for she was too popular for Melba's liking.'

Another gifted pupil of Marchesi had an even shorter career at Covent Garden; this was the soprano Frances Alda, who was born in 1883, in Christchurch, New Zealand, but lived her young life in Australia and considered herself to be an Australian. If she expected Melba to smile on her for that reason she was disappointed.

Frances Alda was all but born on the grand opera stage. She was a granddaughter of Martin and Fanny Simonsen, who ran an opera company of their own in Australia and New Zealand for some years last century. Fanny Simonsen was a singer of distinction, and her granddaughter, Frances, had an exceptional voice and a personality which matched it. Having started her stage career in light opera in Australia, she went to Paris when about eighteen and became a pupil of Mathilde Marchesi. According to one legend, Melba, while visiting the Ecole Marchesi, heard the young Alda singing and acidly said, 'What a pity that girl has no voice to train.' Alda however had a series of successes at the Opéra-Comique, Paris, in 1904, and was then acclaimed at Melba's own operatic alma mater, the Monnaie, in Brussels. She was ready to conquer London – or so she supposed. She made a successful début at Covent Garden in 1906, as a last-minute substitute for Melba in *Faust*, and, having scored an even bigger success in *Rigoletto* with Caruso a few nights later, imagined her position at Covent Garden to be secure. She soon learned her mistake; she had been engaged to sing in eight performances of *Rigoletto*, but was told she would not be wanted for the remaining seven, and paid off. Banished like a failure, she went to Milan, where La Scala took her to its heart. Toscanini was conducting there, and he and Alda formed a close friendship. In 1908 he helped to launch her at the Metropolitan Opera House, New York, whose director, Giulio Gatti-Casazza, she married in 1910. The rest of Frances Alda's professional life was lived almost entirely in the Americas, and for many years she was nearly as powerful at the Metropolitan as Melba at Covent Garden, but possibly more benign.

Few competent judges of the human voice who put their opinions on record at the time believed that Selma Kurz or Frances Alda or any of the other coloraturas who came and went at Covent Garden was quite the equal of Melba; they felt her fears that she might be overthrown were understandable but ill-based. That was until Luisa Tetrazzini, unheralded and practically unknown in England, arrived at Covent Garden for the autumn season in 1907. Tetrazzini sang, and London listened, wondering, entranced. This was the rise of a new and dazzling star. Melba was in mortal peril at last.

5

PETER DAWSON, the Australian bass-baritone, once put the matter in earthy but comprehensible terms. Tetrazzini, he said, 'hadn't a chance of getting in with a tin opener' while Melba was at Covent Garden. Dawson liked Tetrazzini and disliked Melba, so perhaps he exaggerated; but it is true that Melba was ten thousand miles away from London, in Australia, when Tetrazzini burst into Covent Garden for the first time.

It almost seems as if Tetrazzini slipped into Covent Garden while Melba was off her guard. Rosenthal notes that her arrival by 'the back door was yet another proof of the great difficulty many artists encountered in obtaining an engagement at Covent Garden in the days of Melba, Lady de Grey, and Forsyth'. Melba, who always worked hard, had been working harder than usual in the year or so immediately before Tetrazzini's arrival at Covent Garden. She was tired, and had also gone through a troublesome spell of illness. This was understandable. After a heavy season of opera and concert engagements in London in 1906, she went to New York in the December to appear at the Manhattan Opera House which Oscar Hammerstein had opened in competition with the powerful—and, as most Americans supposed at the time, the invincible—Metropolitan. Hammerstein knew he could beat the Metropolitan, which had ruled the New York grand opera roost unchallenged for twenty-five years, only by a piece of showman's wizardry. He did it by engaging Melba, a long-established star of the Metropolitan.

Melba's action in switching from the Metropolitan to the Manhattan has been the subject of much speculation. Some of her admirers say she did it because she loved a fight, while Vincent Sheean, Hammerstein's biographer, says that she was 'extremely kind when her heart was moved, and the available evidence is that Hammerstein had in some way moved her heart.' To suppose either of these reasons to have been more than secondary is ingenuous. One powerful argument which swayed Melba was the fee Hammerstein offered her, $3,000 a performance; another was the knowledge that at the Manhattan she would be the absolute dictator, as she was at Covent Garden. For some years she had been growing steadily more impatient of the Metropolitan management's inclination to tell her what parts she should sing and when she should sing them. She wanted to teach the Metropolitan a lesson, and she did.

The Manhattan, on West 34th Street, opened on 3 December 1906. Business was sagging when she arrived, but the house was sold out when she made her first appearance, in *Traviata*, on 2 January. American opera-goers already knew and admired Melba, but Oscar Hammerstein or the Manhattan, or both, seemed to bring out new beauties in her voice and new hues in her personality. She sang in fifteen performances, although she had been engaged to appear in only ten, and each time every seat was sold. It was an astonishing feat for a prima donna of forty-six, whose figure had settled into outlines which made it necessary for members of her audience to close their eyes if they were to believe that this was the consumptive Mimi or the nymph-like Gilda.

Vincent Sheean says that Melba 'saved' Hammerstein. That has never been disputed. Whatever was to come later, it was Melba who carried the Manhattan Opera House from its ominously shaky beginnings to its first dazzling triumphs. Many other singers – Mary Garden, Luisa Tetrazzini, John McCormack, Alessandro Bonci, and Maurice Renaud, to name a few – were to contribute to the success which culminated in 1910, when the Metropolitan bought Hammerstein off with a cheque for $1,250,000. But Melba was the first and the principal architect of Hammerstein's victory, and worth every nickel of the $3,000 a performance which he paid her.

After making her last appearance of the season at the Manhattan on 25 March 1907, Melba caught a ship to Europe. She landed at Cherbourg early in April, and a few days later went down with bronchial pneumonia. One of her lungs was weak for months afterwards, but she sang at Covent Garden that season, and apparently sang as well as ever. She felt physically flat, however, and soon after singing on 30 July in *Bohème*, the last opera of the season, she left for Australia on a holiday trip. Less than three months later Tetrazzini made her début at Covent Garden, and swept London off its feet.

Tetrazzini, who was one of the best-loved prima donnas in the history of opera, not only by the public but also by her fellow singers, published an autobiography in 1921. The English edition runs to 328 pages, and Melba's name is mentioned only once, and then in a neutral context on page 177. Melba went one better in her autobiography; she did not mention Tetrazzini at all. Thus both the principals in perhaps the most celebrated battle of singing giants in the history of grand opera maintained public silence about the affair once it was over. This is a matter of some interest, since in the world of reminiscing divas, as in the world of reminiscing generals, dog sometimes declines to eat dog, but not often.

Melba must have had some working knowledge of Tetrazzini's singing abilities long before 1907; being sensitive to such things, she perhaps even thought of Tetrazzini at times as a potential rival but while they were far apart this did not matter much. When Tetrazzini came to London, Melba's home ground as it were, the situation took on a new, and startling, complexion.

Tetrazzini was born in Florence on 29 June 1871, and was thus at thirty-six ten years younger than Melba and in her singing prime when she reached London. Her sister Eva, nine years older than Luisa, and also a soprano, had made her début at Covent Garden in 1890 but never achieved more than moderate success in London. Luisa owed something to Eva, who was one of her early teachers, but rather more to the circumstance that Eva married Cleofonte Campanini, the great conductor. It was Campanini, at that time principal conductor at Covent Garden, who recommended Luisa to the management. He was doubtless prompted by a wish to help his wife's younger sister, but he had another reason also; this was rooted in his well-established dislike of Melba, who never hesitated to override his musical authority if she saw fit. He hoped to break her power at Covent Garden.

Luisa Tetrazzini had a long sequence of successes behind her; her reputation was high in her native Italy, and also in Spain, Portugal, Russia, Mexico and Latin America, yet she was known in London only by hearsay, and to a mere handful of grand opera connoisseurs. Although well recommended she did not come trailing those clouds of glory which enable a prima donna to fill the house before her name goes up on the billboards. She had a winning personality but being thirty-six and rotund was no great beauty, and her fees, though below Melba's, were still stiff. Having engaged her, the Covent Garden management began to have doubts as the time for her to arrive drew near. In the sober light of the boardroom she appeared to have too little to justify the cost of bringing her to London – too little at any rate unless she should turn out to be the marvel that her brother-in-law, Campanini, said she was. The season opened on 3 October, with Tetrazzini not listed to sing for another month, and London was not enthusiastic. For a start it was not 'the' Covent Garden season, but only the autumn season, when the stars of the audience, like Lady de Grey and her circle, as well as the singing stars, like Nellie Melba, were apt to be otherwise engaged. Seeing a heavy loss ahead, the management wired Tetrazzini suggesting a postponement of her début until 1908. She refused and so, preferring to risk a money loss rather than fight an action for breach of contract, they resigned themselves to the worst and told her to come to London after all.

She came and, all in a single night, she conquered. She made her début on 2 November, as Violetta in *Traviata* – one of the half-dozen roles recognized at Covent Garden as Melba's special property. The regular old-guard opera-goers were not much excited by Tetrazzini's coming; so little excited, in fact, that many of the more expensive seats remained unbooked a few days before the performance and hundreds were given away to make sure the new prima donna would not sing to a half-empty house. One section of Londoners turned up at Covent Garden in force, however; this was the Italian community who, so one man present at Covent Garden that night recalled, 'had long been waiting for a countrywoman of theirs who could be pitted against the great Australian singer in the Covent Garden where she had queened it so long'. They found her in Luisa Tetrazzini.

That was one of the unforgettable Covent Garden nights. It was not a Melba Night or a Caruso Night but something all of its own, and no bigoted interpretation of the facts can alter them. Tetrazzini carried with her not only her ecstatic compatriots but the whole audience, including the critics. Rosenthal records that the audience, at first apathetic, 'ended by giving the newcomer one of the warmest ovations heard at Covent Garden for many years.' The echoes of 'Brava!' and the hand-clapping had hardly died away when the London morning newspapers appeared, affirming in print everything that Tetrazzini's hearers had expressed in their own way. Some of the critics described her as 'the new Patti'; she had seen that phrase attached to her name a year or two before, when she had sung in a season of grand opera at San Francisco and been hailed by the public and the critics alike. One man, a regular patron of Covent Garden, who did not bother to attend her début, decided on reading the newspapers that he must hear her as soon as possible. Walking to his office, he went by way of Covent Garden, intending to book a seat for Tetrazzini's next appearance, but found a queue stretching right out to the Strand. He did not hear her that season, but had to wait until the summer.

Whenever she sang in the remaining four weeks of that autumn, whether in *Traviata*, *Lucia*, or *Rigoletto*, the house was sold out as soon as booking opened. Black-market prices for tickets on a Tetrazzini Night were dizzy. The company included many other good singers, such as Félia Litvinne, Maria Gay, Edna Thornton, Amadeo Bassi, Giuseppe de Luca, John McCormack, and Mario Sammarco, but it was Tetrazzini who packed the house. She had a voice resembling the flight of a flashing bright-winged bird and a virtuoso's skill in using it; but she also had some other transcendent quality which was all her own. Those who heard her in her prime said that her gramophone recordings never did her justice; although the microphone captured the glitter of her top notes, the perfection of her trill, and all the other fine details of her singing, it missed some extra element which was present when she stood before an audience. Perhaps the only name for that element is 'star quality' – the mysterious thing which makes the difference between a good public entertainer and a great one. Patti had it. So did Jean de Reszke and Caruso. So did Tetrazzini; and Melba. It lifted them high above those about them. It cannot be acquired by the most painstaking study. Like any other kind of genius, it has to be born in the individual.

Melba arrived back in London in good time to make ready for the 1908 summer season at Covent Garden, opening on 30 April. She must have known the biggest test of her career lay ahead, for Tetrazzini was also back in London; her success in the autumn had been so phenomenal that the Syndicate could not have resisted, even to please Melba, the public demand that Tetrazzini should be booked for the summer. There is no evidence that Melba tried to bolt Covent Garden's doors against Tetrazzini. Agnes Murphy published an early biography of Melba (which Herman Klein, the critic and teacher once described as 'nearly, but not quite, an autobiography'), in which she insisted that 'Melba knew little of what had been said and done during her absence,' and 'set her influence against the cultivation of any form of rivalry between herself and her colleagues'. Miss Murphy then went on to elaborate her point (could her adulatory tongue possibly have been in her cheek when she wrote it?) by saying that Melba made her reappearance at Covent Garden on 19 May 1908 in *La Bohème*, 'an opera which allows her practically no opportunity for brilliant vocal display, and which has in it no element to make any special appeal to the enthusiasm of even her wildest partisans'. Since Mimi had long been

Melba's most popular role and was to remain so throughout her life, Miss Murphy's statement must be classed as a piece of benevolent self-delusion. The season was successful, and Melba and Tetrazzini did not come into open conflict, then or later, but among friends neither made any pretence of liking the other. Once, passing a suite at the Savoy Hotel, London, while Melba was practising, Tetrazzini turned to Mrs Kate Butler, the Savoy's lady superintendent, and asked, 'Have you *many* cats in your lovely hotel?'

Tetrazzini scored a series of successes in *Il Barbiere di Siviglia, Les Huguenots, Rigoletto, Lucia di Lammermoor, Traviata* and *Les Pêcheurs de Perles*, and Melba a series of no less brilliant ones in *Bohème, Otello, Rigoletto*, and *Traviata*. The rival prima donnas — for the rivalry was deep and burning, no matter what Agnes Murphy and other apologists tried to pretend — alternated in *Rigoletto* and *Traviata*, and whether a hearer preferred the one or the other came down to a matter of individual taste. The beauty of singing lies as much in the ear of the listener as a woman's beauty lies in the eye of the beholder, and it was a choice between the coruscating coloratura flights of Tetrazzini and the angelic purity of Melba. A few days after Melba's death in 1931, a columnist in the London *Sunday Times*, in recalling the long-ago duel of the prima donnas, wrote:

'I saw and heard [Melba] at Covent Garden about twenty years ago when she appeared on the same evening as Tetrazzini. That grand vocalist was just then the rage on the musical stage of Europe and America. Her execution was wonderful, and she could produce higher notes than most sopranos could reach without loss of quality. I do not think it was the intention of the management to pit the one prima donna against the other; but that was the form the entertainment assumed for most of us in the audience. They both sang the compositions of the Italian masters of the great period which was the best test for both; for Signora Tetrazzini herself never appeared in German opera and Melba's few attempts at Wagner were not very successful. It was a feast of golden and silver notes; and I thought nobody could possibly have rendered that clear, tuneful southern music better than the Florentine artiste — except the Australian! There was a kind of depth and majesty about Melba's singing that seemed to me to surpass all Tetrazzini's vocal gymnastics, amazing as these were.'

Those who heard Melba and Tetrazzini at that time were rarely neutral; they nearly always found persuasive reasons for preferring one or the other. As a generalization, it is probably true that people who enjoyed singing with their hearts first and their heads second tended to favour the Italian, while the more erudite and analytical listeners preferred the Australian.

Oscar Hammerstein, still waging his war with the Metropolitan, engaged Tetrazzini for the Manhattan Opera House in 1908. This was the first time she had been heard in New York, and as in London she unleashed a kind of public madness. The popular effect of her singing on large sections of the public both in London and New York is comparable with nothing in latter-day operatic history; it resembles the mob hysteria which today accompanies the public appearances of some groups of young singers of ultra-popular songs, with the difference that many of the people who screamed, sobbed, and flung their hats in the air when Tetrazzini sang were not teen-agers but mature people living sober and balanced lives. Hammer-stein's biographer, Vincent Sheean, says 'there can be little doubt from the critical accounts given of the two that Melba had the lovelier voice and the more exquisite control, but I have a fairly good idea that if I had been able to hear opera in those days I should have admired Melba but spent my money on Tetrazzini.'

Although Tetrazzini was a star of opera in New York for only four years, from 1908 to 1912, first at the Manhattan, and later at the Metropolitan, she held New York's opera-going public in the hollow of her small and chubby hand from first to last. On her fare-well appearance at the Metropolitan in 1912, as Gilda in *Rigoletto*, with Caruso as the Duke and Renaud as the Jester, two thousand people clamoured to be admitted after the house was full and the doors were closed; the police were able to quell the threatened disorders only by using rugged methods. It is freely agreed that this siege of the Metropolitan was not inspired by the names on the billboards of those two fine artists, Caruso and Renaud; it was a salute to Tetrazzini.

Most of the New York critics admired Tetrazzini, but some of them were less ready than the London critics to see her as a great soprano. When she made her Metropolitan début as Lucia, in 1911, Henry Krehbiel wrote in the *New York Tribune*: 'Mme Tetrazzini was received with much cordiality on her entrance, but after she had begun to sing she was, we fear, made to realize there are different standards of judgment touching the art of song among the patrons of opera in New York . . . there is not much to be said of Mme Tetrazzini's singing that has not been said over and over again in these columns – said in praise and said in mournful depreciation; in praise of her command of artistic device, in dispraise of the inequalities of her voice; in praise of the fine texture of her upper tones, in regret because of the infantile character of her lower; in laudation of skill artistically used and in denunciation of the same skill abused.'

On the other hand Pitts Sanborn, the New York critic, novelist and essayist, writing in 1912, said of Tetrazzini: 'Only Sembrich and Melba in our day have been worthy to be compared with her, and in some respects she is a greater singer than Sembrich, in some not, but in all, save sheer voice, a greater than Melba. One can afford to forget the quibbles and just be thankful that the Metropolitan stage, in days when real singing is all too seldom heard, boasts, if but for a few performances, one woman still in the prime of her voice who can sing like a vicar of song on earth.'

John Amadio, the New Zealand-born flautist, who occasionally played obbligatos for Melba but worked more often with Tetrazzini, whom he accompanied on a number of tours, formed his own estimate of the two and held to it. A few weeks before his sudden death in 1964 Amadio said: 'Melba was unique. Her voice was never big, nor of exceptionally long range, but it was wonderful in quality and perfectly controlled; her intonation was always faultless. She did not have the bravura of Tetrazzini, who was able to throw out the high Es and the low notes with equal effortlessness, but she was the finer singer.'

Tetrazzini went back to London year after year until 1912. That was her last season at Covent Garden, and from then on she concentrated on her career elsewhere, chiefly in America. So her contest with Melba did not finish in a clear victory for one or the other, but at the end Melba was left in possession of the London field.

Whatever their comparative merits, Melba easily outlasted Tetrazzini; she was still singing well, although below her youthful best, when Tetrazzini, her voice worn to a shadow of what it had been, was struggling to fill English concert halls by flaunting the bright shreds of her once-dazzling reputation. Tetrazzini earned tremendous fees in her prime, but she was a woman of spontaneous and unthinking generosity, and no unscrupulous sponger who pitched her a reasonably plausible hard-luck tale went away empty-handed. If she had been blessed with some of Melba's shrewdness she would not have lived her last years, as she did, with debt-collectors always close behind her. Melba was often generous to deserving people, but rarely to the undeserving; she had an almost unerring nose for the glib opportunist. Claude Kingston, who was closely associated with the management of both the 1924 and 1928 Melba-Williamson grand opera seasons in Australia, said: 'Melba would come to my office fairly regularly early in the morning, bringing a bundle of letters asking for help. She was amazingly psychic when analysing such appeals. She would read through every letter carefully, tear up those she considered bogus, and then give me directions about helping the writers of the others. I remember that the amount disbursed came to over £400 one day—fair money then. Her gifts usually varied between five and fifty pounds, according to her reading of the distress signals. In some cases she nominated a certain amount to be paid weekly over a period. In her lifetime she must have distributed a fortune in this way. I, and others who knew of it, were on our honour to say nothing about it.' At times Melba, although not a sentimentalist, would succumb to an impulse to indulge in quixotic generosities. On a concert tour after World War I she was taking a morning drive in Dundee when she saw a woman standing on the kerb selling flowers. She took a hard look at the woman, then told the chauffeur to pull over, got out of the car with her accompanist, Lindley Evans, and walked back.

'I've seen you somewhere,' she said.

'Yes,' the flower-seller replied. 'I've often see you, Dame Nellie. I used to sell flowers outside Covent Garden.'

Evans could see Melba was touched, but she pretended to be gruff. She asked the woman where she lived and, having heard the address, nodded and said, 'Oh, well, I'm glad to have seen you,' and led the way back to the car.

Next day Lindley Evans was sent off to the address the flower-seller had given with a gift from Melba for old times' sake—about ten pounds' worth of groceries packed into the boot of the car.

Melba's generosities were usually more carefully reasoned, however, and it is a pity that Tetrazzini's were not. The end of her life was wretched. Some years after World War I ended her money ran low and she came out of retirement and struggled to keep the pot boiling by making concert tours. Much of the splendour of her voice was gone, and she was hardly more than a travesty of the Tetrazzini who had conquered London and New York. She died at Milan on 28 April 1940, nearly penniless, and forgotten except as a name by most of those who had once flocked to her opera appearances and recitals as to the shrine of a goddess.

6

MELBA sometimes cursed Australia and Australians, but she had an abiding love of her own people and her own country, even if they often enough exasperated her. Having sung to the large cities, she wanted to sing also to the smaller country places, and that was what she did in 1909. She called it a 'sentimental tour'; that was an over-simplification because the tour paid her well, but a series of recitals in the principal cities would have paid her equally well and been far more comfortable.

She had to miss the summer season at Covent Garden, leaving the field to Tetrazzini, but the possible consequences did not worry her; or, rather, she gave no signs of worry. She caught the *Orontes* for Australia at the end of January and bubbled with high spirits all through the trip. An Australian named Florence Laidlaw, who had known Melba and her family for years, was travelling in the *Orontes*. Melba one day pounced on Miss Laidlaw's autograph book and said, without invitation, 'Come on, Flossie, I'll write something in your book for you.' She flipped over the pages, then stopped abruptly; her eyes were fixed on an inscription signed a year or so before by Ruby Armstrong, an English girl whom George Armstrong had married in 1906; their short and stormy marriage had been legally dissolved in 1908, and the circumstances of the divorce were still rankling with Melba.

'Flossie,' said Melba, 'that comes out for a start!', and without further ado she ripped out the page, tore it up and let the fragments go fluttering away on the ocean wind. Having thus cleansed Miss Laidlaw's autograph book, Melba took a pen and wrote: 'Never strike sail to a fear. Come into port bravely, or sail with God the seas', dated it 16 February 1909, signed it with a flourish, and handed the book back to its owner. Miss Laidlaw felt she should make some protest about the violence Melba had done to her autograph book, but then she shrugged and said nothing. Like most of Melba's friends, she had learned to treat such high-handed acts with resignation.

Melba was bursting with energy when she disembarked in Melbourne; this was just as well, because to travel the hinterland of Australia in those days, before World War I, was physically trying for a woman nearing fifty. Melba covered 10,000 miles, in New Zealand as well as Australia; 7,000 miles of the trip was made by railway trains and in small coastal steamers which were often comfortless and sometimes grubby. She sang in towns as remote as Dubbo, Glen Innes and Orange in New South Wales, and Mount Morgan, Townsville and Charters Towers in Queensland. The tour was not sentimental enough to take in Mackay; she passed Mackay in the steamer which carried her and her party on the 540-mile journey from Townsville to Gladstone.

She enjoyed herself, for all the roughness of the going at times. Of course she did everything to make travelling as agreeable as possible. As well as John Lemmone, who was both manager and flautist, and three assisting artists, she had her personal maid, and also a valet to see to the luggage. In trains, ships and hotels she slept between her own monogrammed linen sheets. Two small grand pianos also went along. So, in one way and another, her journeyings had the royal and authentic Melba touch.

Lemmone, a skilled and indefatigable organizer, made the best arrangements possible at all points, but in some of the outback towns he had to be content with makeshifts. In one place a dark and gloomy horse-drawn carriage arrived at the hotel to take Melba to her concert. She looked at it doubtfully and said, 'Funny vehicle we've got tonight!' Lemmone confessed later that it was a mourning coach hired from the local undertaker; no other even approximately suitable vehicle had been available.

Melba basked in the adulation; her appetite for that never became jaded. In every town there was a gala supper at the best hotel, with the local notables and their wives gathered together to drink her health. Small crowds gathered even at wayside stations where her train could stop for only a few minutes, and she always showed herself, graciously accepting the salutations of her subjects.

She made a habit of taking a walk on any morning when she was not travelling. Una Bourne, her pianist, was often her companion, and Melba never failed to stop somewhere to talk with another stroller or a man or a woman in a cottage garden.

'Are you coming to my concert?' she would ask.

The answer was often yes, but if it was not she would say, 'Oh, nonsense! You must come,' snap open her handbag and scribble out a pass on one of her own cards. Every hall was booked to capacity weeks beforehand, and Melba's queenly gesture in issuing free passes all but drove John Lemmone to despair.

'Nellie, you mustn't!' he would expostulate, when someone else arrived at the hall with Melba's card and had to be fitted into a seat.

'Oh, get along with you, John,' she would tell him. 'I've invited them, and you've got to find room for them.'

It was while she was making that 1909 tour that her Australianism took fire. From then onward she always kept one foot in her own country, even though she spent perhaps half of her remaining twenty-two years living and singing and travelling abroad. Although she never failed to start pining for London and Paris and the sophistication of Europe after a few months in Australia, she always liked coming home. At times when she was abroad an almost overwhelming hunger for the sights and sounds and smells of the Australian countryside would attack her. One of the things she liked to do in Australia was to go out alone into a quiet place in the hills near Lilydale and sit, listening to the golden notes of the bellbirds chiming through the bush. Perhaps she listened to the bellbirds with a singer's ear and heard in them a perfection of sound no human singer could ever attain, but it is more likely that she listened to them just with the ear of an Australian going back to her beginnings.

It was in 1909 too, that she showed a practical interest for the first time not only in singing to Australians but also in creating a school of Australian singers trained in what she believed to be the only correct method of singing—in effect, Mathilde Marchesi's method with some modifications of Melba's own. As a first step she formed her own singing classes at the University of Melbourne's Conservatorium of Music; her aim was to give any specially talented young singer the benefit of her knowledge, but above all to train aspiring singing teachers in what was later to become known as the Melba method. She was successful; some able singing teachers, who in the years ahead moulded the singing voices of scores of young Australians, came from those classes. Melba thought she would be hailed as a national benefactress for doing this, but the applause was not unanimous. Cynics said that it was just another piece of self-advertising; she was interested less in producing singers, they scoffed, than in producing limelight for herself. They also said that any girl with a voice resembling Melba's could hope for nothing—Melba wanted no rivals and would go to any lengths to discourage a potential competitor. This campaign of detraction depressed her, and one day she told one of her students, Beryl Fanning, stressing the words with some bitterness, 'I do wish I could find a really high soprano, because they are saying I am too jealous to teach any but contraltos. I am really a good-hearted woman.' It was probably then that Melba began toying with the idea of finding a successor to herself. She never did find one; perhaps, subconsciously, she never wanted to, and knew in her heart she never would. The odds against the world ever producing a facsimile of her voice were, and are, heavy, while any possibility that the world will ever again produce such a voice in the body of a woman having the personality to use it as Melba did are astronomic. It is like expecting another Michelangelo, another Shakespeare or another Beethoven to appear.

She had for some years thought of buying a small country property, and making an Australian home for herself. One day in 1909 she found what she was looking for in Victoria, just outside the township of Coldstream, four miles or so on from the town of Lilydale where David Mitchell had his limestone quarries. The place was about forty-five acres in area, a sweep of grassy paddocks with a little stone cottage. She discussed it with her canny old father before buying and he said, 'Aye, lassie, it's a nice wee property, but . . .', and pointed out that the natural water supply was meagre and that to bring adequate water there would be costly. She said she had thought about that and was willing to pay the cost, and, having satisfied herself of what could be done with the place, she drove up to the cottage one evening and knocked on the door. The owner, Mrs Dooley, answered Melba's knock; Mrs Dooley used the land for grazing while her husband, John Dooley, worked as a stevedore. Melba introduced herself, then cut through to the heart of the matter by saying she wanted to buy the land and the cottage. Mrs Dooley named a price.

'Very well,' Melba said. 'Let me have a piece of paper, and I'll give you a note of it now.'

The light was going, and it was dark in the little cottage. 'Why not wait until tomorrow?' Mrs Dooley asked.

'No,' Melba replied. 'Let's do it now.'

So Mrs Dooley fetched two candles and put them on the living-room table, and there and then Melba scribbled out a home-made contract to buy. She and Mrs Dooley signed it, and the deal was completed.

It was in this way that she came to the Lilydale-Coldstream region which was to become known as 'the Melba country'.

To design her house she called in a Melbourne architect and

civil engineer, John Grainger, a Londoner, who had settled in Australia many years before and made a good name. He was the father of Percy Grainger, the pianist and composer, whom Melba had helped to launch on a career in Europe, but she did not choose him on that account; she simply believed him to be the best man to do what she wanted done. They spent many days together, inspecting the property and discussing ideas. Grainger drew sketch-plans, and she examined these minutely and critically, and made changes here and there, but on the whole she liked his vision of a large one-storey house with wide verandas, built around the Dooleys' old cottage.

The thing began to shape itself in her mind as it would one day be, with terraced gardens, sweeping lawns, a swimming pool, and a high and dense cypress hedge enclosing it all like a great green wall. It would be a quiet place to come home to when she wanted a change from Europe – perhaps some day a place in which she would live her last years in the shadow of what she possessively called 'my hills'. She decided to call it Coombe Cottage, in memory of an historic house at Kingston Hill, Surrey, twelve miles from London, which some years before she had rented from Admiral Lord Charles Beresford, and lived in for one happy summer.

7

THE country surrounding Lilydale and Coldstream is green and gentle, with some low rolling hills, lush and plump. The road from Melbourne, making a long low sweep, curves down into Lilydale around the flank of a hill and the shallow valley unrolls below. The town lies there, with the farms dotted about it, and the valley stretches away to the blue of the Great Dividing Range in the east and the soft contours of the Dandenong Ranges in the south. It is a tranquil place. It had a few exciting years in the 1860s, when Lilydale was a staging-point roughly halfway between Melbourne and the Warburton gold diggings; then the Warburton gold petered out and life settled back to its normal gait, and none of the local people were really sorry.

In Melba's time most of the land was held by small farmers, and except for one or two places it was still held by small farmers fifty years after she found there the piece of country she wanted for herself. Many of the farm families had been there for two or three generations. It was good country, green all through the year barring a month or two at the height of the summer, and most of the farmers were content to go their way at an even jog, making a living for themselves and their children without becoming slaves. They were solid people, warm-hearted people when you knew them, although on the reserved side with strangers. But David Mitchell's girl, Nellie, was no stranger; the valley had known her from the days when she was a tomboyish schoolgirl, kicking up her heels like a young colt. Nobody—except perhaps herself—had dreamed then that she would make one of the great names of the world, and that whenever she came back to Lilydale the main street would be decked with bunting, that mounted horsemen would turn out to escort her into the town, and that the local band would blow its hardest in her honour.

Her father, now an old man, but with an irrepressibly twinkling eye, was one of the pillars of the place, although Doonside, the family home at Richmond, continued to be the main focus of his daily life. At one time he had been a shire councillor for some years. Most of the able-bodied men in the district had worked for him at his Cave Hill quarries, and apart from Cave Hill he had owned grazing properties in the neighbouring hills. At the time Melba bought her land at Coldstream he owned St Huberts, a vineyard where he grew luscious grapes and pressed wine which had a good name with men of palate in Australia and even with some in Europe. He liked the respect which his wine commanded; if he did anything at all he had to do it as well as anyone else, and if possible better. That was one of the things his daughter Nellie inherited from him.

The valley knew and liked all the Mitchells, in particular Charlie Mitchell, Melba's second brother, who lived with his wife and young family at Cave Hill, managing the quarry operations for his father. Everyone knew Charlie Mitchell; he was a great outdoor man, a good horseman and a fine shot, and they said he could outdrink any other man within two hundred miles. Charlie never pretended to be dedicated to hard work like his father. He had a self-protective arrangement with the men who drove the railway train from Melbourne to Lilydale. When David Mitchell was on board, coming up from Doonside to make sure that work at his quarries was going on in the appointed way, the driver would sound

the whistle twice when passing Cave Hill; then by the time the
old man walked across from the station Charlie would be at his
desk, with a mass of papers in front of him and a portentous frown
on his brow, where a quarter of an hour earlier he had probably
been whistling cheerily away as he cleaned his guns, and thinking
of anything but profits and loss on limestone. It did not always
work out like that, but he fooled his father most of the time.

Charlie Mitchell had been an outlaw as a boy and he was an
outlaw as a man, but a lovable one who had the priceless gift of
playing jokes which deflated pompous people and made ordinary
men crack their sides laughing. He must have been a throw-back
to some scapegrace of an ancestor, because he had none of the rever-
ence for business which had helped to make his father and his sister
Nellie successful, nor could he bring himself to be even decently
respectful in the presence of worldly success. Melba was leaving
Melbourne town hall one night after giving a recital at which the
social as well as the musical elect of the city were present. Looking
every inch a queen, she sailed down the great main porticoed
stairway to the street, escorted by her manager and a band of courtiers and watched by the crowd with wide and wondering eyes.
Her Rolls-Royce was waiting at the foot of the steps, and immediately behind it stood a horsedrawn piecart, which had no business
to be there. As the diva reached the bottom step, the mufflered
pieman, peering out from under the peak of his cloth cap and waving
a bottle of tomato sauce, hoarsely invited her, 'Saveloy an' roll,
Mum?' She transfixed him with a lethal glare, then stepped into
her car and was whirled away. Even in her fury, she could not help
wondering how much her brother Charlie had paid the pieman
for the loan of the piecart, the cap and the muffler, and then how
much more he had paid the traffic control men on duty outside the
town hall to let him drive the piecart into position behind her
Rolls-Royce.

She tried to make allowances for his irresponsibility, on the
ground that he was nine years her junior, but did not always succeed.
She never knew when Charlie would embarrass her or her guests,
and his more outrageous practical jokes now and then led to temporary estrangements between them. Some years after building
Coombe Cottage she installed a light on each of the two gateposts
flanking the main entrance. Driving back to Cave Hill after dark
from a shooting expedition, Charlie Mitchell saw the two lighted
globes and could not resist the temptation. He pulled up his car,

got out a rifle, and shattered the globes with two well-aimed shots. Melba vowed she would never speak to him again and even talked of suing him, but they were speaking again in a week or two and the threat of litigation was forgotten.

Some of her more stately friends believed she was unwise to make her Australian home anywhere near Lilydale, since her brother Charlie lived there, but she took the chance, and never regretted buying the place at Coldstream. She always loved it, and although she settled Coombe Cottage on her son in 1915 (and with it an adjoining property of some 500 acres, Coombe Farm, which she bought later), she reserved the right to live there, and did live a good part of nearly every year there for the rest of her life.

The interest she found in establishing Coombe Cottage did not make her forget that she had a professional reputation to keep alive. At the end of 1909 she knew she had been away from London long enough, especially with a rival of Tetrazzini's calibre at Covent Garden, and she was back there, vocally and physically as indestructible as ever, for the opening of the 1910 summer season. Before leaving Australia, however, she laid the foundations of a project she had been revolving in her mind for a long time; this was to take to Australia a grand opera company of international standard and let her fellow countrymen hear opera sung by artists of world stature. The company would be built around her, of course. How could it be otherwise? And she wanted Australians to hear her not just in recitals but in opera, while her voice still retained most of its splendour. She also wanted her father to sit back in a box and hear what she could do as Mimi, Desdemona, Violetta, Marguerite.

The one-time Nellie Mitchell, of Richmond, had conquered Europe and America, and she wanted to complete her conquest of her own country. So the Melba-Williamson opera company of 1911 was formed. It was to leave a lasting impression on Australia's theatrical history.

8

OPERA companies, some bad, some mediocre, and two or three reasonably good, had toured Australia before, but the Melba-Williamson company of 1911 set a new high standard. It was as important a milestone in the history of grand opera in Australia as the visit of Sarah Bernhardt, twenty-odd years before, in the history of straight theatre. The company was not the equal of a Covent Garden, a Paris Opéra, a La Scala, or a Metropolitan Opera House company, of course; no entrepreneur could have recruited such a company, transported it to Australia, and staged a season of opera without ending in the bankruptcy court. But it was a collection of fine artists.

Melba and the American-born Australian theatre magnate, J. C. Williamson, joined forces to run the season. Neither could have done it alone and each knew it. Melba and John Lemmone recruited the artists. Lemmone spent most of 1910 in Europe, moving from opera house to opera house with an ear cocked for promising singers, then going back to Melba in London, Paris or wherever she happened to be to discuss his findings with her. While conducting the search, he and Melba managed to fit in concert tours of Europe, the USA, and Canada, with Lemmone playing her obbligatos and also consolidating his reputation as a solo flautist. In America they took time to make recordings of Melba singing to Lemmone's fluting. Considering it was hardly more than a decade since the gramophone had ceased to be an inventor's bad dream these records were astonishingly good. At the same time Lemmone made a solo flute recording of the Metzger composition, *By the brook*. This is interesting for a special reason: Melba played the piano accompaniment.

The company, which reached Australia in August and began rehearsing for the opening of the season at Sydney early in September, included as well as Melba some impressive figures of the grand opera stage. The one who was to go on to make the biggest name, excepting only Melba herself, was John McCormack. He had gone back to Covent Garden every year since making his début there in 1908 and his reputation had steadily grown. But in 1911 he loomed little, if at all, larger than the other stars of the Melba-Williamson company, such as the American mezzo-soprano Eleanora de Cisneros, the Polish dramatic soprano Janina Korolewicz-Wayda, the Italian baritone Angelo Scandiani, and the Canadian bass Edmund Burke.

Melba had chosen McCormack not because she liked him personally but because she thought he sang well, and he had accepted the engagement not out of affection for her but because the fees were good and he wanted to see Australia. As ever, they were apt to strike fire from each other whenever they were together. To Melba, McCormack was a gifted but brash young man, with much yet to learn; to McCormack, Melba was a domineering prima donna, who supposed that her lightest remark should be listened to in awed silence. His acting was even stiffer and more stilted than hers, but he shot venomous glances at her at rehearsals when she criticized his stage deportment; when she questioned his singing he fairly flamed. While they were rehearsing *Roméo et Juliette* she interrupted him in the middle of a phrase, 'No, no! Jean sang it like this,' she said, thinking back to Jean de Reszke, her first Roméo, and as she always believed her best. Before she could sing the phrase as Jean de Reszke had sung it, McCormack spat at her, 'I'm John McCormack, and I sing it like this!' He did so there and then, and continued to sing it like that for the rest of the season. Their strained relations were not soothed when as the season progressed McCormack showed himself to possess a business sense no less lively than Melba's own. He had signed a contract to sing in three operas a week, but after eyeing the packed houses he contrived to find the Australian climate so hard on his voice that his third weekly appearance nearly always became impossible unless he was compensated by an extra fee of £100. Since Melba and J. C. Williamson were sharing the profits of the season this meant that every time McCormack gouged more money out of the management half of it came from her pocket.

One night when his voice was troubling him and she and Williamson had refused to soothe him with an extra £100, she sang *Bohème* with a second-string lyric tenor, Guido Ciccolini, as her Rodolfo. Ciccolini had a pleasant voice but sang only fairly well; for one thing his sense of tempo was sketchy and whenever Melba found an excuse to do so she would embrace him and keep him in time by tapping on his back. After the final curtain Ciccolini gallantly bowed to her and said, 'Madame, you still sing beautiful!' She might have passed over it if he had omitted the word 'still', but at fifty she could not accept the implication. She gave the tactless Ciccolini one withering look, then turned on her heel and strode away. Finding the operatic heights beyond him, Ciccolini turned to vaudeville, and some years later electric lights blazing in front of the Palace Theatre, New York, proclaimed him to be, on Melba's authority, the greatest living tenor. She would have fumed to know that he of all people had appointed her his musical fairy godmother.

The memories of knowledgeable listeners who heard her sing in the 1911 season leave no doubt that Ciccolini was right; she still did sing beautifully, and on some nights she fell only a little short of the best she had done in her first golden decade at Covent Garden. A man named Ladislas de Noskowski, who arrived in Australia from his native Poland a few months before the season opened, and settled in Sydney, was a close friend of several of the principals and heard most of the performances. A student of singing, who was later to write music criticism for various Sydney periodicals, he came of a music-loving family, and one of his uncles, Zygmunt Noskowski, was a symphonic composer. Looking back more than fifty years later to the entries in his 1911 diary, he recalled that in *Roméo et Juliette* Melba 'sang her high notes from A flat upwards with care, and not as spontaneously and freely as she must have sung them formerly', but added: 'Nevertheless her coloratura was faultless, the trills and runs being admirable. Later, in her despair at losing Roméo, Melba's Juliette, however, was exactly the same as her Gilda, her Violetta, and her Marguerite.' After a performance of *Traviata* he noted in his diary: 'The limpid and unique quality of her lovely voice seems to fill every corner of the theatre with effortless ease, but the voice is rather cold. Of her acting the least said the better. Her movements are brusque and often seem to lack refinement.'

The audiences were dazzled by the showy spectacles and enchanted by the fine singing, and knew nothing of the storms which blew up behind the scenes. Even when Melba and McCormack were not bickering the backstage regions were rarely calm; perhaps the backstage regions of any opera house are never calm for long. Brushes between Melba and the Polish soprano Madame Wayda were frequent. After a performance of *Madama Butterfly*, in which the singing of Wayda and McCormack roused wild enthusiasm, a slanging match developed between her husband, Dr Wladyslaw Wayda, and Hugh J. Ward, who was in charge of J. C. Williamson's operations in Sydney; the cause of the dispute was an order Melba had given restricting the presentation of flowers.

'You bad manager!' Dr Wayda howled at Ward. 'This is not theatre! This is vaudeville! What do I care about Melba? I don't care about Melba!'

Melba was doubtless jealous of Madame Wayda on one count. Melba had long yearned to sing the role of Tosca, and intended doing so in Australia in 1911. She could have sung it years before had she insisted, either in London or New York, but she was secretly a little frightened, not of Tosca's music, but of the histrionic demands of the part; in fact, she recorded *Vissi d'arte* in 1907, and in the opinion of some good judges it is one of her best discs. She once told Mary Garden she had been studying the part. Mary Garden later commented: '. . . she never could sing Tosca – and never did. She just wasn't made for Tosca.' Most people with any knowledge of opera agree, but *Tosca* had never been performed in Australia, and Melba resolved to put it on in 1911 with herself in the title role. A few days before the first performance she fell ill in Sydney; Wayda took her place and was so successful that Melba abandoned any thought of singing Tosca later in the season. This did not strengthen her liking for the Polish girl.

Wayda reciprocated Melba's dislike. She lived a long life and made a big reputation both as a singer and an actress, in Europe and America, but her antipathy to Melba never diminished. In an autobiography, published in Poland in 1958, three years after her death, Wayda had little good to say of Melba in the many pages she devoted to the 1911 Melba-Williamson season in Australia. She went so far as to attribute Melba's success in London largely to her connections with aristocratic patrons, and in particular to the beneficent influence of Edward VII, and wrote: 'Her artistic powers bore no relation to her fame; she had a beautiful voice and was a good singer, but she was no phenomenon. . . . By nature she was unpleasant, off-handed and brutal, very sure of herself, conceited and spoilt. . . .'

Wayda told in her book how one of the Italian principals, Vito Dammacco, a bass, who had made a good impression with the Sydney critics and public, fell gravely ill early in the Melbourne season. The twenty-eight-year-old Dammacco, whose young wife and their only child were with him in Australia, had no means but his salary. 'Wanting to assist him,' Wayda wrote, 'we asked Melba to take him under her protection. She advised that he should be put in hospital, and this was done, but the all-powerful Melba did nothing to help him. Dammacco was young and, like all artists starting their career, had no money. He lacked funds for medical care, and did not even know whether his salary would be paid during his illness. He was placed in a big ward with about forty other patients, and died after ten days' suffering. The artists paid for his funeral, which was arranged by the theatre manager. His widow did not know English and was nearly prostrate with grief. . . . The day after the funeral Signora Dammacco went to see Melba to find out about her position. Melba was very short with her and offered her twenty francs—truly, twenty francs.* The unfortunate widow was so upset that she took the twenty francs, which she should have thrown at Melba's feet.'

Whatever antagonisms existed between Melba and some of her fellow singers, the stagehands and the gallery patrons swore by her; she showed them an aspect of herself which her professional equals or near-equals rarely saw. Perhaps it was mere showmanship but it worked.

When she paid a visit, well before the season started, to Her Majesty's Theatre, Sydney, the stagehands stood all about staring at her, hardly able to believe they were looking at the great Melba in the flesh.

'Like to hear me sing, boys?' she asked.

She spoke a few words to the conductor, and the orchestra went into the opening of *Ah fors' è lui*. Melba sang it through to the end, and walked off into the wings, then came back and bowed to the stagehands. They were her devoted slaves ever after.

She also won the hearts of the gallery in Sydney with a like gesture. The gallery was packed out by two o'clock every afternoon for the evening performance and the management found a corner there for a piano, so the waiting people could entertain themselves. Melba was persuaded to climb to the gallery one afternoon and show herself. It was a tiring climb but she recovered her wind by the time the ovation died down. Then she sat on the piano-stool and, playing her own accompaniment, sang while the gallery sat, hardly breathing. When she got up to go they stood and yelled their adulation.

She had one favourite among the principals of the company. This was Edmund Burke, a tall and handsome Toronto man, who had started out to study law but changed to singing, and made a success at Covent Garden and on the Continent in such roles as Mephistopheles, Prince Igor, Amfortas, and Abimelech. Burke, then in the middle thirties, was a striking figure, and Melba liked going about with him as her escort. Time had not lessened her

* At that time the exchange rate was twenty-five francs to the £.

disposition to arrange the lives of members of her own family, always with the worthiest of intentions and in what she believed to be the best interests of the individual concerned. She decided that Edmund Burke would, in the fulness of time, make an ideal husband for one of her nieces, Nellie Patterson, then a retiring and diffident schoolgirl, who was fascinated but rather overawed by the world of grand opera as she glimpsed it from a privileged position at her aunt's side. Nellie Patterson was always to remember with horror how she sat, unable to say a word for herself, listening to a discussion between her Aunt Nellie and Burke as to whether he should wait the eight or nine years which would have to pass before the trembling child would be ripe for marriage. She did not remember what decision Aunt Nellie and Burke reached, but she supposed they must have written the idea off in the end. At all events it was one of Melba's cherished projects which came to nothing.

9

THE 1912 season at Covent Garden seemed incomplete; Melba was not there. For most of the year she was busy with her own affairs in Australia. She probably wished also to serve notice on the Syndicate that she was tired of finding Tetrazzini at Covent Garden year after year. If so, the gesture was effective. Tetrazzini sang her familiar roles at Covent Garden in 1912, but it was her last season. The Syndicate managed her departure without any fuss. For one thing, although she was still popular in London, her coloratura flights had become familiar and lost much of their original power to dazzle; for another, the feelings of her brother-in-law, the conductor Campanini, no longer had to be considered because 1912 was his last Covent Garden season also; early in 1913 he became director of the Chicago Opera House, where Tetrazzini joined the roster of prima donnas.

Melba found plenty to do in Australia for most of 1912, first in trimming off the loose ends left by the opera season, and after that with more personal affairs. Coombe Cottage took up much of her time. Many lovers of fine buildings considered the rambling mansion which John Grainger built to her instructions to be a mediocre example of architecture, but it was comfortable and spacious, and she poured into it the pick of her possessions, which she shipped out from Europe; jewellery presented to her by kings and queens, antique furniture bought wherever she had come upon it (Melba had an eye for quality in antique pieces and a sharp nose for a bargain), pictures by fashionable European and Australian artists, and other of her treasures all went into the making of Coombe Cottage.

She had her own ideas on interior decoration as on everything. Some years after Coombe Cottage was built she called on a Melbourne bookseller, Edgar Harris, and asked if he had a batch of books with brown tooled-leather bindings; she wanted them, she said, to complete the decoration of a guest-room. Harris happened to have in a storeroom a job lot of books with impressive bindings of the very kind she described. He had picked these up cheaply on an order from a theatrical producer who needed them as stage furnishings for a play he was putting on in a Melbourne theatre. The play had a long run and when it ended the books came back to Harris who thought of sending them to the destructor; he knew nobody would buy any of them to read, for they were collections of sermons by long-dead divines, old-fashioned essays rich in beautiful thoughts, and a few dreary Victorian novels. He showed them to Melba, who took one look at the bindings, said they were precisely what she wanted, and bought the lot. Harris sometimes wondered with a shudder if any literate house-guest at Coombe Cottage ever tried to read any of them as a bedtime book.

Europe seemed ineffably gracious to Melba when she arrived back there early in 1913, and London positively enchanting. She looked about her, and nothing seemed to have changed, everything to be as she had left it. A handful of men who refused to take life as it came but insisted on peering below the surface for hidden currents and submerged shoals had doubts. They believed a collision between Britain and Germany to be inevitable; it could be only a matter of time before this strutting megalomaniac, Kaiser Wilhelm II, would precipitate a conflict with his paranoiac shouting that 'the bayonets of Europe' were directed against his country. Such pessimists commanded little attention, however.

And in 1913 Melba had other and better things to think of than the political situation in Europe. Twenty-five years earlier, on 24 May 1888, London, as she remembered when she looked back, had shown little enthusiasm for her singing, nor any inclination to fall down at her feet and worship; now she was the great prima donna, whose name on the billboards was enough of itself to ensure that every seat would be sold at the highest price, and it was only right that the twenty-fifth anniversary of her coming to Covent Garden should be fittingly celebrated.

A great burst of publicity attended her appearance in *Bohème* on 22 May. Few sopranos, few singers of any kind, husbanded their voices so well that they were still worth listening to—by Covent Garden's standards at any rate—after a quarter of a century, but Melba's star had hardly dimmed. Every reserved seat was booked days beforehand, and queues waited all night for unreserved seats. The London *Daily Telegraph* reported next morning that her voice had rarely sounded 'richer, fuller or more attractive'. John McCormack, the Rodolfo of the night, was overwhelmed. Although he never formed a warm affection for Melba (and on at least one occasion called her 'an interfering bitch'), McCormack said some years after singing in her twenty-fifth anniversary night at Covent Garden that he counted that appearance with her as one of the great events of his life. He added: 'I believe—in fact, I know—that I sing better with Melba than with any other soprano.' Many singers found they excelled themselves when they sang with Melba; Jean de Reszke and Caruso also had this power to make singers about them do better than they believed they could do.

Melba did not try to hide her satisfaction with her own performance. This was not vanity; she could be arrogant, despotic and aggressive, but she was never vain; she always knew when she had either fallen short of her own level or risen to the height of it. After one of the last concerts she ever gave, late in the 1920s, a woman told her in quivering tones, 'You were wonderful tonight. You have never sung better.' Melba replied, almost between clenched teeth, 'I can assure you, madam, I have.' The public and the critics might be wrong about her singing, but Melba could not fool herself even when she wanted to.

She sang well again at Covent Garden in 1914. Although she turned fifty-three in the first month of that season only the most critical listener could detect any signs of ageing in her choirboy's voice; time had hardly yet begun to darken its pearly sheen. Even when, opening the season in *Bohème*, she sang opposite the twenty-eight-year-old tenor Giovanni Martinelli, she was, for all the difference in their ages, at least his vocal peer. The time had now come when her Rodolfos, her Otellos, her Roméos, her Fausts were men as young as her son George, or younger, but the magic of her voice and her mastery of it ensured that she was still the star of any opera in which she appeared. The years might have caused her strongly-made body to thicken and the skin of her neck to acquire a tracery of fine lines, but opera-lovers went to hear her, not to see her, and what they heard delighted them. She might not look like Gilda or Mimi or Marguerite or Desdemona until she began to sing; but then the enchantment worked and the woman on the stage was not an ageing prima donna, but a young girl in the bloom of youth.

Seven kings and queens (some of whom were to see their thrones swept away for ever in the war which began a few months later) were in the audience of a Covent Garden gala performance in which she sang in 1914. No suspicion crossed her mind then that it was to be five years before she or anyone else would again sing opera at Covent Garden, nor did she dream that when she came back the map of Europe and the life of Europe would be irrevocably changed, and that what she saw as the pushful plebeian upstart would be shouldering the old-style aristocrat into the background. Many of the things she took for granted would have disappeared never to return: a tiara would no longer be a commonplace at Covent Garden, even on a Melba Night. But the 1914 summer flowed smoothly on and she did not even glimpse the consequences when a Serbian assassin's bullets struck down the Archduke Franz Ferdinand, heir to the Austrian throne, at Sarajevo on Sunday 28 June.

The Covent Garden season lasted until nearly the end of July. Melba caught a ship for Australia some weeks earlier. She wanted to get back to Coombe Cottage, but she was chiefly driven by anxiety for her father. David Mitchell was eighty-five, and his health had been poor for some years; the tough Scottish mind was as alert as ever but the tough Scottish body was failing. He was awaiting her at Doonside when she reached Australia early in August. He had been operated on a few months before for papilloma of the bladder but, though still ailing, could manage to crack a dry joke at need.

At the beginning of August, with Germany and Russia already at war, France mobilizing, and the world waiting on Britain's decision for or against war, a special reporter of the Sydney *Sunday Times* called at Coombe Cottage. It was winter in Australia, and the hills surrounding Lilydale and Coldstream were flecked with snow and bright with the gold of wattle in bloom. Melba told the reporter, 'I feel like a child with a new toy, whenever I come near this place. Look at the view, look at those hills, the snow; ah! it's good to be home again.' She led her caller about the house, chatting of the treasures it held, of the future of music in Australia, of opera in Europe, of her hope of bringing another opera company to Australia in the near future. Before the interview was printed Great Britain was at war with Germany, and so also was Australia. The article about Melba and Coombe Cottage seemed unreal as the war, which was to cost more than ten million lives, to remake the map of Europe, and to generate forces which would change the world, lumbered into its stride.

10

THE outbreak of war took Melba by surprise, but when she thought about it she was not really astonished that war had come. As she liked to tell her friends, the Kaiser was an insufferably rude and dictatorial person. She recalled the time, fifteen years before that she had sung to him at the Imperial Opera House, in Berlin.* She was summoned to the Imperial salon after a performance of *Faust*, and received by Wilhelm II, resplendently uniformed, and the Empress Augusta. The Kaiser, who fancied himself an authority on opera-singing, as well as military strategy and tactics, international politics, and all other matters which came under his eye, congratulated Melba on her performance, but then demanded, almost accusingly, 'Don't you think, Madame Melba, you took the Jewel Song at much too fast a tempo?'

'No, your Imperial Majesty,' Melba replied, at least in her own version of the episode, 'I do not. I sang the part of Marguerite according to the instructions of the composer himself, M. Charles Gounod, who was pleased to express his entire satisfaction with my interpretation and to compliment me on it.'

The Kaiser's spiky moustaches bristled, his eyes flashed, and he turned on his heel and strode to the door, snapping his fingers for the Empress Augusta to follow him.

A man who would talk and act like that to the reigning prima donna, Melba implied, was exactly the kind of power-drunk madman to suppose he could conquer the world by force of arms.

* In *Melodies and Memories* Melba gives a somewhat different account of what is obviously the same incident.

Having accustomed herself to the idea that the war, far from ending in a few weeks or a few months, would go on for two or three years, or perhaps even four, Melba settled down to make the best of it. It was terrible for mankind, and damned inconvenient for her personally, but she knew in her practical way that nothing was to be gained by brooding over it or wanting to put the clock back; she simply had to live with it.

She wanted to help in any way she could, and this she did chiefly by organizing concerts for war charities; most of these were held in Australia, but she also earned tens of thousands of pounds by singing in the USA and Canada. She said later that she raised £100,000 for World War I charities, and the figure has never been disputed; if anything, it is on the low side.

Melba's first wartime concert party included one other celebrity of world stature; this was the great English actress Ellen Terry, then in her middle sixties, who had been on a professional tour of Australia and was staying at Coombe Cottage. Ellen Terry was one of the few women of the time whose personality transcended Melba's, and perhaps the only woman to whom Melba was ever content to yield the foremost place, in a way nearly every woman did to her; this was not a grudging surrender of priority, but a willing, even an eager, stepping aside, as if in this one woman Melba recognized a psychic force greater than her own. Ellen Terry's opinion of Melba was also emphatic. To a friend she wrote at that time:

'She is a splendid woman—always working and doing everything herself—at home, I mean; goes to bed early, gets up early; eyes everywhere, always using her senses; her profile (when you get to know her face) is very fine, and she has a grand eye. She is full of fun, and yet is very serious. She expects a lot from people—useful service, I mean, but gives so much herself. . . . So entirely self-forgetting, she compels one to disregard one's bodily discomforts, weariness, pains, morbid thoughts, and to "press on" and do one's utmost. Bless her!'

Melba took a positive joy in going out to sing in small and primitive country halls, as she often did in wartime. She could relax on such nights as she was never able to when she gave a formal recital in an Australian, a European or an American city; she always strove for perfection no matter where she sang, but when she sang to audiences in small Australian country towns, particularly to the people of 'the Melba country', she knew that every note and phrase was not being analysed by critical and expert listeners secretly hoping she would make a slip. She never took liberties, however. She once told a student, 'Remember, you might think you are singing to an ordinary household or an unschooled audience, but there might be one person there who thoroughly knows what you should do and how you should do it. You always sing for that one person.'

The wartime concerts she gave in the small public hall at Lilydale and the far smaller public hall at Coldstream had almost the intimacy of family gatherings. To those audiences Melba was their own prima donna, in a way their own property, and they took whatever she gave them and loved it. Those concerts were informal as evening-gown and starched-shirt affairs could never be. One night, near the end of a concert at Coldstream, Melba looked down from the platform to where a local farmer, Bill Lawlor, and his wife were sitting; the Lawlors' small farm was opposite the gates of Coombe Cottage and they and Melba were old friends.

'What would you like me to sing, Bill?' she asked, standing up before them all, magnificent in cream satin.

'*Home, sweet home,*' he answered.

She sang it and that ended the concert, and as she went down from the platform to leave the hall she stopped in front of Bill Lawlor and clasped his two hands in hers.

'I thought,' she said, pressing his hands, 'that you'd have blisters on your hands, the way you clapped!'

Apart from running patriotic concerts and singing in them, she knitted socks for soldiers until an outspoken friend persuaded her to stop; her knitting was distinguished by verve rather than skill, and her friend suggested that if she sang as badly as she made socks she would be arrested for causing a public nuisance. She bowed to this advice but bullied friends and acquaintances into forming knitting clubs and sewing circles, and whooped them on when their enthusiasm flagged, even though she left the routine work to them. Some Australian frontline soldiers of World War I continued for years to treasure handwritten notes scribbled by Melba and pinned to socks, flannel shirts and other garments delivered to them in Red Cross parcels which they received on the Gallipoli Peninsula, on the Western Front, and in other war areas. These notes, enjoining the recipient to 'show the Germans how the Australians can fight' or something of the kind, carried an authentic whiff of Melba's personality.

She would have been driven to despair had she been anchored in Australia for the duration of the war. For twenty-five years she had moved about the earth pretty much as she pleased, never staying for more than a few months in one place, and she was too old to change her ways. Travel between Australia and England under the rigours and restrictions imposed by war conditions was difficult, as well as dangerous, but visits to America were managed easily enough. Although German warships operated in the Pacific from time to time, notably in 1917 when the raiders *Wolf* and *Seeadler* were active, the danger to any fast steamer was small, and Melba made three visits to the USA and Canada, in 1915, 1916–17 and 1918. She gave a series of concerts each time, thus preventing the moss from taking root on her professional reputation. She also seized any chance that offered to impress the Americans, until they entered the war, with the sacred character of the British Empire's crusade against the Kaiser and German imperialism.

For a time in World War I she seemed to see herself as Public Enemy No. 1 of Germany and to imagine that the Germans saw her in that light also. On one American tour she had a series of minor but irritating misadventures, and with her talent for self-dramatization she saw these as the work of German agents out to assassinate her and thus, presumably, strike a damaging blow at the Allies. She was stunned for some minutes and suffered a cut leg and bruises when a section of scenery fell on her while she was singing in one theatre, and later had a rough ride when her private railroad car broke away from a train and was stranded in the middle of a busy complex of tracks near Chicago. None of her accidents seemed to be the product of human wickedness so much as human fallibility, but she fell into a highly nervous state and for a time developed an impediment in her speech. If German secret agents were out to murder her, however, they were remarkably incompetent about it.

Melba was for the most part an unsubtle patriot of the hang-the-Kaiser school, but she had some close friends of enemy birth and could not persuade herself that they would have been parties to the atrocities supposedly committed by German troops in Belgium and France. It was well for her peace of mind that Joseph Joachim, the great violinist had been seven years dead when the war began; he had been one of her most admired friends, and as a man she ranked him with Jean de Reszke and Ignace Jan Paderewski. Although Hungarian by birth, Joachim was German-trained and one of the great figures of pre-World War I German music, and the thought that her country was at war with his would have made Melba's wartime state of ambivalence almost unbearable. Even as it was there were difficulties. In 1915 she sang in Boston with the Boston Symphony Orchestra, whose conductor was a German, Dr Karl Muck. Dr Muck and his wife had been friends of Melba for many years; she had first sung at the Imperial Opera House, Berlin, under his baton. Neither the Mucks nor Melba tried to argue the merits of the war when they met and talked in Boston, but confined themselves to saying how terrible it was, recalling happier days in times of peace, hoping the fighting would soon be over, and weeping a little. Then Melba went out on to the platform and sang exquisitely to the orchestra's playing under Dr Muck's direction. The music they made together was a melancholy obbligato to the thunder of distant battles in which her people and his were slaughtering each other.

11

THE war did a service for Australian singing by giving new force and new direction to Melba's ambition to create a school of Australian singers using their voices as she used hers. Although she had worked for some years to indoctrinate the singing teachers and pupils of the University of Melbourne Conservatorium of Music with her method, her efforts had been spasmodic and irregular, because in peace she was much of her time abroad. Wartime restrictions on travel made her stay more in Australia, and she worked at teaching with some continuity.

She caused surprise at the time by setting up her classes not at the University Conservatorium but at the Albert Street Conservatorium, a private music school in East Melbourne. She had for some years taken a deep practical interest in the University Conservatorium and had worked hard to raise money to provide it with an adequate building; this had been officially opened in 1913 and named Melba Hall in her honour. The natural thing would have been for her to develop singing classes there, but she found what seemed to her to be good reasons for preferring the Albert Street Conservatorium.

The Albert Street director was Fritz Hart, a graduate of the Royal College of Music, London. An Englishman, Hart had come to Australia some years before as conductor of an opera company and, liking the country, had stayed. In 1915 his conservatorium faced a crisis which threatened to close it down; two key members of the staff, Madame Elise Wiedermann, a singing teacher, and Edward Goll, a pianoforte teacher, gave Hart notice that they intended leaving him to join the University Conservatorium staff at the beginning of 1916. Both Madame Wiedermann (who was, ironically, the friend whose letter of introduction had taken Melba to Madame Marchesi) and Goll were natives of Austria-Hungary, and Melba was incensed to think they proposed leaving Hart at a time when he would find it all but impossible to replace them, because of a war in which their country was ranged against the British Empire. So, having interpreted their defection as an attempt by two enemy nationals to injure a true-blue Englishman, she went to Hart's aid.

She barely knew him, and he was astonished when his telephone rang one day and a woman's voice said: 'Fritz Hart, what would you do if I offered to come to the conservatorium and teach singing?' The caller was Melba and Hart did not hesitate; his only fear was that she might change her mind before he could say yes.

She held her first classes within a week or two; they were only for girls. Her singing girls at times numbered nearly a hundred and came from every state of Australia, with sometimes one or two from overseas. She never took a penny for teaching. Ruth Ladd, an Albert Street Conservatorium student and later a leading teacher in Sydney, said, 'She had a feeling of passionate love for the human voice, and no length of time, and no test of patience was too much for her when dealing with a voice. I shall never forget the pains-taking care with which she re-established voices that had been badly trained and strained.' Another student named Marie Bremner, who became a star of the Australian musical theatre, was on the ground floor at the conservatorium one day when Melba came up the front steps. A girl was having a lesson upstairs, and Melba let out an anguished 'Ow!', and went leaping up the stairway shouting 'Stop that girl! She's singing off her soft palate.'

Melba has been charged with sometimes trying to screw a fee out of a student, but such stories make little sense against the back-ground of what she did for the Albert Street Conservatorium and its girls. At Albert Street she tested the voices of many aspiring prima donnas and never charged a fee. This does not mean she tested the voice of every hopeful singer who sought her opinion;

she would have had no time for herself if she had listened to every singer of supposed promise who wanted a hearing, and candidates had to come to her responsibly recommended.

The Victorian inland city of Ballarat discovered a girl whom local opinion placed as a contralto with a great future. The girl's backers wrote to Melba, asking her to hear the prodigy, and she replied naming a day and time at Coombe Cottage. A small committee escorted the girl to Coldstream, and arrived there to find Melba painting a fence. She led them to the music-room and, sitting down at the piano, tested the girl's voice. Her report to the committee was succinct. She said: 'First, voice: good. Second, appearance: fair. Third, intelligence: nil.'

The singing school she started at the Albert Street Conservatorium in 1915 lasted until her death; in a sense it still survives, because although the youngest of the girls who learned her method then are ageing now some of them are still teaching, and many passed their acquired knowledge on to younger generations of singers and teachers. So what Melba did is never likely to be completely lost. It is true that the Melba method has not yet produced one great singer, but many of her girls have distinguished themselves in opera, in oratorio, in concerts and in operetta.

Except when she was travelling outside Victoria, she would sweep up to the front door of the conservatorium in her chauffeur-driven car on at least one morning a week, often on two mornings, and sometimes on three. She would arrive about nine o'clock or a few minutes afterwards, having left Coldstream soon after eight. She rarely managed to enter the conservatorium unnoticed, even when she came unannounced, nor did she expect to; she had a well-developed sense of the respect due to the world's greatest prima donna.

Students who shared in the lessons Melba gave at Albert Street never forgot them. Week in and week out every girl worked under her own teacher on the conservatorium staff, but had to be ready to sing if called on at a Melba assembly. Only a few could be heard in the three or four hours Melba was there, but she got her message over to the whole class by criticizing each of those who did sing in terms which made the principles of her method clear to every hearer.

Some people who knew Melba in other fields called her a bully, but she never bullied her singing girls. She had a knack of putting frightened beginners at ease. 'Forget you've got a voice,' she would say. 'Just sing as though you were humming about the house.' If a girl forced her voice, Melba would clap her hands over her ears and cry, 'You mustn't scream like a cat! I can't bear it!' But there was never any sting in the words; they were the kindly advice of the veteran to the beginner, and when she said them she was doubtless hearing in memory Mathilde Marchesi's words to her, all those years ago at the house in the Rue Jouffroy, 'Why do you screech your top notes? Can't you sing them *piano*?' She always said that if a singer could not sing any note *pianissimo* it was the beginning of the end.

To sing with complete relaxation was the essence of her method. 'The great thing in singing is relaxation, not only of the muscles of the throat, but of all the muscles in the body,' she said. 'Anyone who stands rigid can never hope to sing well. You must relax the same way as a prize-fighter does before he enters the ring.' She herself was always completely relaxed when she sang. 'Good singing,' she often said, 'is easy singing.'

Her power to relax was one of the things about her that impressed other musicians. A Melbourne violinist, Annie Oliver, cherished a vivid memory of a rehearsal for a big concert. Melba came on to the platform, pulled a chair forward, sat down, arranged herself comfortably, signalled to the conductor of the orchestra, and presently started to sing. In the middle of her aria she took off her wrist-watch, glanced at it, and wound it up, singing all the time out of a completely relaxed body.

Although not a physical fitness crank, she was careful of what she ate. She liked walking and walked a great deal, swinging along with a brisk stride. She believed one of the best ways of reducing weight was to roll on the floor, and now and then demonstrated it to her classes, rolling back and forth without regard for the dress she happened to be wearing, whether it was a London-tailored tweed or a Paris-styled silk. All her life Melba had to fight fat. Her niece, Nellie Patterson, was with her for some months in Honolulu in 1915. About seven o'clock every morning Melba, wearing a swim-suit, would knock at her niece's door and they would go down to the beach for a pre-breakfast swim, and always Melba would put in a few minutes rolling on the sand.

She believed bodily well-being was indispensable to the ability to sing. To a girl whose voice she tried Melba said, 'Watch me take a breath, and then hit me.' The girl hesitated to punch Melba in the ribs as bidden but at last she did it. It was a solid punch with all her strength behind it, and, she said, 'was like hitting against concrete'.

Nobody was ever in doubt who was running one of her classes; she would pause now and then to ask Fritz Hart a question or invite his opinion, but she alone was in charge. A girl singing an aria was apt to be waved to a stop, and Melba would say, 'Fritz, I don't like that cadenza. Will you write this down?' Then she would pick out the notes of her own cadenza on the piano or hum it through while Hart, standing by with paper and pencil, jotted down the basic points. Unless she was accompanying a student on the piano, as she sometimes did, she usually listened on her feet, moving round at the back of the room, hands thrust into the pockets of her coat, head bent, missing nothing, formulating her criticism and advice. Sometimes she would give a student a word of praise, but she was always sparing with praise; she felt a little of it went a long way with young singers or with anyone at all for that matter.

Even when she brought a carload of social and music celebrities with her to see how she ran a class she did not put on prima donna airs. Perhaps that was the secret of her rapport with her students. 'She seemed to mesmerise them,' said Ida Scott, for many years an accompanist at the conservatorium, 'and their voices would soar up, perfectly relaxed, head notes where they had never been before and probably never would be again.' Her naturalness was spontaneous and irresistible. One day a lesson was going on when a barrel-organ in Albert Street outside struck up a popular tune of the day, *Yes, we have no bananas*.

'I can sing that,' she exclaimed. And did.

The spirit of the Richmond tomboy was never deeply submerged under the grandeur of the prima donna. One of the memories that a woman took away with her from a visit to Coombe Cottage was of afternoon tea on the lawn, with Melba presiding over a battery of tea things after a butler and footman carried them out, and singing, not a snatch of opera or even a ballad, but *Pop goes the weasel!*

She had a knack of giving people apposite nicknames, and many of her singing girls carried these through life – Rabbit, Little Brown Mouse, The Duchess, the Little Victorian Lady, and so on. Years later Ruth Ladd, when applying for a teaching appointment at the New South Wales Conservatorium of Music, mentioned that she had studied under Melba. The director, Dr W. Arundel Orchard, said, 'If I were to cable her, do you think she would remember you?'

'Not if you call me Ruth Ladd,' Miss Ladd said, 'but if you ask whether she can recommend The Duchess I think she will say yes.'

Miss Ladd was right.

Melba was generous to girls she liked. Often one of them, booked to sing at a concert and too poor to buy a suitable frock, was whisked off to one of Melbourne's best shops and outfitted for the night at Melba's expense. One girl was sent in to Melbourne's most costly hospital for an operation to remove a bone partly blocking her nose, and Melba paid the bill.

She had an eye for a student's temperamental as well as vocal qualities. The soprano Marie Bremner first sang for her at seventeen years old. When she finished Melba said, 'Come here, gal! Let's see your legs.'

Miss Bremner lifted her skirt and showed a pair of shapely legs and two pretty knees. 'H'm,' said Melba, 'you've got good understandings! You'll go a long way. You ought to go into musical comedy.'

Marie Bremner's heart was set on grand opera at that time, but a few years later she admitted that Melba had been right, and proved it by becoming a star of Australian operetta and musical comedy.

Melba was never a musical or a theatrical snob. To her light music had its place no less than classical music; all she asked was that an artist should sing whatever had to be sung as well as possible, but she realized that often the owner of a fine voice was not psychologically equipped to meet lofty musical demands. Marie Bremner was one example; another was Gladys Moncrieff, whose powerful and beautiful voice and dark gipsy-like good looks made her Australia's queen of operetta between the two world wars and kept her on that pinnacle until the 1950s. When someone asked if Miss Moncrieff would be suitable for opera, Melba replied, 'No. She wants a quick return.' It was not a criticism, but a recognition of a fact. Gladys Moncrieff, who was more than thirty years younger than Melba, liked the diva for her directness and bluntness; there was, she found, no possibility of misinterpreting Melba's meaning. Miss Moncrieff was an established star when, walking off the stage during a rehearsal of The Merry Widow in Melbourne, she was confronted by Melba in the wings. She had just finished singing the Waltz Song, and thought she had sung it rather well.

'Listen, my dear,' said Melba, 'LUV not LOV.'

She nodded and strode away, leaving a rather flustered Gladys Moncrieff to digest the advice.

Melba at one time had high hopes of José Collins, the famous

English light opera singer of World War I and the 1920s, who created in London many of the roles that Gladys Moncrieff was later to play in Australia, notably Teresa in *The Maid of the Mountains*. Convinced that Miss Collins had the temperament as well as the acting ability, the looks, and the vocal excellence to become a great opera singer, Melba wanted her to play Carmen at Covent Garden, and would have sponsored her there. This would have guaranteed her success if any extraneous aid could have done so, but Miss Collins had to refuse. To accept Melba's offer she would have had to abandon a musical play which depended on her and turn her back on a salary, immense for those days, of £225 a week free of income tax. She would also have had to learn French. And so perhaps the grand opera stage lost one of its great Carmens – possibly another Calvé.

Melba expected her singing girls to work hard, and most of them did so, but it was not work all the time. Now and then one or two or three of them would be invited to stay at Coombe Cottage for a week-end; these visits were ostensibly social occasions, but Melba took the opportunity to study each girl's social deportment and diplomatically lecture any whom she found wanting. She drummed into them the need to speak, to dress, and to carry themselves correctly, as an indispensable part of making a professional success, and none of them ever seems to have felt embarrassed about it, much less resentful; on the contrary, they listened and many of them profited. Some of them came from homes in which table manners were casual, a bathmat was a rarity and fingerbowls were unknown. Melba would take any such girl for an early-morning stroll in the rose-garden and give her a quiet homily on basic etiquette. 'If you are going to succeed in the world,' she would say, 'you must know the right way to do things.'

(She always had a strong didactic instinct, as many other people besides her singing girls were made to realize. Late in her life she interested herself in the career of a young Australian journalist named Harold Eather. He and his wife visited her at Coombe Cottage, and while they were taking afternoon tea in front of the fire in the billiard-room Melba gently reproved him for speaking with an Australian drawl. 'Not Satur-day,' she said. 'Satur-da'.' Then she recited the days of the week – 'Sunda', Monda', Tuesda', Wednesda', Thursda', Frida', Saturda'.' Eather felt like a small boy in knickerbockers, but for some reason did not resent the lecture.)

Sometimes the whole class would be summoned to Coombe Cottage for the day, and Melba would put on a 'chop picnic'. Wearing a chef's tall hat and brandishing a long-handled fork, she would stand over the open fire grilling steak and chops for her songbirds. Even at functions of that kind she was apt to be dictatorial. At one picnic a girl refused meat and Melba demanded to know why.

'I'm a Catholic,' the girl said, 'and this is Friday.'

'Oh, rubbish!' said Melba, thrusting a sizzling steak at the objector. The girl still refused to eat meat, and after jollying her along for a minute or so Melba gave in. 'I admire you,' she said. 'There's somebody else here who shouldn't be eating meat today!', and she shot a darkling look at another girl who, although a Catholic, felt she must not risk Melba's displeasure by refusing meat.

She designed a uniform for her singing girls; this was distinctive but hardly elegant, and the girls, who called the uniforms their 'long white nightgowns', wore them only to please her. She also designed a badge, to be worn on the hat and the left breast-pocket of the uniform. The badge had the letter M in blue, surrounded by a laurel wreath, and above this a representation of a dove with a spray in its beak, and underneath a scroll bearing the words 'Con amore'. This expressed Melba's love of singing and what she hoped was her students' love of singing also; it did express the feelings of most of them.

Perhaps Melba was trying at that time to assure the survival of her name when death should silence her. It is hard to know; she was a woman who rarely bared her inmost thoughts even to intimate friends, and anybody who had dared to question her on so personal a matter would have been snubbed. It was then that she started to search for her successor, or appeared to be doing so at any rate.

She believed that Australia was a land of good singing voices and once told a magazine interviewer, 'At the conservatorium in Melbourne I can find a hundred good voices as easily as I could find ten in the same number of girls in London. So fresh! Such quality! Australia is a nest of singing birds.'

Whether she really hoped to find a soprano whom her crown would fit is a matter of dispute, but on the surface at least she pressed the search long and hard. In her will she left £8,000, directing that the income should be used for a scholarship, to be known as the Melba Scholarship, at the Albert Street Conservatorium 'or if that institution ceases to exist then at the University of Melbourne Conservatorium of Music'. She said in her will that she was establishing this scholarship 'in the hope that another Melba may arise.' The bequest has not yet justified that hope.

12

For Melba the years of World War I held both personal sorrow and personal joy.

When she returned to Australia in 1914 she guessed, if she did not know, that her father's life was coming to its end; when she saw him and, holding his hard-working hands in hers, felt the thinness of the flesh covering the bones and the once-strong muscles, she had to admit to herself that his time was running out. The thought lay heavy on her. They had always been so close, had always understood each other without words.

His death did not seem to be at hand, however, when she took ship late in 1915 for a singing tour of the USA and Canada; if there had been any immediate reason for alarm she would not have gone. All through that Australian summer he continued to supervise his business affairs, and if his old body was slower in movement his mind was still as sharp as a well-honed blade. But disease was eating at him, and late in March 1916 he had to go into hospital. Nellie was on her way home across the Pacific and expected early in April and he wanted to wait for her return, but surgery could not be delayed. The shock of the operation was too much for the old man and he died on Saturday 25 March. He was buried two days later, a week before Melba's ship docked in Sydney. The news hit her hard. She was not a crying woman, but she cried then. Although he was an old man, eighty-seven years of age, his death left a blank in many lives, including hers. Whenever he had gone to one of her concerts he had sat near the front, and often her eyes had met his and she had watched his face light when she sang a Scottish ballad and memories of his homeland crowded in on him. Now she would sing to him no more.

Until David Mitchell died his children had only been able to guess at the size of the fortune he had made in the years between the day he landed in Melbourne in 1852, with the legendary sovereign in his pocket, and his death in 1916. They knew it must be a large fortune but that was all; he always kept his money affairs to himself. His eldest daughter observed the same canny principle. He once asked her, on her first visit home in 1902, if she had saved any money.

'Yes,' she replied, 'a little.'

'How much?'

'Perhaps twenty thousand pounds.'

'Well, lassie,' he said, fibbing as hard as she was, 'you're much richer than I am.' Neither said anything for a moment. Then he fixed her with his twinkling eyes and said, 'You're quite right, lassie. Never tell anybody what you've got. Not even me.'

He left an estate worth £299,717, bequeathing it equally to his seven children and forming a trust to manage it.

David Mitchell was lucky in one thing; when he lived Australian taxation was insignificant, and this enabled him to build a fortune worth at least £1,500,000 in terms of money values fifty years later. He would have writhed under the obligation to pay heavy taxes, as his daughter Nellie was to writhe after the war at what she saw as a conspiracy by the British and Australian tax-gatherers to impoverish her. For years she waged a running battle, not through accountants and solicitors, but in her own person, with what she called 'the Tax Man', as if he were some kind of ogre in a cave whose business it was to plague and pauperize her. One day a friend met her in London, dressed not only from head to toe in black as if she were in mourning, but in shabby black for good measure. It turned out that the threadbare mourning was not for a loved one untimely dead but on account of her income tax assessment.

'The amount they want me to pay will ruin me,' she groaned.

A week later the friend, finding her looking happier and no longer mournfully garbed, asked what she had decided to do about her tax assessment.

'I'm paying it,' she said. 'The doctor told me that if I kept on worrying about it I would kill myself.'

She was given to these periodical bursts of self-dramatization. But even her fondest friends could not summon up a tear for her; they felt she was doing nicely, the Tax Man notwithstanding.

The pain of her father's death left no visible marks on her; she was too robust for that. And with her work for war charities she was making a name of a kind she had never had before; and she rather liked seeing herself, and being seen, as a benefactress of the British Empire and of the men who were fighting to save the world from being overrun by a new barbarism. Few people worked harder in their own way for the Allied cause in World War I, and in 1918 King George V recognized her efforts by creating her a Dame Commander of the British Empire.

She was travelling across the USA at the time, on a concert

tour. The party woke one morning after Melba's private railway car had been parked overnight at a siding in the small city of Walla Walla, Washington. She breakfasted alone that morning in her own room, sitting up in a negligée with a copy of the local newspaper for company. Afterwards she went to the bath through the dining section of the car where the others were sitting late over breakfast. Passing the table she said to her private secretary, Freda Sternberg, an Australian journalist, 'You like newspapers. Here's one for you,' and went on. Miss Sternberg came on a headline, 'King Honors Melba', over a paragraph reporting that Melba had been created DBE. Miss Sternberg said nothing to any of the others, but folded up the newspaper and went to Melba's room. She knocked, and, invited to go in, did so and found Melba stark naked.

'Did you see this?' she asked.

Melba took the paper and glanced at the paragraph indicated by Miss Sternberg's forefinger.

She read it through, then began to caper about the room, chanting, 'I'm a Dame! I'm a Dame!', pretending that the newspaper paragraph was the first word she had had of the honour.

Melba was following her usual custom of drawing as much drama as possible out of the situation. The British practice since Victorian times has been to inform people in advance that they are to be honoured; this is done to give them a chance to refuse the honour if they wish, but they are sworn to secrecy. Any likelihood that, war or no war, the practice was varied in Melba's case is remote.

She pretended to be facetious about her title, but she valued this royal acknowledgement of what she had done with her life and savoured it to the full. The tomboy from Richmond had come a long way since she had played on the Burnley river-flats, beside the slow-flowing Yarra. Not that her pleasure was allowed to be unalloyed. Like every successful man or woman she was a mark for neurotics who try to compensate for their own failures by writing anonymous abuse to those who succeed; soon after she got back to Australia an unsigned, hand-printed letter came to her: 'We think the honour the King bestowed on you, DBE is very suitable— Damned Bad Egg!' She laughed over the letter, but not with much mirth.

Some of her intimates believed she was secretly disappointed that the honour was not of a higher grade; if so, she was consoled in 1927 when she was promoted to be a Dame Grand Cross of the British Empire.

Whatever her reservations about her DBE it helped to make her 1918 American tour memorable for her, but another piece of news which reached her soon afterwards was perhaps even more welcome; this was in a letter from Australia which told her that her son's wife, Evie, was expecting a baby. Melba had long wanted a grandchild, and now at last if all went well she was to have her wish. Mrs Armstrong had borne a son earlier, but the child had lived only a few days and his death had been a heavy blow to Melba as well as to his parents. Perhaps this time the luck would be better.

George and Evie Armstrong spent much of their time travelling and living with Melba, but made their permanent home at Coombe Cottage from the beginning of World War I. They had married in London in 1913 after George's first short and unhappy marriage had ended in divorce. For his bride, Evie Doyle, a Brisbane girl, it was the first marriage. They were well suited, although temperamentally opposite in some respects. She was a talented mezzo-soprano singer and a good violinist, and could have built a sound professional name had she chosen to make a career of music rather than marriage. Occasionally in wartime charity concerts she sang on the same programme as Melba and was well liked by audiences; those who heard her in 1914 at one of Melba's Lilydale concerts remembered her warm and lovely voice long afterwards. George Armstrong, on the other hand, had no special liking for music and no voice worth mentioning; one of his close friends for many years never heard him sing anything but hunting songs in company with boon companions; he preferred riding and hunting to musical soirées, and liked working among farm animals on Coombe Farm.

Melba—Dame Nellie now—swept on through her American tour, warmed by the thought that within a few months her grandchild would be born. That tour had its harsh moments, though, and some of these were generated by Melba's irritation with the popular success that the Italian soprano Amelita Galli-Curci was scoring in America just then. Galli-Curci was twenty years younger than Melba, and pretty well in her vocal prime. American concert-goers were raving over her astonishing vocal agility in the famous coloratura arias and in showpieces such as *Lo, here the gentle lark* (which Melba was apt to consider her own personal property without having any good reason to do so except that she sang it extremely well). In Meyerbeer's *Dinorah*, at the Lexington Theatre, New York, on 28 January 1918, Galli-Curci had moved the audience to the verge of frenzy; they recalled her twenty-four times after the Shadow song and sixty times at the final curtain. Melba was respectfully heard when she appeared at the Lexington in *Faust* a few days later, but where the house rewarded her with ripples of admiring handclapping they kept their thunders of ecstasy for her younger rival. The American response to Galli-Curci was faintly, and disturbingly, reminiscent of the acclaim which had greeted Tetrazzini in both London and America a decade before, and Melba did not relish it. She knew Galli-Curci was not another Tetrazzini, whatever hypnotized admirers might temporarily suppose; nor was she another Melba. Yet her singing did have a dash, an exciting quality, a youthful glitter which brought audiences to their feet shouting her name.

The two women detested one another, and Melba had no advantage of Galli-Curci in her capacity for prima donna one-upmanship. They once went from Boston to New York in the same train; through a booking oversight Melba had to travel, not in a drawing-room, but in a public compartment. The train was hardly under way when Galli-Curci came out of her drawing-room and walked with slow and stately tread past Melba's compartment. Presently she came back, still stepping with queenly deliberation, while Melba sat, staring frozenly ahead, trying to pretend she did not see this upstart rival. Boston and New York are about 160 miles apart, and Galli-Curci had time to execute her manœuvre three or four times in the course of the journey. Never once glancing at her, Melba hissed at her companions each time Galli-Curci appeared, 'Don't look at that woman!' The waves of dislike passing between the two were all but tangible.

One of Galli-Curci's pet gibes was: 'To hear Melba sing *Lo, here the gentle lark*, when she has finished you would think it was a turkey.' Melba had little to say – in public – about Galli-Curci at any time, but she made one statement which appeared in several American newspapers: 'Galli-Curci, I suppose, is wonderful. I have only heard her once and on the road. I know that I have the most beautiful voice in the world, and as long as I know that, I shall keep on singing.' She was more precise in private. 'That woman,' she said, 'sings either flat or sharp. She never has been able to sing.'

When the tour ended Melba rented an oil millionaire's house at Santa Barbara, California, and moved in there, but she could not rest. One day she realized what was wrong; she was homesick. She wanted to be back at Coombe Cottage, seeing the blue hills which she loved, even though to many eyes – English eyes in particular—they were gaunt, unfriendly, a little forbidding. She also wanted to be able, if she fancied it, to order out the car and go off to a quiet gully where she could hear the bellbirds singing. Above all, she wanted to be with her son and daughter-in-law as the time for the birth of her grandchild drew near. Melba knew she could do nothing that skilled obstetricians and nursing sisters could not do better, but she had the egoist's mystic conviction that any affair in which she was interested would run smoother merely if she were there. She decided to catch the next ship home. The steamer *Niagara* was to leave Vancouver a few days later; within hours everything was arranged and when the *Niagara* put to sea Melba was on board.

It was winter in Australia, and again there was snow on the hills around Coldstream and the wattles were in bloom. It reminded her of her homecoming four years earlier. Since then Europe had been torn asunder and millions of men had died, but now the war and the horror could not last much longer.

Melba's grandchild, a girl, was born on 12 September. Melba was captivated, and wanted to lose no time whatever in implanting in the child the seeds of musical appreciation. She told the nursing sister, Clyne Mackay, to bring the baby in her pram every day and leave her on the veranda outside the windows of the music-room, so she could hear her grandmother practising. Sister Mackay did not dare to refuse, but she told George Armstrong it would never do to let the baby be kept awake by Melba's 'screeching'. If Armstrong was startled by the word Sister Mackay chose to describe the singing of the world's greatest prima donna, he did not dispute it, and she supposed he persuaded his mother that the objection was valid; at all events Melba's order was withdrawn.

The baby was christened Pamela Helen Fullerton on 14 November; it was a coincidence, but a pleasant one, that the christening ceremony should have taken place in the first days after peace returned to the world. The ceremony was held at Coombe Cottage. Melba's singing girls came up from Melbourne and sang as a choir, and her old friend John Lemmone played a flute solo. Melba sang Mendelssohn's *O for the wings of a dove*. Those who listened forgot that the singer was a woman of fifty-seven. Her voice sounded like a girl's.

EVENING

1918-1926

1

THE Christmas of 1918 was a time of glorious anticipation for Nellie Melba; she was making ready to go back to London, the city she loved above all cities. She pictured it in her mind as she had left it in 1914, but shocks awaited her when she once more trod its streets in February 1919. London was dirty, unkempt, shabby and war-stained. There were human changes, too. It was nearly five years since she had seen England, and many of the men she had known as gay companions had died on the Western Front or in other war theatres; other old friends, among them the Marchioness of Ripon (the former Lady de Grey) and Alfred de Rothschild, were also gone to their graves.

Sadness and fear seemed to overlie the great city still. 'London just then, to one who had known it at its best and come back to see it in its worst,' she wrote later, 'provided a constant succession of shocks.' She suffered one shock on her first visit to Covent Garden; she threw open the door of her old dressing-room to find that it had been newly repainted green. She was furious, not so much perhaps because the shade of green offended her as because the painters had been brought in without her leave. Sir Thomas Beecham was artistic director at Covent Garden that year, and she stormed into his office, demanding an explanation. Her temper cooled when Beecham diplomatically offered to repaint her room any colour she might choose. After that, according to Beecham, they 'soon became excellent friends', but it is to be doubted that their regard for one another ever went below the surface. They had in common too many human characteristics, such as arrogance, masterfulness and aggressiveness.

Beecham was not an unmixed admirer of Melba's singing. In his autobiography he said that her popularity was 'confined to England and those other Anglo-Saxon communities where the subtler and rarer sides of vocal talent are less valued,' and went on: 'Melba was a singer who had nearly all the attributes inseparable from great artistry. Her voice was beautiful and bright, of uncommon evenness throughout; and she handled the whole range of it with absolute mastery except in measured coloratura passages such as those at the end of the Waltz song of *Roméo and Juliet*. She was extremely accurate, insisted on her fellow artists being equally so, was punctual to the tick at rehearsals and while at work was a shining example in discipline to everyone else. But there was always some element lacking in nearly everything she did, and it is not easy to say just what it was. It was hardly absence of warmth, because many an artist has had the same deficiency without one being made uncomfortably aware of it. Of the mysterious quality known as temperament she had certainly a little, and her accent and rhythm were both admirable. I am inclined to think that she was wanting in genuine spiritual refinement, which deprived the music she was singing of some virtue essential to our pleasure; and perhaps it is for this reason that in the maturer musical culture of the Continent she had comparatively little success.'

On her side, Melba, as she told friends, liked neither Beecham nor his work. Her dislike of him might well have been rooted in his unconcealed lack of interest in Italian opera, which was her forte, the thing she sang with unfailing and surpassing success. It would have been astonishing if she could have called up much enthusiasm for an artistic director who was not only indifferent to *Bohème*, *Lucia*, *Traviata* and the like, but even mildly scornful of them.

Her spirits revived a little when she reopened Covent Garden as Mimi on 12 May. The reopening was a milestone in the history of the great theatre (which had been used as a furniture storehouse throughout the war) and in Melba's career; Beecham's companies had presented opera seasons in London in 1915, 1916, 1917, and 1918, but these had been staged in other theatres and, although musically admirable, had lacked the social imprint which only Covent Garden could give. There were tiaras, bare shoulders and stiff white shirts in Covent Garden on the night that grand opera — and Melba — came back, but there were also sartorial shocks for Melba and other sticklers for the old and once inviolate customs. 'Can you imagine in the old days,' Melba asked, 'men walking into Covent Garden on a Melba Night, or any other night, and sitting in the stalls, in shabby tweed coats? Yes, that is what I saw on this night, and though I have no objection to brown tweed coats, or to shabbiness, I could not help feeling a sensation almost of resentment that men who could afford to pay for stalls could not also afford to wear proper clothes.'

Melba had not realized that World War I was a war not only of nations but also of philosophies. She did not understand then, or ever, that the world had undergone a social revolution since 1914 and would never be the same again. She never made any pretence of where she stood socially; she loved titles and used to say, 'I'm a damned snob!', and that was true even though she was never obsequious and never let those she cultivated exploit her beyond a predetermined point. One of the things that made her heart ache when she reopened Covent Garden in 1919 was the fear that grand opera was no longer to be the shining jewelled toy of the rich and titled but was being brought down from its high place to the level of tweed-coated men in the stalls.

The 1919 season held some rewards for her. One was the singing of a Lancashire-born tenor, Thomas Burke, who was her Rodolfo on the opening night. She did not see him as a new Jean de Reszke, of course (for Melba, nobody ever approached dear Jean), but she told all her friends that he put her in mind of the young Caruso, and she made him promise to go to Australia if she took another opera company out there. Burke remained a favourite at Covent Garden for some years, but when Melba's next Australian opera season came round, in 1924, he was not in the company. He never quite fulfilled her early hopes of him, and it is astonishing that so perceptive an ear as Melba's should have heard in his singing a quality which made her extol him so largely, while she remained lukewarm about another young tenor in the same company, Fernand Ansseau, a Belgian. Ansseau, who in that 1919 season scored a success opposite Melba in *Faust*, had a more delicate voice than Burke and was a finer artist. Perhaps Burke's aggressive masculinity touched an emotional chord in 'Melba which the reticent Ansseau could not reach.

The 1919 season gave her something else also; that was the lasting admiration of a young man named Eugene Goossens, who was to become one of the most noted orchestral conductors of his day and to be knighted in 1955. Although he had inherited his talent from his father and grandfather, who were both operatic conductors of distinction, and been schooled by Beecham, Goossens in 1919 was merely a promising young musician who had yet to prove himself. He was conducting in Manchester, but by the merest fluke happened to be in London one day when Albert Coates fell ill; Coates was listed to conduct *Faust* at Covent Garden that night and Goossens was asked to take his place. The formidable Melba was the Marguerite, and an hour or so before the curtain was timed to go up Goossens went to her dressing-room to discuss the performance. Melba was in a negligée, and throwing a light wrap about her shoulders she plunged into a technical discussion of the opera. Goossens asked if she made any changes in the traditional *tempi*.

'None whatsoever,' she said. 'I sing it exactly as Gounod wrote it. And I hope you conduct it the same way.'

He hastened to assure her that he did, doubtless remembering that Melba had a reputation among composers for singing their music as they had written it, not as she believed they should have written it. Giacomo Puccini himself had told her once, 'You sing my music. You don't sing Melba-Puccini.'

'Her singing of the role [Goossens was to write] turned out to be a most refreshing musical experience. With none of the kittenish tricks and simperings elderly *prime donne* usually indulge in when they're playing a youthful role, the incomparable singer realized Gounod's Marguerite to perfection, and made our task in the orchestra pit easeful and unapprehensive. Only once, in the quartet, when Mephistopheles' *rubato* threatened to get out of hand, did she give that gentleman a baleful glare which carried a warning not to be ignored. At our final curtain-call together, she plucked a rose from her bouquet and thrust it in my shirt-front with a spontaneous gesture which carried as pleasant a tribute as I shall ever know. Nellie Melba was the *grande dame* of singing, unaffected and charming. The purity of vocal style which was her great characteristic remained unimpaired to the end.'

For the benefit of cynics who might suppose that Goossens had an eye on his professional future when he wrote of Melba in those terms, it should be said that he published that tribute in 1951, twenty years after her death.

2

LONDON in 1919 was alive with uniforms, many worn by sailors, soldiers and airmen from the Dominions waiting to go home. Two of the soldiers were nephews of Melba, Douglas and Gerald

Patterson, sons of her sister Belle. Douglas Patterson, then twenty-six, was a ranker in an Australian infantry battalion; his brother Gerald, aged twenty-three, was a captain in a British artillery regiment and had won a Military Cross for an exploit on the Western Front in 1917. Gerald Patterson was also a brilliant lawn tennis player, and when Melba returned to London early in 1919 he was being mentioned by discerning judges as likely to be the next Wimbledon champion.

Melba, who was apt to complain that for some reason none of her family but herself ever made a splash in the world, enjoyed her share of the limelight beating on her nephew Gerald. One day she went out to watch him play at Surbiton, twelve miles from London, where he was sweeping all before him in a tournament. Douglas Patterson also went to Surbiton that day, but Melba paid little attention to him. 'I must have my photo taken with my famous nephew,' she said and beckoned a hovering press photographer. The picture of her standing beside Gerald Patterson appeared on the front page of a London daily next morning. It did not include another figure who had obligingly stood to one side; this was Douglas Patterson, who thereafter sometimes spoke of himself, with a mixture of ruefulness and irony, as 'Melba's infamous nephew'.

Douglas Patterson liked his Aunt Nellie, but found her unpredictable. Soon after she returned to London he had four days' leave and went to see her. She gave him a warm welcome and an excellent dinner, and when he was leaving slipped a pound note into his hand. 'Remember, Douglas, I'm your mother's sister,' she said. 'I don't want you to treat me as a great person. Any time you want anything you are to call on me.' He acted on that invitation when, broke, he was in London for pre-embarkation leave, before returning to Australia late in 1919. Melba was in a prickly mood that day. She snapped at him, 'Why do you always come to me for money? Your brother Gerald doesn't pester me like this.' Next thing he knew he was outside, walking down the street and thinking to himself that prima donna temperament was no mere myth after all.

Gerald Patterson had no reason to complain of his Aunt Nellie. He won the Wimbledon singles title in 1919, and nobody blew his trumpet harder than Melba did; she wanted all her friends to know that he was her sister's son, and she went about saying with her tongue only partly in her cheek, 'Gerald used to be known as

Melba's nephew. Now I'm known as Gerald's aunt.'. Soon after winning Wimbledon, Gerald Patterson went back to Australia. He was not a moneyed man and, wanting to get a firm business footing in his home city, Melbourne, he had not thought of returning to England in 1920 to defend his Wimbledon title. Melba however cabled his parents, urging that he should go back for the 1920 Wimbledon, and offering to pay all his expenses, supply all his tennis uniforms, let him stay with her, and give him pocket-money. Her persuasions were always hard to resist, so Gerald Patterson went and was at Wimbledon again in 1920. He was beaten by the American, William T. Tilden.

Melba revelled in being in the full whirl of affairs; she had for so long stood on an eminence above most other mortals that she would have been miserable if she had found herself just one of the crowd. And, unlike most ageing prima donnas, she was not passed by, unheeded, ignored. Her personality as well as her singing saw to that; it was prodigiously strong as Clemence Dane tells in *London Has a Garden*:

'I met her once just after the First World War at a dinner party given by an American publisher. We all met in an impersonal sitting-room at the Savoy; the evening was chilly, and the Thames and the Embankment Gardéns could hardly be seen for mist. The company was literary, and I was new to that sort of gathering. I was introduced to one or two gods, but hadn't the nerve to be talkative. Cocktails came. They didn't help.

'Suddenly a bustle in the doorway–Melba was entering all in one movement as if on roller-skates. She wore a dress of scarlet gauze liberally spangled with minute dewdrops. She was stoutish. She had eyes like a hawk or a headmistress, and they at once took in the room and the situation. She beamed inclusively, missing nobody, and from that moment the party was a party. She was a heavenly woman that evening, jocund, gleaming, wicked. We were her ninepins, and she bowled us over one after the other.

'When we went down to the restaurant for dinner she began to clown, shamelessly and endearingly. A new dish was brought to her and she was told that it had been specially invented for her that very evening and was to be named after her. She was delighted. The surrounding tables stared, fascinated, till she flung her napkin over her face and besought her host to "stop them!" I have never seen anyone enjoy herself nor make others enjoy themselves so much.

'But she wanted all of us, our whole attention, our united admiration, and unluckily I had been placed next to an elder god whose books I knew by heart, and I suppose I had got a little too much absorbed in him and his charm. For suddenly Melba wailed across the table: "I've been telling my best story, and there's Clemence Dane won't look at me, and isn't even listening."

'She won, the smiling, rollicking, she-egoist. There was only one thing to do—surrender, and I did, and he did, and we all did, and enjoyed her more than ever. She was such wonderful theatre as a human being that it was impossible to believe that three hours earlier one had thought of her solely, and with awe, as a Voice.'

Most of those who knew Melba would endorse Clemence Dane's words about her. She never tried to hide her light under a bushel, and she rarely failed to overshadow everybody around her. As a privileged friend of every governor-general and state governor to hold office in Australia for the last twenty years or so of her life, she was often invited to stay at one or another of the official residences. Someone once asked a state governor's wife how Melba showed up as a house-guest.

'Delightful!' the governor's lady said, with just a hint of acid in her tone. 'You know, she does allow you to feel so much at home in your own house!'

If many of those who remembered the Melba Nights at Covent Garden before the war felt, when she came back in 1919, that her voice had lost a little of its shining magic, they were bound to admit also that more than enough of the unique splendour remained to hold an audience spellbound. She could still fill Covent Garden or any concert-hall in England, not because those who remembered her in her prime did not want to hurt her feelings by staying away, but because she was still, even at fifty-eight, a great singer.

She had evidence enough of the adulation she inspired. In one of the large English provincial cities a woman wearing a chinchilla coat was in a front seat; Una Bourne, who was touring with Melba as solo pianist, kept wondering all through the concert what the coat had cost. Afterwards Melba and Miss Bourne drove back together to their hotel where a crowd of admirers was waiting on the footpath. They got out of the car, and the woman in the chinchilla coat forced her way forward, took off her coat and, like a female Raleigh, flung it on the ground, inviting Melba to walk on it. Melba exclaimed 'Oh!' Her frugal Scottish soul was shocked at the thought of walking on so costly a garment, but she went forward and, stepping as lightly as she could, passed over the coat and into the hotel. Miss Bourne was about to follow her, but as she moved to do so the chinchilla woman swept the coat up into her arms, exclaiming, 'Only for her feet!'

As a singer she was no less relaxed than she had ever been when she went back to England after the war. She never fussed before a concert, or indulged in temperamental outbursts, or practised the gargling and lusty throat-clearing which some singers apparently find necessary. While dressing for a performance she would probably sing a few arpeggios, then limber up with a sequence of soft and delicate trills, but her preparations were never showy. Her habit when she was singing was to eat a light meal about five o'clock, perhaps fish, perhaps an egg dish, with nothing to drink. She was at that time addicted to playing dominoes, and after the evening meal she and Una Bourne would settle down to an hour or more at the game. Melba was a superb whistler, and all the time they were playing dominoes she would whistle, not her own repertoire, but Miss Bourne's.

'Dame Nellie,' Miss Bourne asked once, 'why do you always whistle my repertoire?'

'Well, you see, Una,' she said with a warm kind of wistfulness, 'I wanted to be a pianist, but then I discovered I had a voice.'

She probably meant the words when she spoke them, but even if she could have turned the clock back she would not have changed her singer's career for a pianist's. She gloried in the acclamation that went with the prima donna's life; it was like bubbling wine to her. She would never have raised such ecstasy as a pianist, and she knew it.

She had lost none of her talent for commanding the affection and the loyalty of people whom she liked, such as Una Bourne, nor her gift of annihilating with a glare and a word or two any fatuous or impertinent person who thrust himself under her notice. She was about to go out on to the platform in one of her London concerts when a representative of her agents burst into the artists' room. He was purple in the face over some minor crisis, and demanded that Melba should hear about it there and then.

'Go out!' she told him in an icy voice, fixing him with her eye. 'I think you are about to have an apoplectic fit.'

His jaw fell and he stumbled from the room, leaving her to sail out on to the platform, completely self-possessed.

She never found it easy to suffer fools gladly, but at times she managed to do it. In a provincial city the mayor, a pompous little man, kept addressing her as Dame Melba.

'You shouldn't call me Dame Melba,' she said.

'What should I call you?'

'Dame Nellie.'

Evidently supposing this to be a prelude to unmentionable intimacies, he sidled up, almost leering, and asked, 'Isn't that rather familiar?'

Her eyes blazed for a moment. Then she closed her lips hard and said curtly, 'Well, it's usual!'

Her sharp business sense told her she must pass over such stupidity. It would never do if word were to get about that she had acted as David Mitchell's girl Nellie must have been tempted to do and told his Worship the Mayor, 'Don't be a damn' fool!'

3

THE salient way in which Melba betrayed her worry about the march of the years was by insisting that it did not worry her.

'There is no Anno Domini in art,' she told a newspaper interviewer. 'I have the voice of a genius. Then why should I not always sing beautifully as long as I always take care of it and do not forget what I have been taught? Why should I not sing for a thousand years?'

While talking in that strain she could almost without pausing to draw breath announce that she was looking for a successor to herself and was determined to find one. In London and on her travels about England in 1919 she often named a young Australian, Stella Power, as the soprano destined to take her place. She told people in public and private wherever she went that she was arranging for the girl to make her London début about the end of the year, exclaiming, 'Just wait till you hear her!' Thus was the way prepared for Stella Power, the so-called Little Melba, to conquer London and then the world—if she could.

Opinions differ whether or not Melba ever hoped deep within herself to find a young woman endowed with a voice, an intelligence and a personality matching her own. Some of her admirers think she really tried, others that she only believed she tried—in short, that the search was a piece of elaborate self-delusion. Her enemies do not think she tried at all, but merely went through the motions as an act of showmanship. The only inarguable fact is that since her death no true successor, whether an Australian or a singer of some other nationality, has appeared.

Thorold Waters, the Australian music critic, who believed that 'the child in Melba made her singularly impulsive in taking up young singers when they came to her', wrote:

'Never in the history of great singers has there been one who permitted herself to be so needlessly interested—if only fleetingly—in so many lesser singers from her own and other lands. . . .

'The expectation of so many that the successor to Adelina Patti would be able to push them forward became pathetic. The wonder was that she lent a temporary hand in one after another of these cases. A woman in her exalted place had nothing to gain by it; in some ways, it was inevitable that she should lose, for of a truth it led to a deal of misunderstanding, some of it very wilful, among her fellow-Australians as to the efforts Melba should or should not, have made for them.

'. . . it really is no use at all going out to seek reputation in the arcades of music unless you are able to stand on your own two feet. If a Melba will lend you an arm for a while, well and good, but that is not to be expected of her indefinitely. And few arms were more friendly to young singers than Melba's.'

Melba did help many young women to singing success. The most notable of these were not Australians but Americans, Elizabeth Parkina and Elena Danieli, both good sopranos of the second flight. Parkina died young, but Danieli had a long singing career and always remembered Melba's help. As Helen Daniel she was a student in Paris in 1925 when the American tenor, Charles Hackett, took her to Melba's apartment. Having heard her sing Melba said, 'You may not have a phenomenal voice, but there is a tear in it, and I believe you will make a career.' She pushed Miss Danieli's career in the most practical way in Europe, America and Australia.

Among Australians her most successful protégée was possibly a Melbourne soprano, Gertrude Johnson, who had a good London career and sang with solid if unspectacular success at Covent Garden after World War I. A woman of determination and personality, Gertrude Johnson returned to Australia in 1936 and, having settled in Melbourne, founded and undertook the direction of the National

Theatre Movement of Australia. Melba helped her as a student, and helped her also in her career abroad, but always seemed to have some restraint in her attitude to the girl; perhaps they had too many traits of character in common, notably a burning determination to do what they wanted, whether anybody else liked it or not. Strong-minded people are apt to find their similarities the reverse of endearing.

Those close to Melba in World War I believed that she genuinely supposed herself to have found her successor in Stella Power. Stella Power was born, like Melba, in Richmond, but into a working-class home. She was one of a family of three girls and two boys whose mother died when they were young. In childhood she had little chance to become familiar with even the names of the great personages of music, but an early experience made her aware of Melba. This occurred in 1911 at a time when the little girl was a boarder at a Richmond convent which specialized in housing and educating girls of poor families who had lost one or both parents. She and her classmates were taking their Saturday afternoon walk under the supervision of two nuns and Melba drove by in her car while they were marching across Princes Bridge, the main city bridge over the Yarra.

'There goes Champagne Nell,' a man said, parrotting John Norton, and the bystanders guffawed.

Stella Power, who had heard Melba's name but never before seen her, brooded on the words for the rest of the day and went to sleep that night still thinking of them.

In 1915 she won a singing scholarship to the Albert Street Conservatorium of Music, and a week after that Melba went there to hold her first class. The girl, gauche and agonizingly shy, was pushed up to the piano. Melba struck a chord, and Stella sang, 'Aaaah!'

Melba glowered at her. 'What do you mean, Aaaaah!' she mocked, making it sound like a sheep's bleat. 'Don't do that!'

They started again, and Melba took her up the scale, then said, 'Do what your teacher tells you and you'll be all right,' and called for another student.

A week later Melba came again and, sitting at the piano, said, 'Where's that child who got high F last week?' Fritz Hart beckoned Stella forward, and Melba took her up the scale. 'You've got a natural voice,' she said. 'I'll teach you.' She told the girl to get *Voi che sapete*, Cherubino's aria from Act II of Mozart's *Le Nozze*

di Figaro, adding, 'I'll teach you to sing it.' That was the beginning of an association between the ageing prima donna and the raw
young soprano which might have produced something resembling
Melba, but didn't.

The quality of Stella Power's voice was never in question. It
was a small voice, with an impeccable *legato*, and many of her
fellow students believed it to be nearer to Melba's voice than any
other they ever heard; when she sang hearers were reminded,
as with Melba, of Dresden china. Some of those who knew her
doubted that she was temperamentally equipped to succeed in
opera, much less to succeed Melba; they found her too gentle, too
feminine, too compliant, and altogether lacking in those indispensable qualities of character which Melba once expressed in a
remark tossed off to Fritz Hart: 'Fritz, if I'd been a housemaid,
I'd have been the best in Australia—I couldn't help it. It's got to
be perfection for me.' Those who doubted Stella's capacity to touch
the heights felt that while she would have been a decorative and
pleasant housemaid she would not have been the best in Australia
but only one among thousands, and were afraid she would turn
out to be only one singer among thousands also. Few of them
dared mention these doubts to Melba once they realized she had
taken the girl up, but a Melbourne flautist, Alfred Weston Pett,
one day bluntly said, 'Madame, you're backing the wrong horse!'
According to Pett Melba snapped back, 'Yes, I know, but I don't
want you to tell me.'

Many of Melba's friends believed her to be a poor judge of
character; they felt she often over-estimated the qualities of those
she tried to help but, once committed, would not drop the favourite
even when the shortcomings were apparent to her, not so much
out of kindness as because she hated to admit that she was wrong.
'The trouble was,' one of her friends said, 'that she so often tried
to turn little ugly ducklings into swans. She was always rather
disappointed when the transformation did not come off.'

Stella Power was a hard-working student, and Melba saw her
as the flower of the Albert Street Conservatorium class; nor did
she hide her good opinion. When leaving Australia in November
1916 for a professional tour of the USA, Melba told her, 'Stella,
I am conferring a very great honour on you. I have told the Taits
to advertise you from now on as the Little Melba.' The Taits
meant J. and N. Tait, the Australian firm of concert managers, who
on Melba's instructions were arranging for Miss Power to give

her first individual recital in Melbourne in 1917. The girl was touched by the honour; she—and doubtless Melba also—did not realize that the label, with its implication that here was a smaller and a lesser Melba, would hinder rather than help her career. Melba appeared to be delighted with the idea. To a newspaper interviewer in Sydney just before her ship left she said that three or four of the girls in her Melbourne classes were 'bound to achieve big careers for themselves in the near future'. Then she added, with a liberal sprinkling of operatic licence as to the strict facts: 'One of the four is Miss Stella Power, and her companions call her "The Little Melba".' This was not so; that label was Melba's inspiration.

Stella Power's Melbourne début in August 1917 was successful, and nobody listened more raptly nor applauded more warmly than the real Melba. On the face of it this seemed to be the beginning of a good career, perhaps a brilliant one. Melba went to America again a few months later, and toward the end of 1917 cabled the girl a summons to go to New York, escorted by her conservatorium teacher, Mary Campbell. When they arrived Melba took one swift and horrified glance at her putative successor's clothes, starting with the button-up boots, and exclaimed, 'Oh, child, what a horror!' She was living in an hotel, but had an apartment waiting for them, and as soon as they were settled she took them shopping; within a few days Stella Power, who had arrived looking like a backwoods wench in her Sunday best, was transformed into an elegant young woman of fashion. Melba paid for the clothes, as she paid the fares and was paying the rent of the apartment; when she wanted to do something she never skimped.

Stella Power toured the USA with Melba, finishing in California, and sang at every concert as a supporting artist. Melba would lead her out by the hand and introduce her to each audience, saying, 'I hope you will love Stella as you have loved me.' Americans liked her singing, but she was always less a singer in her own right than a minor satellite of Melba's. Her earnings were good, however; to dress, to live and to travel cost her nothing, and Melba paid her a good fee for every concert. And now and then there was a wind-fall. One afternoon in New York, Melba took her to a party at the home of Charles M. Schwab, the steel magnate. Melba sang, and then Stella. When they were about to leave Schwab put a cheque into her hand; it was for $500, the biggest fee she had ever earned. Thinking how she would spend the money she showed the cheque to Melba who took one look at it, grabbed it, and said, 'Give me that! That goes straight into the bank until you get home.' Melba had not frittered money away in her struggling student days, and she was determined that her protégée should not do it.

Stella parted from Melba in California and was back in Australia in June, a month or two ahead of the diva. She was a more sophisticated girl than the one who had left six months before, and mildly intoxicated with her taste of professional success and her hopes of the career ahead of her. Then she did something which must have made Melba wonder if this was really the girl who was to succeed her; she got married – not a reprehensible act for any normal young woman, but perhaps illtimed for one working for a singing career.

The wedding, to a young man named William O'Rourke, took place in St Patrick's Cathedral, Melbourne, in the December; both O'Rourke and the Little Melba were Roman Catholics. Melba appeared to give the match her blessing by going to the ceremony and the reception, even though she had a concert that night and always tried to avoid exertion before making a professional appearance. But she cornered O'Rourke at the reception and told him threateningly, 'Stella isn't going to give up her singing. Get her to London as soon as you can.'

Melba herself started out for London a few weeks later, and on the trip she must have done some serious thinking about her protégée's future; her own broken marriage was a constant reminder to her that marriage and a singing career are hard to combine, but she let herself hope for the best.

The O'Rourkes were some months behind her; they reached London about the end of October 1919 and moved into a modest hotel. Melba was touring the provinces, but she scribbled a note of welcome from Leeds, telling Stella that arrangements for her London début were in hand. She returned a week or so later, and William and Stella O'Rourke went to see her at her house in Dover Street. Melba was surrounded by personal friends and business associates, and there was little chance for free talk. This was trying for Stella who wanted to discuss a matter of some intimacy. Even apart from that the meeting did not come out well.

When Melba saw O'Rourke she demanded. 'What are you here for?' – as if he, a husband of less than twelve months, had no business to be with his young wife.

He said, 'You told me to bring Stella as soon as I could, didn't you? Well, I've brought her.'

Melba turned her shoulder to him with a grunted remark which implied that he was a damned nuisance, and said to his wife, 'You're having your audition at the Albert Hall, but he's not to be there!'

O'Rourke muttered a few angry words, but he and Stella left without an explosion, and she began practising for her audition.

When she arrived at the Albert Hall a few mornings later—without her husband, as Melba had commanded—she found a few people waiting to hear her; one was Lionel Powell, the entrepreneur. Melba's accompanist, Frank St Ledger, was late, and Melba, never patient, sat down at the piano and played the opening bars of *Una voce poco fa*. Stella Power stood there, preparing to launch her voice into the great empty hall. Then, suddenly the accompaniment stopped.

'Are you going to have a baby?' Melba asked her.

'Yes, Madame,' she replied. 'That's what I've been trying to tell you.'

Melba sprang up from the piano and stamped across the stage calling to Lionel Powell. When he came she said, 'The bloody little fool is going to have a bloody baby.'

Stella burst into tears. She could not guess how Melba knew. She was about two months pregnant, and did not dream that anyone could see she was with child.

Just then St Ledger arrived and strolled on to the platform to be confronted by a tableau which might have come straight out of grand opera—the pretty blonde girl crying, the matriarch glaring, the others staring and lost for words. St Ledger picked up the essentials of the story in a few seconds and walked across to Stella.

'Come on, come on, come on!' he muttered. 'Pull yourself together! You've just got to do it.'

'I can't,' she mumbled through her tears.

'You've got to,' he repeated, and sat down at the piano and started to play.

The sound of the notes was like a dash of cold water on her face. She mopped her eyes, cleared her throat, walked to the edge of the platform and sang. She was never quite sure afterwards what she had sung or how she had sung it, but she knew it must have been satisfactory, because when the audition was over Lionel Powell said to Melba, 'She'll make her début in two weeks.'

The O'Rourkes were half-afraid that Melba would show her displeasure by calling the whole thing off, but she saw it through. She was furious, though, and wrote a blistering letter to poor

Fritz Hart, in Melbourne, demanding to know why he had let the girl leave for London when she was pregnant. Hart knew nothing of the inopportune pregnancy until Melba's letter reached him, nor did he see what he could have done about it if he had known. All he could do was to write a soothing reply and hope the storm would subside.

The Little Melba made her London début in a Sunday afternoon concert at the Albert Hall on 23 November 1919, supported by an orchestra conducted by Landon Ronald. London was polite, but not deeply impressed. *The Times* did not think 'the Albert Hall was the place to hear her in; it sounded too much as if she was singing in Australia and we were listening to her on a relay-telephone. . . . There are singers whom the Albert Hall exactly fits, but Miss Power is not one of them.' The *Globe* believed 'she would have been heard to greater advantage in the concert rooms one associates with *musique intime*.' That was the consensus.

Melba must have been downcast. She had been foretelling a brilliant career for the Little Melba, and now her enemies would snigger with knowing winks, 'The old grey mare ain't what she used to be!' She did not abandon Stella Power, however; the girl had a charming voice and used it well, and in the next few years she was to tour as assisting artist with the violinist Jan Kubelik, the violoncellist Jean Gerardy, and the pianist Wilhelm Backhaus, and to build a sound but unexciting reputation. But a career, even a minor career, in grand opera eluded her; in fact, she sang only once in opera, when she took the secondary soprano role of Micaela, in an Australian performance of *Carmen* in 1924. Melba, who could have forced open Covent Garden's doors to her, belatedly realized that, whatever qualities of temperament are essential to a prima donna, the Little Melba lacked them—she was too little a Melba ever to find and keep a place in the fiercely competitive surroundings of a great opera house. Nothing revealed Melba's resigned state of mind better than a note she wrote in 1920, when the O'Rourkes' son was born in London. The note was short but warm: 'I am so very glad your little son has arrived and send you my sincerest congratulation. I shall try and come and see you in about a week. God bless you.'

Stella Power's singing career lasted until the 1950s, and she made a small name in Britain and some European countries, and in the USA, Canada, and New Zealand, as well as in her native Australia. Although perhaps vocally endowed to succeed Melba she was psychologically unsuited to do so. Melba, knowing the inexorability of her own will to succeed, was apt to suppose that the same consuming purpose drove others also, and was always surprised when events proved her wrong. Stella Power was one of her disappointments.

In 1925 a few months before her formal retirement she told a newspaper interviewer in London: 'It is no use having a perfect voice unless you have brains, personality, magnetism, great willpower, health, strength, and determination. If they are to find a woman to take my place, she must have all these qualities – and such women come only once in a century. I have been trying to get a successor – but I have not seen one.'

She had evidently concluded that a Little Melba was not enough; her successor had to be another Melba without any reservations.

4

MELBA was wrong if she thought Covent Garden had reached its nadir when men wore shabby tweed coats in the stalls. For a time, early in the 1920s, it teetered on the verge of extinction as an opera house and its prospects were bleak. After the 1919 reopening Melba did not sing at Covent Garden for nearly four years, and when she did so – with a somewhat patronizing air that irritated a few people – it was in a season of the British National Opera Company, which was fighting for survival.

Beecham and the Syndicate were again partners in the 1920 summer season at Covent Garden, but Melba told a friend, 'I dislike Beecham and his methods. I'll sing only if the King commands me.' The King did not command her so she did not sing. There was no opera at all at Covent Garden in 1921, except for an eight-weeks season put on by the Carl Rosa Company in October–December, and when the BNOC staged its first Covent Garden season in 1922 Melba would not risk her status by appearing, even though the company included a good leavening of distinguished singers and conductors. She might have taken the risk more readily if she had been thirty years younger, but she probably felt that, at past sixty, she could not afford to have her friends, not to mention her enemies, shrugging and saying among themselves that Nellie Melba had fallen from her pinnacle and was reduced to singing in a company which was not of world standard. She was still acknowledged as the supreme prima donna of her time, and she intended holding her place.

The directors of the BNOC knew the company's reputation would rise if it could put on a season at Covent Garden with Melba singing there. Even if it was true that her voice had lost something of its young beauty, even if she could no longer encompass the great coloratura roles, even if she avoided the soaring high notes which she had once taken in her vocal stride, she was still Melba, the incomparable soprano, the woman whose singing had enchanted kings and commoners and could enchant them still. Her name had magic; so had her voice, although she was an ageing woman and would soon be old. The concert tours she continued to make in the British Isles and on the Continent were evidence that she could still fill any hall; her name, the one word 'Melba' on the posters, was enough. And those among her audiences who went to hear her out of curiosity, doubting that this woman whose name as a singer had been a household word for thirty years would still be capable of producing anything but a sorry ghost of her once angelic voice, found themselves staying to listen, enchanted. So it was a great day for the BNOC when Melba at last said yes. She chose *Bohème*, and the company would not have had it otherwise; Mimi had always been her best role as well as her favourite, and the public loved her in it.

She went back to Covent Garden, not in a summer season, but in the BNOC's 1922–3 Christmas season, appearing in *Bohème* on 17 January. Fog wrapped London that night and crept into every corner of Covent Garden, but it did not dull Melba's voice. Eugene Goossens found her performance 'unforgettably touching', and the London *Daily Telegraph* critic wrote that her voice 'rang with that serene purity of tone which has always been her most priceless possession.'

It was like an old-style Melba Night (although the tiaras and the stiff white evening shirts were fewer), and after the last curtain she made a speech to the capacity audience. She said: 'Dear friends, I am so happy. It is good to be home again. I have always considered Covent Garden my artistic home, and I hope it will always be my artistic home. We cannot afford to let this beautiful theatre go, as it is suggested it should go, and I for one will do everything I can to keep opera going in England. I am proud of the work this brave little band of singers is doing. That is why I am singing tonight, and that is why I hope my darling public will come and help them. If you do help them they can go on; if you do not, they cannot. So please me and come.' If the words smacked of queenly condescension they were at least widely reported and must have helped the cause. Perhaps the *amour-propre* of some of the 'brave little band of singers' was slightly ruffled, however; the company included such artists as Maggie Teyte, Florence Austral, Edna Thornton, Muriel Brunskill, Norman Allin, Walter Hyde, Frank Mullings, Robert Parker and Robert Radford.

Melba did not speak merely for effect when she called Covent Garden her artistic home; with her no other opera house counted for nearly as much. She went back for the BNOC's big summer season, beginning in May, and appeared in *Faust* as well as *Bohème*. Although she must have known her career as a prima donna could not last much longer she did not let sentimental reflections steer her into unbusinesslike actions. Her earlier *Bohème*, in the January, had been broadcast by the British Broadcasting Company (later superseded by the British Broadcasting Corporation, which was established by royal charter on 1 January 1927), but Melba rejected a proposal that the *Bohème* she sang on 1 June, in the presence of the King and Queen, should also be broadcast. Some of the published comments on her refusal were indignant, and some of the unpublished ones suggested she was a ruthless money-grubber who did not mind depriving tens of thousands of listeners of their pleasure so long as her pocket did not suffer. She was not visibly shaken by these wordy slingstones; she believed her earnings as a concert singer would suffer if radio listeners could hear her for nothing, and she did not intend to let that happen to please anyone.

She had an old acquaintance among the BNOC singers; this was the Australian bass-baritone, Frederick Collier. He had often sung in Melba's wartime concert parties in Australia and, having gone to England soon after the war with his wife, Elsy Treweek, a soprano, was beginning to make a name in Europe. Collier liked Melba for a number of reasons, but chiefly because she was no humbug; she was, he found, always delighted if the audience applauded another singer on the same programme as herself, but only so long as it applauded her louder and longer. One of his first meetings with her had been in November 1914 when her party gave a patriotic concert in Adelaide. Collier opened the programme with the Handel aria *Arm, arm, ye brave,* and the audience clapped and roared its approval. He went back on to the platform time after time, bowing, then going off, but he was not allowed to sing an encore; Melba was singing next and nobody was allowed to take an encore before she sang. She stood in the wings, lips tight-pressed, foot tapping, growing more and more impatient as the ovation for Collier rolled on and on, and at last exploded, 'Damn them! Why don't they stop?'

Collier was glad to see her again, and she seemed well pleased to see him. To his ears her voice had lost little if anything of its old quality, and he quickly discovered that Melba herself had not changed. They were rehearsing one day at Covent Garden, and after she had sung an aria he came face to face with her in the wings.

'You're still it!' he said, meaning every syllable.

'I'm going to be it!' she replied, also meaning every syllable.

Collier, a forthright man, could never bring himself to treat Melba with the deference she commanded from many singers; he believed that those who let her browbeat them were lost, and acted on that conviction. The company was rehearsing *Bohème*; the Colline was missing, and Collier, who was Schaunard, was giving Melba Colline's cues, so the rehearsal would flow more smoothly. He made a mistake and gave her a cue in the wrong place, and she snapped at him, asking him what he supposed he was doing. Collier, who had the physique of a heavyweight wrestler, saw red. He strode across, gripped her shoulders with his powerful hands, and snarling, 'I'm only doing it to help you', shook her hard. To his astonishment, Melba did not order him to take his hands off her. She laughed, and Collier, feeling a little foolish, let go of her shoulders and walked back to his place. The rehearsal went on as if nothing had happened.

5

AUSTRALIA and the approval of Australians meant more to Melba in the last decade or so of her life than ever before. It almost seemed as if she wanted to build up a reserve of good-will for herself which would last her through eternity. Although she had an unquenchable hankering for Europe and managed to go abroad every year, she spent more time in Australia and lost no chance to make Australians remember her.

It is true that Australians infuriated Melba at times, and in private she was outspoken about it. Beverley Nichols, the English writer, who was closely associated with her in her last years, has written:

'If only the Australians could have heard how Melba herself used to rail against her own country! If only I had possessed a gramophone record of the mocking, bitter invective which she poured out upon Australia and everything Australian! By comparison, Mrs Trollope's assaults on Victorian America were the sweetest milk of human charity.

'I found myself in the curious position of having to defend her own countrymen against her onslaughts.

' "They may be crude," I would say, "but they're incredibly warm-hearted and hospitable, and they're obviously anxious to learn."

'She brushed such protests aside:

' "They're hopeless . . . hopeless!" '

For some reason she held a special fascination for those of her own people who take a delight in proving that home-grown celebrities are unregenerate sinners just like lesser folk, but rather more so. She knew most of her own failings, but she resented being constantly damned in her own country not only for sins she had committed but also for sins she had never been tempted to commit.

Norman Lindsay, who suffered both as an artist and a novelist at the hands of Australia's official and unofficial prudes, once discussed the subject with Melba. She burst out, 'Oh, the horrible people of this country! Everywhere else in the world I am respected. Here I am insulted!' Thirty years after Melba's death Lindsay recalled her 'simmering indignation at the things said about her in Australia—that she was half her time drunk and indulged in indiscriminate amours.' He wrote in a private letter:

'She could not enter a hotel dining-room without hearing the splenetic hiss of whisperings and titterings all around her. It really did outrage and confound her that she should get that sort of thing in the country of her birth, when in all other countries she had the social elect, from crowned heads downwards, paying royal obeisance to her. I was pretty splenetic myself at that time, over the sort of stuff I was getting from the newspapers and the public, so we had a mutual theme to chant exasperation over the village parochialism of the Australian national ego of that era. I remember pleasing her by saying, "At least when you are on the stage you have the satisfaction of knowing that you dominate them and they are your subject creatures!" '

Melba was not censorious of other people's morals but she expected them to be discreet. One day in the 1920s the Sydney artist, editor and critic, Sydney Ure Smith, asked her to lunch with two of his friends, whom he described as a brother and sister. In fact they were lovers, the man being encumbered with a wife, but the good chance that they bore the same surname helped them to promote the fiction of their blood relationship. The man, a wealthy middle-aged member of Sydney's commercial world, and his putative sister were living in an attractive little house in a fashionable suburb, and there on the appointed day Melba and Ure Smith arrived and were graciously received. Melba was charmed. When she and the young woman retired at the end of lunch, she sang the praises of the meal and the company almost in grand opera terms; then, passing on to the qualities of her listener's 'brother', she dilated on the reports of his business genius which, she said, she heard on all sides. This was too much for the young woman, who suddenly burst into tears and sobbed, 'I'm terribly sorry, Dame Nellie, but I'm afraid you are under a misapprehension. I'm not his sister. Our relationship is a quite different one.' Melba frowned as she heard the confession but presently told her hostess to dry her tears and forget all about the deception, and when the two guests took their leave a little later Ure Smith had no inkling that Melba knew the truth. She enlightened him in the cab on the way back to the city. Flushing, he cleared his throat and tried to explain but Melba silenced him. 'I don't mind her living with him,' she gritted. 'What I do object to is that you should make a damn' fool of me!'

Being about as positive a character as it would be possible to find, she naturally roused antipathy as well as liking. David Low, the cartoonist, who had a studio in Melbourne for some years until he went abroad in 1919 and settled in England, remembered her as 'a bullying woman who ate a good deal and swore a lot'. On the other hand Dr A. E. Floyd, organist and choirmaster of St Paul's Cathedral, Melbourne, formed a friendship with her after the war which lasted until her death, and found her always ready to go out of her way to do an act of practical kindness, the quality of which was never diminished for him by the gruff brusqueness of her manner. His wife mentioned to Melba in passing conversation that one of the children had a persistent cough. A day or two later she came banging at the Floyds' door, waving a prescription for a cough mixture which, she said, was infallible. It quickly cured the Floyd boy's cough at any rate.

She wanted to be favourably remembered by Australians in general as well as by individuals, and nothing else she ever did so lifted her mass popularity as her Concerts for the People, which she gave in Melbourne and Sydney in 1922. The idea came to her after she had given a series of recitals, at the customary gilt-edged prices, in Australian state capitals. Taking a rest after her exertions, she found her mail heavy with letters and telegrams from people who told her they wanted to hear her sing but could not afford to pay two guineas or a guinea, or even half-a-guinea, for a seat. Melba talked it over with John Lemmone, and they decided to put on a series of concerts for which the seats would be 5s. 6d. and every seat would be reserved. She did her best to shame affluent music-lovers into staying away from the Concerts for the People, so that those with little money could get seats, and she largely succeeded. Thirty-five thousand people heard her in the fifteen Melbourne concerts and more than 36,000 in the fourteen Sydney concerts.

Both in Melbourne and Sydney long queues would begin forming outside the booking agencies at dawn or thereabouts whenever seats for any of the Concerts for the People were to be sold. The Melbourne agency, Allan's, tried to help early arrivals by giving them coupons establishing their places in the queue, so they could go away for an hour or two and come back just before booking began. One morning George Goldie, the Allan's man with the coupons, strolled up about eight o'clock. The long queue went wild at sight of him and, breaking up, chased him across the street yelling for coupons. They cornered him on the steps of a bank opposite and tore his coat and waistcoat. Fearing that his trousers would go next, Goldie threw the coupons in the air and let the mob dive on them, then ran for his life.

The success of the concerts astonished some people but not Melba; she never had the slightest doubt that many thousands of Australians wanted nothing so much as to hear her sing, and on the evidence she was right. But she did not hide her pleasure. She kept a close eye on the booking, and at times made rather a nuisance of herself. A girl went into Allan's for two seats. The woman booking clerk behind the counter told her all the seats were sold, and she was turning away when a voice demanded, 'What about those two seats there?' It was Melba who had come up and stood with a forefinger tapping two seats not marked off on the box-plan.

'I'm sorry, Dame Nellie! They're sold,' the booking clerk stammered.

'Give them to this girl here,' Melba ordered. The booking clerk said she couldn't, and repeated that they were sold. 'I tell you to give them to this girl here,' Melba said. 'Whose concert is it? Yours or mine?'

The battle ended with the two seats handed over and Melba marched away, head high. She believed it was no good being an empress unless you acted like one. The girl who got the seats never discovered if they had been booked or if the booking clerk was holding them for some privileged customer.

For an autocrat—and, when the spirit moved her, a harshly domineering one—Melba could be quick to understand the troubles of lesser folk. Her friend, Beryl Kingsley-Newell, who acted as her secretary for the Sydney series of Concerts for the People, was with her in the greenroom of the Sydney town hall one night when she heard a baby crying nearby. In the corridor outside she found a tired young woman, looking desperate, with a crying baby in her arms. The young mother said she had travelled from a country town many miles from Sydney and could not get a seat. 'I can't go away without hearing her sing,' she said. Mrs Kingsley-Newell went in to Melba, told the story, and asked, 'What are we going to do?'

Melba thought for a moment, then said, 'Oh, well, bring them in here.'

The baby was bedded down on the greenroom sofa with his bottle and presently went to sleep, leaving his mother free to take a seat arranged by Melba and hear the concert through.

Melba never made any pretence of not enjoying the power that her position and her money gave her. She approved the way in which monarchs acted and liked to emulate them. One royal custom which she copied was that of issuing warrants to selected trades-people, certifying that they had served her and her family faithfully and well; a framed specimen of a Melba warrant, austerely engraved and bearing her dashing signature, was to be seen many years after her death hanging on the wall of a Melbourne fishmonger's shop.

Some years before World War I she established what her friends facetiously called Melba's Order of Knighthood. The emblem was a tiepin with a head in the form of a capital M. These pins were made by a London jeweller to Melba's own precise specifications. There were different grades. The lowliest was of gold with the M picked out in enamel and a small diamond set in the centre; the next was in ruby chips; the highest was of platinum with the M worked in diamonds. She never distributed these pins indiscriminately, but presented rather more of them to loyal and deserving subjects in her later years; she was always sparing with the platinum-and-diamond grade, reserving specimens of it for men who gave outstanding service to her cause. Most of the recipients of the Melba pins treasured them, but there were exceptions. She presented one to a young tenor whom she sang with soon after the war. They fell out later, and while crossing to America for a professional engagement he wrenched the pin out of his coat lapel in a burst of petulance and pitched it into the Atlantic. Melba heard what he had done and never forgave him.

She did not keep her tiepins only for professional associates. To a conductor of the Melbourne–Sydney express train, who went beyond the line of duty to make her comfortable whenever she travelled with him, she presented a pin of the third grade. He valued it far above any money tip.

A few people sniggered at her royal pretensions, but never let her see them doing it, and the chosen members of her order of knighthood usually gave her lifelong loyalty. In 1923 her brother Charlie Mitchell and his wife Blanche took a holiday in Europe. Passing through Brussels they tried to book seats for the Monnaie, where Nellie had made her début, but were met with shrugs and polite regrets; Toscanini was conducting *Pagliacci* and *Cavalleria Rusticana* that night and every seat had been booked weeks before. Not realizing the magnitude of her reputation in Brussels (which even called a street Avenue Nellie Melba, after the 'distinguished singer and philanthropist'), they did not use her name and returned, disconsolate, to the Grand Hotel, in which they were staying. They were sitting in the lounge when the manager bade them good afternoon and asked if they were comfortable. They told him they were, and he was turning away when Blanche Mitchell noticed he was wearing a Melba pin (ruby class) and remarked on it.

'Dame Nellie Melba is the most famous person to have stayed in this hotel,' he said. 'You know, of course, that she also is an Australian?'

'Yes, we know,' said Charlie Mitchell. 'I'm her brother.'

For a moment the hotel manager was speechless. Then words poured from him. Why had they not told him before? It was unthinkable that the brother of that wonderful woman should be staying in his hotel and he not know of it! Surely, but surely, there was something he could do to show his delight at their presence? They had only to name it and it would be done. Blanche Mitchell spoke up. They wanted seats for the opera, she said. They had tried to book and failed. Could he, perhaps, arrange it for them?

The manager smiled. Seats at the Monnaie? Nothing. . . . He snapped his fingers, and hotel servants raced to do his bidding.

That night Charlie and Blanche Mitchell were welcomed at the Monnaie as honoured guests. The manager of the theatre made a little speech and presented Blanche with a sheaf of flowers, then escorted them to a box where they sat to hear the opera like a visiting king and queen.

6

A RATHER unexpected aspect of Melba disclosed itself as age settled upon her. She had never been a deeply spiritual woman or taken much interest in orthodox religion; now and then when visiting Australia she had sung in Scots Church, Melbourne, but this had been rather to please her father than from any sense of compulsion to do an act of worship. Perhaps it was always the theatrical element in the practice of organized religion which appealed to her most, but at all events she showed a desire in the 1920s to identify herself with church observances, particularly those of the Church of England.

One day she invited the then Archbishop of Melbourne, Harrington Clare Lees, to lunch at Coombe Cottage, and with him Dr Floyd, and their wives. As they sat down to lunch Archbishop Lees, an urbane and cultured English prelate, remarked, 'Well, Dame Nellie, you have a lot of beautiful things here!'

'Do you know,' she answered him, speaking almost wistfully with her head slightly on one side, 'there's one thing I'd love to possess.'

'Indeed, Dame Nellie! And what is that?'

'A private chapel.'

Her hearers had no doubt of her earnestness, but Dr Floyd at any rate felt that her histrionic instinct was at work. He reasoned that, seeing Lees on one side of her and himself on the other, she had conjured up a mental picture of herself entering her own private chapel in the grounds of Coombe Cottage with the archbishop in attendance as her private chaplain and Dr Floyd making music as her private organist.

One night Floyd was a dinner guest at Government House. He found himself seated next to Melba and wondered why. Presently the reason became plain.

'I'd like to sing in your cathedral,' she told him half-way through the meal.

'That,' he said, 'would be very nice! But it isn't in my jurisdiction.'

'Whose jurisdiction then?'

'The Archbishop's.'

'I'll call on him tomorrow,' said Melba, never a woman to let the grass grow under her feet.

A day or two later Archbishop Lees asked Floyd if Melba could be given a solo to sing in the anthem one Sunday. Floyd said this could not be done; by tradition the cathedral choir provided music for the statutory services on Sunday morning and Sunday evening. He suggested instead that he give a Sunday afternoon organ recital with Melba singing nine or ten songs.

Floyd had never worked with Melba until they began rehearsing together for the recital. They rehearsed both at Coombe Cottage and in the cathedral, and he found her scrupulous in her preparations and almost pedantically exacting in the demands she made on herself. They were rehearsing in the cathedral one day, he at the console of the organ and Melba standing a few feet away in the men's choir stalls. She was singing a sacred song, *Into the woods*, for which Floyd had composed the music, using the words of a poem, *A ballad of trees and the Master*, by an American poet, Sidney Lanier (1842–81).

> *Into the woods my Master went,* [she sang]
> *Clean forspent, forspent.*
> *Into the woods my Master came,*
> *Forspent with love and shame.*
> *But the olives they were not blind to Him*
> *The little gray leaves were kind to Him . . .*

She stopped abruptly and said, 'Did you like the way I sang the word, "kind"?'

'It sounded all right to me,' he told her.

'Let's go back and do it again,' she said.

They started again and went through the verse once more, this time to the finish:

> . . . *The little gray leaves were kind to Him:*
> *The thorn-tree had a mind to Him*
> *When into the woods He came.*

Floyd noticed that she made an almost infinitesimal pause before articulating the first letter of 'kind'. Although a tiny thing it improved the delivery of the line. He realized then that to Melba the smallest detail mattered.

Few people heard her rehearse in the cathedral, but one who did was Marie Bremner, then still a student at the Albert Street Conservatorium although moving fast toward a career in operetta. She contrived to slip into the cathedral and hide behind a pillar, listening. Only a few other people were in the cathedral, and she was not interested in them nor were they in her.

For the rest of her life she remembered a discussion between Melba and Dr Floyd. Melba began to sing the Liza Lehmann song *Magdalen at Michael's gate*. Her voice soared out into the cathedral, carrying every syllable with complete clarity.

' "*Magdalen at Michael's gate tirléd at the pin. . . .*" ' She stopped. ' "Tirléd!" ' she said. 'It's an unfortunate word. Do you think they'll hear it? Do you think they'll understand it if they do hear it?'

'Of course they will,' Floyd assured her, 'if you sing it.'

'Tirléd! . . . What does it mean anyway?'*

Then, without waiting for a definition, she nodded to Floyd and sang the song from beginning to end. Marie Bremner lurking behind her pillar felt as if lifted on wings.

The cathedral could have been filled many times over on the afternoon of the recital, and the loftiness of the building seemed to invest Melba's voice with a kind of ethereality. The cathedral boys' choir supported her in some of her songs. When rehearsing with

---

* Webster's New Twentieth Century Dictionary (Cleveland, Ohio, and New York City, World Publishing Company, 1943) identifies 'tirl' as a Scottish word and describes it as a 'variant of twirl'. The definition goes on: 'To tirl at the pin; to twirl or rattle the door-latch, as a courteous signal to the inmates that a person desires or intends to enter; an old practice which prevailed when house doors could be readily opened from without, and when they were not provided with bells and knockers as they are now.'

her and in the recital itself the boys found her anything but awesome; she seemed to them to be more like a cheerful and appreciative aunt than a prima donna. She was also a generous one. From time to time in later years she would appear in the choir vestry after a Sunday night service to say how much she had enjoyed the singing and to leave a few pounds to be distributed among the boys.

Melba did not always compel the affection of adults, and some who sang with her even spat when they spoke her name, but the St Paul's choirboys had no reservations about her. She found the way to their hearts.

7

COOMBE Cottage and the surrounding country loomed large in Melba's scheme for the last decade of her life. To travel abroad every year, keeping her place as an international celebrity and seeing her friends in London, Paris, Rome, Monte Carlo, New York, Boston, and other cities of the world was necessary to her; but so, as a counterbalance, was life at Lilydale and Coldstream.

The district always made a great occasion of a homecoming by Melba when she had been away for some months. A few of the local people disliked her, feeling that her smiles and her inclinations of the head as she moved among them were too queenly, even a shade condescending; and once there was some heartburning when a sheaf of flowers, presented to her by local schoolchildren in Lilydale, was found by the roadside halfway between Lilydale and Coldstream. But most of those living in 'the Melba country' took an almost possessive pride in her fame and drew vicarious excitement and satisfaction from reading newspaper reports of her meetings with the great ones of the earth.

She gave a concert now and then in Lilydale or Coldstream, and when she did so the smallish halls were never able to hold all the people who wanted to hear her. The committees managing the halls always did their best to make the surroundings worthy of Melba. Once when she wrote from Europe, promising to give a homecoming concert in Lilydale, the committee commissioned a local artist to paint a new backdrop. He laboured over it for weeks and it was put up only a day or two before the concert. When the committee inspected it they were horrified; the central item was a nude woman, unmistakably a representation of a handsome young woman of the district. The artist was summoned and told to paint clothing on the girl's nakedness. While grumbling at such bourgeois narrow-mindedness he obeyed, and his backdrop was unexceptionable when Melba walked out to sing in front of it, although the odour of fresh paint still hung heavy on the air.

Melba liked to entertain her friends at Coombe Cottage, to show them her treasures, to sing to them when the spirit moved her. There as nowhere else she could shrug off the pressures of life, but even in her most relaxed moments she was still the empress, ruling her own domain and everyone who came under her eye.

She was always willing to listen to the experts and consider what they said, but nobody ever talked her down about the furnishings, the design of the wallpapers, the way a picture should be hung, the layout of the gardens, or any other detail of the arrangements at Coombe Cottage. Unless she was persuaded she was wrong (which could happen, although it rarely did) she always had her way, experts or no experts. She had a grasp of practical things astonishing in one who sang Mimi's Farewell with the pure detachment of a disembodied spirit. One day painters were redoing the inside of the swimming pool. Not liking the shade of colour they were using Melba climbed down into the empty pool with them, mixed paints until she had the hue she wanted, then painted a section of the wall of the pool as expertly as a tradesman, and told them to do the rest like that.

She was never unduly patient if somebody she employed was slow to understand precisely what she wanted. An interior decorator, renovating one of the rooms at Coombe Cottage, gave the ensemble a finishing touch by fitting to a hanging light a rather gaudy pink-and-white shade. He was up the ladder admiring his shade when Melba came into the room. She gave the shade one appalled look.

'Take it down,' she said.

'But, Dame Nellie . . . !'

'Take the bloody thing down!'

The interior decorator nearly fell off the ladder in his hurry to obey.

Some of Melba's servants stayed for many years in her employ and swore by her. Her butler, John Mitchell, an Englishman, began working for her before World War I and was with her, either in

Australia or abroad, for the rest of her life. Many of her servants were terrified of her, however. They said they could recognize the danger-signals when Melba was angry or exasperated—for example, even by the tone in which she hummed to herself as she took an early-morning stroll in the garden—and then the prudent ones would keep out of her way if possible. One day after breakfast she sacked the whole Coombe Cottage staff, with the exception of John Mitchell and two or three other old retainers, and packed them back to Melbourne at once, having telephoned for a new set to arrive on the evening train.

She never took excessive trouble to see that abstract justice was done in her household; if something important went awry and she could not determine pretty well at once where the guilt lay she was apt to sack the staff *en masse* and replace them. Yet she could be forbearing at times. A footman named Arthur Anton was in the scullery at Coombe Cottage, carrying a valuable English tea-set on a tray. Melba walked in just as Anton, who had been working for her only a few weeks, caught his toe and tripped. The tea-set cascaded on to the floor, and practically every piece was smashed. Anton expected to be sacked on the spot, but she merely looked at the mess of shattered china and said, 'Ah, well, I suppose you couldn't help it!' He saw many flashes of her temper, but after that he doubted that she was so terrifying as some of his fellow servants believed.

While Melba could pass over an honest accident of that kind she was never tolerant of incompetence in a servant, except when harshness might damage a social relationship which she prized. She once told a man working as her private secretary to engage a new gardener. He telephoned an old-established Melbourne firm of nurserymen, Law Somner and Company. On their recommendation he hired a man and put him to work, then reported to Melba what he had done.

'I don't think much of the new gardener,' she said to him some weeks later. 'I can't understand Lord Somers recommending him.' At that time Lord Somers was governor of Victoria.

'Not Lord Somers, Dame Nellie,' the secretary said. 'Law Somner's.'

'Good God!' she exclaimed. 'Then sack him at once.'

Like any man or woman well in the public eye, Melba was often pestered by cranks. Most of these were just nuisances, but now and then a spectacular one found his way into her presence. Cyril

Dillon, the artist, was sitting with her in the Coombe Cottage music room one afternoon when he heard raised voices at the front door, and then the trample of feet in the hallway. The music room door was flung open and one of the handsomest men Dillon had ever seen stalked in with the butler trailing behind him, expostulating. The intruder, about six feet tall, had a leonine head and was immaculately dressed.

'Is Dame Nellie in?' he demanded. His eyes roved about the room and lit up as they fell on Melba. 'Take my hat, my coat,' the man said. The dazed butler obeyed, and the man advanced toward Melba with outstretched hands, saying, 'How are you, Nellie, darling?'

'I don't know you,' she flashed.

'Of course you do, darling,' he said. 'I'm ——— ———.' He was no masquerader; the name he gave was his own, and Dillon recognized him for a brilliant but mentally unstable South Australian barrister. He had been called to the Bar in 1873, when he was twenty-one, and had become a Queen's Counsel twenty years later, only to be certified insane in 1898 and committed to a mental hospital. He was released after a few months and lived until 1927, often straying over the brink of insanity. He earned a living by doing certain kinds of legal work, and was helped in the last years of his life by a pension paid to him by other Adelaide legal men.

Although the afflicted man was about seventy on the day he called at Coombe Cottage he was still a striking figure, erect and active, and when Melba said, 'Keep between me and this man', Dillon edged forward rather charily, knowing this powerful fellow could brush him aside with a sweep of one hand.

'I've written a sermon and I want to read it to you,' the caller told her.

'I don't want to hear your sermon,' she said.

He ignored her and, taking a sheaf of paper from his pocket, began to read. He had a fine rolling voice and read well. Dillon listened, dazzled by the words and the way they were delivered. Melba listened also, because she could do nothing else. The reading went on for about twenty minutes. Then the intruder lowered his papers and, saying he wanted to get something from his car, excused himself and strode out.

Melba sprang to her feet and said, 'I'm going. When that man comes back tell him anything you like,' and she fled from the room.

A few minutes later the man returned and at once asked, 'Where's Dame Nellie?' Dillon said she had asked to be excused. The man shook his head in sorrow and chagrin. 'Very rude,' he said. 'Very rude indeed! You tell her I said so.'

With that he shuffled his papers together, stowed them away in a pocket, and took his leave. Dillon had enjoyed the interlude, but he was rather glad the man went before being stung to an act of perhaps homicidal violence.

Such episodes were blessedly rare at Coombe Cottage. For the most part life moved along smoothly there, whether Melba was in residence or when, travelling abroad, she left the place to her son and his wife. Once or twice, in periods when she was away, her friends were astonished to meet an unexpected house-guest there; this was an ageing man with piercing blue eyes, white hair and white moustache who, even when he was in the late sixties, could still ride a horse as if he had been born in the saddle. The man was Charles Armstrong who had settled down to live out his life in Canada, in a cottage standing on some twenty acres on the shores of Shawnigan Lake, British Columbia.

Anyone who supposed—as some friends of Melba's did—that Armstrong had slipped into Australia and gone to Coombe Cottage for a more or less surreptitious holiday while his ex-wife was away was wrong. Melba encouraged the young Armstrongs to invite him when she was away, just as she often told friends visiting Canada, 'Go and see Charlie! See how he's getting on.' So it seems that the emotional flame he lit in her at Mackay never quite died. Nieces and nephews of Melba who had previously known Charles Armstrong merely as a name discovered his indestructible charm when they met him on his visits to Coombe Cottage; they began to understand why, as a twenty-three-year-old sugar planter, he had captivated their Auntie Nellie and why the ghost of that old long-ago romance continued to haunt her.

8

MELBA looked upon gracious living as her right, and at Coombe Cottage she lived graciously and saw to it that her guests did also.

Even in her sixties her energy seemed to be inexhaustible and she was always out of bed long before breakfast, wandering about the garden and physically limbering-up for the day ahead, before going in to the piano about eight o'clock for singing practice. A house-guest waking in the morning would find on her morning tray a rosebud or some other flower, still with the dew on it, and a note scribbled by Melba, 'My dear. What would you like to do today?' Melba would have picked the flower with her own hand.

Afternoon callers would be served tea in traditional English style with Melba herself, surrounded by all the orthodox paraphernalia, making the tea on the spot in a shining silver teapot. (Notwithstanding John Norton and his allegations that she was a wine-bibber, Melba's favourite drink all her life was tea. She carried a little silver tea-kettle wherever she went, in Australia or abroad, so that she or her maid could brew the kind of tea she wanted wherever she chanced to be. The kettle came to be almost a talisman, and in her will she bequeathed it to her granddaughter, Pamela.)

Dinner guests would sit down to a meal which nearly always included some unusual item—perhaps quail or plovers' eggs shipped from England, or asparagus grown at Coombe by an Italian gardener, Augusto Olivieri, who ripened it green in the Italian style as Melba liked it.

To Melba her performance as the lady of the manor at Coldstream was no less important than her performance as Mimi or Marguerite on the stage of Covent Garden, and she saw to it that the background was right. Driving home one afternoon she noticed many bits of waste-paper littering the main street of Coldstream. Visitors were coming up from Melbourne next day, so early in the morning she routed out of bed one of her nieces, Mary Patterson, who was staying with her. They drove down to the township and, each armed with a walking-stick fitted with a prong, ranged the main street, stabbing and collecting every scrap of paper they saw. After an hour's work Melba was satisfied that Coldstream was fit for her friends to drive through on their way to Coombe Cottage.

She was dressed for that scavenging expedition in a squirrel coat and knee-high Russian boots but Coldstream people, knowing her well, were not startled. She always wore expensive clothes, though not always suitable ones, and in the street often appeared badly or at any rate carelessly turned out. She rarely went wrong, however, in dressing for a formal night occasion – that is, in what she called *pomposa* dressing. The Italian word *pomposa*, meaning 'full of pomp', was one of her favourites. Close friends knew when she told them before a dinner-party, 'We're going to be *pomposa* tonight!', that she had arranged a specially elaborate meal with vintage wines, including French champagne.

Guests continually came and went at Coombe Cottage whenever Melba was in residence. She was not given to solitary meditation, nor did she read much excepting light novels and now and then a non-fiction book of ephemeral character, and human companionship, always necessary to her, became indispensable in her later years. Music was by no means the only entertainment offered at Coombe Cottage; music never dominated the life of the house. Melba had a croquet lawn and liked to play. She also had a lawn tennis court on which social titans as well as tennis immortals performed.

Many of her guests were, naturally enough, musicians and singers. One with whom she formed a warm friendship was the Russian-born pianist Jascha Spivakovsky, who made a series of recital tours of Australia in 1921–2, and later went back from Europe to settle in Melbourne. Melba was present at most of his Melbourne concerts and usually rounded off the night by taking him and a few other friends to supper in a private room in an hotel. Snooping waiters were one of her pet aversions; she hated thinking that her conversation was being eavesdropped on and would presently be repeated, with appropriate ornamentations. One evening she said, 'Look, Jascha, tonight we're going to talk a language that neither you nor I understand.' He comprehended her idea at once, and when the waiters came in broke into a stream of gibberish which sounded convincing enough to be a foreign language; Melba replied with an equally eloquent flow of meaningless sounds. The waiters' eyes popped with astonishment, while Melba and Spivakovsky rattled on with their idiot dialogue, and that night, instead of loitering about, retired as soon as the food and drinks were served, leaving the party to talk freely in plain English.

She often took personal trouble to help a visiting musician who was finding Australian audiences unresponsive. She admired the Russian violinist, Efrem Zimbalist, and was indignant when he toured Australia in 1927 and played to half-empty houses. She took him and his wife, Alma Gluck, the soprano, under her wing and had them to stay with her several times at Coombe Cottage. She also–unpaid–gave a concert with Zimbalist in Melbourne, as if to tell Australians, 'This man is a great artist. See what I, Melba, think of him!' The concert was a huge success with some five hundred people turned away from the hall, but Zimbalist without

Melba on the programme played to meagre houses for the rest of his tour. A friend who saw Melba in her dressing-room after that concert thought she looked exhausted. She was slumped in an armchair with lines of strain etched deep on her face.

Skill as a musician or even a routine appreciation of music was not essential to a friendship with Melba. One of her best friends in the 1920s, Cyril Dillon, did not know a note of music and could hardly have told the difference between a basso profundo and a coloratura soprano. One day in the music room Melba turned to him and asked, 'Which of my songs is your favourite?'

Never having noticed what she sang he closed his eyes and, hoping for the best, blurted out, 'Oh, the Gentle Lark.'

She sat down at the piano there and then and, playing her own accompaniment, sang *Lo, here the gentle lark*, while he tried to look soulful but was really congratulating himself that he had been able to identify even one of her songs.

Daryl Lindsay, at that time a struggling young artist but later to become director of the National Gallery of Victoria and to build a sound reputation as a painter, was another visitor to Coombe Cottage whose response to Melba's singing was less than flattering. He and his wife were there on a night when Melba, who was giving a concert at Coldstream, asked after dinner, 'Now, who's coming to hear me sing?'

Lindsay, a fine horseman and a lover of horses, who liked talking horses with George Armstrong, replied, 'If you don't mind, Dame Nellie, I'd rather stay here by the fire and talk to George.'

If her prima donna's vanity was ruffled she hid it. She walked up to Lindsay, playfully slapped his face, and said, 'Do exactly as you like! George, give him some whisky. He's the only person who has ever told me to my face he doesn't want to hear me sing.'

For a woman who liked to command the esteem of persons of exalted rank Melba could be unconventional enough when it suited her. One afternoon, accompanied by an Adelaide friend, Lorna Cowell, who was staying with her, she drove from Coldstream to Melbourne on a household shopping expedition. They went into the city's biggest department store, Myer's, to buy the two utensils necessary for a chop picnic—a gridiron and a large billycan. The salesman was slow in making out the invoice and Melba, impatient as always, seized the unwrapped billycan and, with Mrs Cowell trailing behind carrying the unwrapped gridiron, led the way out into the busy heart of Melbourne at the height of the afternoon shopping rush. Either unaware or unconcerned that she was being smirked at by other shoppers, she took her way along the crowded street to her car, the billycan swinging in her hand. Luckily, Mrs Cowell knew Melba's knack of doing the unrehearsed —and, for anyone with her, sometimes the embarrassing—thing. They first met in Adelaide, and Mrs Cowell took Melba to lunch at the exclusive Queen Adelaide Club. The meal went along well enough until Melba spread butter on a roll and bit into it.

'This butter is bad!' she exclaimed in a loud, clear voice which, to Mrs Cowell's ears, seemed to echo and re-echo around the dining-room.

A little later Mrs Cowell was summoned to the secretary's office and called to account for her guest's intolerable behaviour. Nobody, the secretary told her, no, not even Dame Nellie Melba, might enter the Queen Adelaide Club as a guest and outrage the sensibilities of members and their guests by making noisy complaints against the food. Mrs Cowell crept away, wishing that the voice which had laid a spell on the world were not quite so audible when its owner saw fit to find fault with the Queen Adelaide Club's butter.

9

ALTHOUGH Coldstream lay twenty-six miles from Melbourne nobody ever declined an invitation to one of the parties Melba gave there on account of the journey. She had the showman's instinct for knowing what would make a party succeed, and when she found what she needed the cost of getting it never discouraged her.

One night in 1924 she and some friends were at a Melbourne night-club, Admiralty House, and Leslie Ross, the leader of the small dance band, played several popular numbers at her request. A fortnight later she asked him to call and see her at a Melbourne hotel where she was staying overnight. When he presented himself she asked without any preliminaries, 'What nationality are you, young man?'

'I'm an Australian with a dash of Scottish,' he said.

'Good,' she said. 'Come on! Sit down.'

She told him she was planning 'the greatest party ever held in Australia', and wanted his band to go to Coombe Cottage for the night and play. What would it cost? He made a quick calculation and named what was a tremendous figure then.

'Young man,' Melba said severely, 'you want more for one performance of your band than I pay my grand opera orchestra to play for a whole week.'

'Well,' Ross said, 'if I were giving a concert in the Melbourne town hall I could get fifty fine sopranos, any one of whom would be glad to sing for a guinea. If I want you to sing at the town hall it will cost me a thousand guineas.'

'I see the point,' she said. 'Very well, it's a deal!'

Ross went overseas within a year or two as leader of a jazz-playing act, billed as the Three Australians, which made a big name in the leading variety houses of Europe and America, but he never met any entrepreneur who clinched a business arrangement with less talk than Melba. Every detail was settled in a few minutes.

On the day of the party Melba sent her chauffeur-driven air-cooled Franklin to pick up Ross and his four bandsmen in Melbourne and take them to Coldstream. They arrived at Coombe Cottage about three in the afternoon to find a small army of electricians stringing up lights all through the garden. Melba was striding around, supervising everything. She had a red bandanna handkerchief on her head and wore an apron; at first glance she might have been a servant, but nobody could have mistaken her for anything but the mistress of the house after standing by for a minute or two and hearing her crack out commands like a general directing a battle.

She took Ross and his men inside and gave them tea, then showed them all over Coombe Cottage. Leading the way into one room with an enormous bed in it, she said, 'This is the holy of holies — Melba's bedroom. Everyone wants to say they've lain on Melba's bed. Go on, lie on it!' Ross did so, and found the bed uncommonly comfortable.

She had booked him and his men in at a Lilydale hotel, and presently she summoned the car and sent them off there to change into dinner suits and have a meal. When they got back to Coombe Cottage, Melba was transformed. The red bandanna and the apron were gone, and she was wearing an evening dress of shimmering white satin and a diamond tiara.

The music and the dancing were still going and champagne corks were still popping long after midnight, and Ross and his men settled down, expecting the revelry to last until dawn and probably after that. They did not know Melba. At three in the morning she sent her butler through the house and out into the grounds, calling, 'Will guests please assemble in the ballroom!' A few minutes later the last stragglers edged into the ballroom, and then the butler strode ceremonially to the grand piano and set down on it a lighted candle in a silver candlestick. The lights all over the ground were slowly lowered, then went out, and presently the whole house was plunged in darkness, except for the light of the single candle on the piano. Melba sat down on the piano-stool and played the introductory chords, then sang *Home, sweet home*. Her voice fell into the darkness like a thread of bright silver, and Ross, although a jazz man to his fingertips and never interested in any other kind of music, felt a cold shiver running down his spine as he listened.

Afterwards Melba told the band to wait, and when she had bade farewell to the last of her guests she walked over and put her arms around Ross and said, 'You've been wonderful! You must be hungry. Come along!' She led him and his men to the kitchen, and there rolled up her sleeves and cooked them bacon and eggs. Ross ate his food, wondering if this efficient cook, with her sure and practical hands, could be the same woman who half an hour earlier had made the hair rise on the nape of his neck with her singing of that hackneyed but wonderful old ditty, *Home, sweet home*.

10

MELBA had always remembered her 1911 opera season, both for the personal triumphs and the handsome profits it had brought her. It was no sooner over than she felt it would be worth repeating on both counts. World War I forced her to postpone a second season, but she did not forget the idea and began making plans once the post-war world settled down. So, in 1924, another Melba-Williamson opera company took the stage in Australia. Largely recruited in Milan, the company was particularly strong in young singers. The coloratura Toti Dal Monte stood out; others who were later to make good reputations overseas were Lina Scavizzi (soprano), Apollo Granforte (baritone) and Dino Borgioli (tenor).

Melba had little hand in picking the singers. She went to Italy in 1923 with Nevin Tait, a director of J. C. Williamson Limited, and John Lemmone, but had to hurry back to London and undergo surgery for an intestinal ailment before recruiting began. Tait and Lemmone did the searching, helped by Henry Russell, who had agreed to go to Australia with the company as an artistic adviser. Melba herself had selected Russell, but she did not so much like him as respect his musical sagacity. She told a friend in London, 'He is a clever, dangerous man, and a Jew, but I can keep him in order.'

Melba sang a number of times in the 1924 season, notably in *Bohème*, *Otello* and *Faust*. One writer has said that, in 1924, Australians had the opportunity to hear her 'fill the entire theatre with the famous floating high C at the end of Act 1 of *Bohème*', and her singing inspired some extravagantly rapturous writing, but other critics felt she had lost something. Henry Russell, always an admirer of Melba but a realistic one, noted after hearing her in *Bohème* that her upper register had 'naturally suffered from the enemy no mortal can resist', but found no fault with the beauty of her medium notes. 'It will always seem to me a pity,' he wrote, 'that hundreds of young people who heard Melba during that season should have been born too late to hear a great voice in its full perfection.'

The season did not run altogether smoothly. Only an innocent of innocents would expect any grand opera season to be free of quarrels, outcries and upheavals and this one was no exception. Apart from the more or less routine backstage ructions, there was a minor industrial storm over what chauvinistic Australians called the cold-shouldering of Australian singers. A number of Australians were included in the company. One, the tenor Alfred O'Shea, was a principal, and a dozen or more Australians sang secondary or minor roles, while Melba's singing girls from the Albert Street Conservatorium were the female chorus and became, in Henry Russell's judgement, 'one of the best female choruses I have ever heard'. A rather tentative effort to form a male chorus in Australia having failed, a chorus was hurriedly recruited in Italy and shipped out. Murmurs against the importation of singers when, as it was claimed, equally good ones, or better, were unemployed in Australia strengthened to a raucous shout. Newspapers were flooded with letters, most of which took the tone that the importation of 'Melba's dago singers' was not only a slight to Australian singers and a subtle blow at the roots of Australian trade-unionism, but also a denial of the well-established fact that Australians could do anything as well as anybody else, and probably better. The author of one letter pointed out with a triumphant flourish that since Australia could produce good cricketers it must also be able to produce good singers. This reasoning was widely endorsed. Nevin Tait, Russell, Lemmone and the others ignored these strictures, even when they came from men of influence such as Labour parliamentarians and trade-union officials, but Melba was worried. She was instinctively conservative in politics and, having no understanding of political realities, went through the later years of her life dogged by a fear that red-ragging socialists would at any moment seize power and proceed to strip her of everything she owned, making her spend the rest of her life in penury. One morning she found her secretary, who was about to leave her to go to a newspaper job, typing on his own portable typewriter.

'You had better sell me that typewriter before you go,' Melba said.

'All right,' the secretary agreed. 'But why?'

'Well,' Melba replied, 'I might lose all my money, and if I do I can learn typing and earn my living.'

The secretary looked hard at her and saw she was not joking. She never joked about losing her money. To her that was a subject not to be mentioned in jest.

So when she was publicly assailed over the Italian chorus she set her jaw and resolved not to be intimidated, but her face wore a troubled frown and she half-suspected that the day on which the proletariat would arise, throw off its chains and destroy its betters was at hand.

She was completely at ease with members of her own domestic staff, stagehands, and workmen in her father's quarries at Cave Hill when she met them as individuals, but wage-earners in the mass took on for her an appearance of menace. Any Labour member of parliament or secretary of a trade union was, in her mind, a red revolutionary intent on dispossessing her and her kind. Yet if need be she could nearly always make friends with a given individual, wherever he might stand in the social scale. The store-man at His Majesty's Theatre, where the 1924 opera season went on in Melbourne, was an example. The management set aside an old storeroom on the third floor of the theatre as a rehearsal room for the chorus. Strict orders were given that nobody was to be admitted without clear authority. One morning Melba arrived at the theatre to attend a chorus rehearsal. She found her way to the antique hand-operated lift, let herself into it, and grasped the rope and pulled. The lift shuddered drunkenly upward. She got out at the third floor to find the storeman barring her way.

'Where are you going?' he demanded.

'To the rehearsal.'

'You're bloody well not! I've got strict instructions, and nobody gets by here.'

Melba did not bother to find out if he knew who she was. She answered him in blunt terms, and words flew back and forth between them, growing fiercer with each exchange. The storeman would not budge and at last Melba, raging, retreated into the lift, lowered herself to the ground floor, and stormed over to the executive offices of J. C. Williamson Limited on the other side of the street. She burst in upon the then general manager, Charles Wenman.

'What's the trouble, Dame Nellie?' Wenman asked.

'It's that storeman over there. He wouldn't let me in to the chorus rehearsal.'

'I'm terribly sorry, Dame Nellie!'

'And what's more he called me a bloody old bitch!' Wenman made no comment, and she thought about it for a moment or two in silence, then half-smiled and said, 'I'm inclined to think he was right!'

The storeman was horrified when Wenman told him that the woman he had refused to let in was Dame Nellie Melba. He sat down and wrote her a letter of apology at once, and she, having read it, took another ride in the shuddering lift to see him. He was nearly speechless with embarrassment, but she laughed him out of it in a few seconds and won his heart by giving him a smacking kiss as a gesture of forgiveness.

She made another lifelong conquest in that 1924 season. One of her frequent places of call in Melbourne was Allan's, a large and old-established music warehouse, whose principal, George Allan, was among her closest friends. A salesman named George Nicholls, working behind Allan's counter, soon found it was easy to have a relaxed conversation with the supposedly terrifying Melba. Having learned that he was a semi-professional singer, she encouraged him to talk about music, and listened to what he said with evident interest and respect. At the start of the season he went to hear her in *Bohème*, and when she was next in Allan's she asked how he had enjoyed it.

'Well,' he told her, 'I was so excited I didn't sleep all night.'

'Will you be going to any more of my operas?' she asked.

'I'm afraid not, Dame Nellie,' he said. 'I've got a family of four children. I couldn't afford to go again.'

She looked at him and said laconically, 'You'll be all right,' and went away.

John Lemmone walked up to Nicholls's counter a day or so later and handed him two tickets for Melba's next performance; for the rest of the season two seats were kept for him on every night she sang.

The J. C. Williamson directors found Melba a good business woman who knew what she wanted but made no unreasonable demands and was always co-operative. There was never any question whether or not she would sing as advertised; she made her commitments, then kept them. Among other things she was her own best press-agent and had no scruples about the means she used to get headlines. Claude Kingston, who was in charge of publicity for the Sydney section of the 1924 season, travelled to Sydney with her in the express train from Melbourne a few days ahead of the main company. Reporters of the Sydney newspapers were to board the train at Moss Vale, about ninety miles from Sydney, and Melba asked Kingston to prepare a handout for them. He drafted something, a conventional statement, but when she read it she scoffed, ripped it up, and tossed the torn paper in the air.

'You have a lot to learn,' she said. 'I'll speak to them.'

At Moss Vale Kingston listened in amazement when Melba met the reporters and said not a word about the forthcoming opera season but told them the train was alive with fleas; she had, she said, been bitten all over and offered to lift her skirt to prove it.

The Sydney newspapers not only splashed the story of 'Melba's fleas' but featured it on their posters. The Victorian and New South Wales railway commissioners were ruffled, and promised to have the train fumigated at once. Kingston never found out whether Melba's fleas were mythical or not, but he knew she had brought off a masterstroke of publicity. Everybody in Sydney was aware that evening that she had arrived—flea-bitten or not—to launch her opera season.

Sir Frank Tait, one of a group of brothers long prominent in Australian theatre and concert management, speaking in 1965 as managing director of J. C. Williamson Limited, said: 'Melba was an extraordinary combination of business woman and artist. She went in for no prima donna antics. Most opera singers are like overgrown children—they have a gift for singing, and that is the end of it. Melba was much more than just a great singer. She called a spade a spade, and some people disliked her on that account. She'd tell a singer to his face whether he was good, bad or indifferent, and that kind of directness often makes one unpopular. She erred at times in recommending artists, but she would have been super-human if she hadn't.'

In one thing only did Melba seem superhuman, and that was in the unique character of her voice. Otherwise she was wholly human; her feet of clay balanced the wings of a dove which she wore when she sang, and they never left the earth for long.

11

THE ageing Melba liked young people with talent and ambition; perhaps when she looked at them she saw herself as the young Nellie Armstrong going out to conquer the world. At all events she nearly always responded to a girl or a young man who seemed destined to succeed. She was often wrong but sometimes right, and she never stopped looking for the fire of genius in young eyes.

She thought she saw it in the eyes of a young man named Beverley Nichols when he tracked her down one day in 1923 at the Empress Club in London, where she was staying. Nichols, then lately down from Oxford, was a Fleet Street reporter, and his newspaper sent him to talk with Melba about a notorious murder trial of the day, the Thompson-Bywaters case. One of the accused was a young woman, Edith Thompson, who with her lover Fred Bywaters was found guilty of murdering her husband and subsequently hanged, and Nichols's editor wanted Melba to put her name to an article giving 'the woman's angle'.

Having got himself into the Empress Club, Nichols found his way to a suite where Melba sat at the piano playing her own accompaniment and singing the Addio from *Bohème*, in a voice 'less like a sound than a light, a silver beam of light that hovered in the air, tracing patterns of unearthly beauty'.

'Who the devil are you?' she demanded.

'I've been ringing for two days. . . .'

She looked him up and down, then laughed. 'You're a sticker at any rate. Will you dine with me tonight?'

How much of Melba's cordiality at that first meeting should be attributed to her recognition of Beverley Nichols's incipient literary talent and how much to his good looks, his dash, his wit and *savoir faire* can only be surmised. At any rate he dined with her, and a friendship was begun which lasted until her death.

She took him up and introduced him to a number of socially exclusive English homes which might have stayed closed to Beverley Nichols, the Fleet Street reporter, but were wide open to Beverley Nichols, the young man for whom Melba was forecasting a dazzling future. Never one to understate any case she espoused, she described him as 'the most brilliant young man I have met since Oscar Wilde'. Their friendship ripened in the few months that passed between their first meeting and Melba's sailing for Australia early in 1924 to do her part in organizing the Melba-Williamson opera season. Back home in Australia she missed his gay presence and lively tongue, and one day cabled asking him, as he put it, 'to go out and help her run her farewell opera season'. He caught a ship for Australia, notwithstanding 'the arrival of a number of anonymous letters kindly suggesting that I must be her lover'.

He stayed at Coombe Cottage and was constantly with Melba on her comings and goings. They were a striking pair—the handsome young man-about-town and the ageing prima donna who, for all the sagging of her face and the thickening of her body, remained a stupendous personality. As she had done in England, Melba saw to it that her literary lion cub was welcomed into the homes of all her friends. She took him to visit, among others, Norman Lindsay, the most controversial Australian artist of the day, at Springwood, in the Blue Mountains of New South Wales. She whirled him across to Adelaide and called with him on her friends, W. J. Cowell and his wife, at their house in the Mount Lofty Ranges, where he knelt before her—the worshipping neophyte before the enthroned goddess—in laughing obeisance while someone snapped a camera and took a curiously pathetic picture. He found nothing about Australia to like and was 'bored to distraction, particularly at nights', but many Australians were charmed by the slim and elegant young Englishman. One day Melba swept into the Albert Street Conservatorium for a special session of her singing class, accompanied by a party which included Beverley Nichols; that day some of the singing girls tried harder to catch his eye than Melba's and were disappointed when he paid no heed to any of them.

He did not perhaps do much to help Melba run her opera season, but he was not idle in Australia and gave much of his time to ghosting Melba's autobiography, *Melodies and Memories*. This work is a typical example of prima donna autobiography – smoothly and competently written, in a craftsmanlike style that admirers of the forty-odd books Nichols has published under his own name will readily recognize. In a letter written forty years after he hammered out the book on those long hushed days at Coombe Cottage, Nichols remarked of his work on it: ' "Ghosted" is a very apposite word, because she was so anxious to appear as an angel of sweetness and light that all the guts and humour had to be taken out of it.' It seems a pity Melba did not let him set down her memories with candour rather than diplomacy; then *Melodies and Memories* might have had lasting value as a picture of her life and times. As it is, the book's only value lies in the significance of what it omits.

Nichols went back to England without regrets, but his friendship with Melba continued. They saw each other whenever she went abroad, meeting in London, in Venice, in Paris and in other cities. She took pride in his growing reputation as a writer, but as the years went on discovered that she harboured some reservations about him; to more than one friend she said she was disappointed that he had allied himself with what she saw as a school of cynical young writers.

On his side Beverley Nichols had some reservations about Melba, and he revealed these when he published a satirical novel, *Evensong*, in January 1932, less than a year after her death. The central character is an ageing prima donna, Madame Irela, who is past her best as a singer but cannot bear to retire from the world which she has ruled for so long, and relentlessly destroys anyone who threatens her supremacy. Although Irela is by no means a photographic portrait of Melba but essentially a novelist's creation, the details of her story and some salients of the character leave no room for doubt that Melba was the model. Nichols himself never denied it.

Evensong had been only a few days in print when the storm burst. Details of the theme and extracts were cabled to Australia and published in the newspapers, and the outcry was immediate. John Lemmone said, 'I cannot understand why he has done it. It is quite unpardonable.' John Tait, one of the chiefs of J. C. Williamson Limited, said Nichols was a very clever young man but 'devoted to his own interests'. Norman Lindsay said, 'Mr Nichols has not even glimpsed the greatness of Melba's personality. Her very faults were those of a strong character beyond Mr Nichols's comprehension.'

The anger against Nichols originated in Australia, and nobody but Australians ever showed much concern with his sin in writing *Evensong*. The indignation of Melba's friends and business associates was natural enough, although in retrospect they seem to have given the matter rather more importance than it deserved; but the anger of all kinds and all classes of Australians, most of whom did not know Melba, had an overlay of irony considering the enthusiasm which many of her fellow countrymen had shown for vilifying her while she lived. Perhaps they felt that, however damagingly an Australian might be permitted to talk about Melba, a mere Englishman—'a bloody Pommy pen-pusher'—who took similar liberties must be squashed.

The Melbourne *Herald*'s London representative interviewed Nichols who said: 'The whole of the book originated in a conversation I had with Dame Nellie Melba, in which I said, "I should like to write a book about the sort of woman you might have been if you had not been you." She replied, "Go ahead. Everybody will say it is me, but I don't care a damn." Dame Nellie would not have cared a damn if she had read the book today because, although the background is hers, the story and characters are nine-tenths imagination. A writer cannot be held responsible for the manner in which his characters act.'

The controversy blazed in Australian newspaper headlines for weeks but gradually subsided and was relegated to the back pages, then more or less died. Echoes of it are still heard now and then, in talk among Australians or when a reminiscent article about Melba appears in an Australian newspaper or magazine, but most of the heat has gone out of it. At its height Beverley Nichols could not have shown his face in Melbourne or Sydney without being tarred and feathered, but he would be safe now. *Evensong* was one of his most successful books; it had large sales as a novel, and was later turned into a stage play and a film, and later still became a television play.

Those familiar with the personalities and events of the 1924 opera season in Australia found many parallels in the supposedly fictional story of *Evensong*. One of the important secondary characters is a young and brilliant Spanish soprano, Baba Letoile, whom Irela sees as a threat; Baba Letoile is said to be a slightly edited portrait of Toti Dal Monte, the Italian coloratura, who, having begun to make a name at La Scala, was brought to Australia in 1924 to share the big roles with Melba and became the idol of Australian audiences. The clash between Irela and Baba Letoile as described in *Evensong* is doubtless based on the conflict between Melba and Toti Dal Monte, although neither of them ever admitted in public to anything but a warm regard for the other. In a private letter from Venice in 1964, Madame Dal Monte, then retired from the theatre and devoting herself to teaching, wrote that Melba was always 'very affectionate' to her, and gave her many gifts and much sound advice. Some backstage onlookers, however, believed that when Melba and Dal Monte were together strong currents of antipathy ran just below the surface of their seeming affection.

The 1924 season opened in Melbourne on a Saturday night with Melba in *Bohème*; the audience was ecstatic. Dal Monte appeared for the first time on the Monday night in *Lucia di Lammermoor*. It was a triumph, and two or three times her singing stopped the performance. Melba was seen to applaud as warmly as anyone, but when the curtain calls were being taken at the end she left her box and presently sailed out on to the stage. She took Dal Monte's hand and kissed her on the cheek, gesturing as if to say to the audience, 'Well, what do you think of my protégée?' – which Dal Monte never had been and never was. Seeing Melba bestowing her accolade on the newcomer, the audience bellowed its approval, while she bowed her acknowledgements. She could afford to bow; she had stolen the scene from under Dal Monte's nose and made it her own.

Whether *Evensong* is a book about the sort of woman Melba would have been if she had not been Melba or a true portrait of Melba as Beverley Nichols saw her is a tantalizing question. Madame Irela is a harsh, egocentric, avaricious, mean-souled woman with no compensating generosities, and few of the people who knew Melba remember her like that; they believe that Nichols chose to be the reverse of the complaisant biographer who writes a sweet and flattering book about his subject, and went as far wrong in the opposite direction by writing one which exaggerated all Melba's faults of character—if Irela and Melba are conceded to be one and the same—and totally ignored her merits. They agree however that he did her justice when he wrote of Irela's voice:

'And then the voice came. It stole through the room like a spirit . . . there was, indeed, the sense that some radiant and exquisite child had come to them from another world, and was unfolding silver scrolls of song on whose pages the pale notes glittered. Oh, the futility of words, of printed words, that flutter like dead leaves in the breath of that voice! And yet, the voice, even in memory, compels those words to flutter from the lips of those who heard her . . . compels the one to compare it to a flower unfolding, the other to a moonbeam dancing . . . and will compel all men in whose ears it echoes to search their souls for metaphors, until the last echo in the last soul is stilled and even the memories of that beauty which she created are lost in the ultimate Silence.'

That description might not suffice for a musician or a music connoisseur, but it says something to a layman which is lacking from descriptions of Melba's singing written by musically wiser men. The somewhat breathless tone of it might make a literary purist feel uncomfortable, yet the words go far toward capturing the magic of the voice which enraptured the men and women of Melba's time. That those words should have appeared in *Evensong* is not the least of the ironies associated with the history of that light-weight, yet durable, tale.

12

THE years did not diminish Melba's personality, but they took their inevitable toll of her physical being. Although the strength of the features made her face remarkable to the end of her life, the rather bold good looks which in middle-age took the place of her youthful comeliness began to slacken and fade about the time of World War I. Worse, her figure thickened, and when she turned sixty much of her one-time physical distinction was gone.

One of the most successful Australian portrait painters of the day, Sir John Longstaff, did several portraits of her in the 1920s. The best of these, with Sydney harbour at night as the background, belongs to the National Gallery of Victoria, Melbourne; but neither it nor any of the other Longstaff portraits is other than pedestrian, although conscientious and factually accurate. A journalist, Mrs. J. D. Brown, who was later to make a reputation, under her maiden name of Nina Murdoch with a succession of books, including a biography of Longstaff, was travelling from Sydney to Melbourne in the overland express in 1923. She was sitting at breakfast when Longstaff came into the dining-car.

'I didn't know you were coming to Melbourne just now,' she said.

'I'm bringing Melba down,' Longstaff replied. 'She's in the van.'

'What did you say?' Mrs Brown exclaimed.

Longstaff, shouting with laughter, said, 'Oh, not in the flesh of course! Heaven forbid! It's quite enough to have to face her in the studio without having her on the train,' and explained he was taking to Melbourne a portrait of Melba which he had been painting in Sydney. He then went on to say how hard it was to put on canvas 'the majestic air' which she could acquire during an operatic performance; he complained that she was 'definitely dumpy', and had even 'a rather commonplace look'.

Later in Melbourne Longstaff persuaded the housekeeper of one of his friends, Sir Keith Murdoch, the newspaper proprietor, to stand as a model for Melba's figure in a portrait he was working on. The housekeeper was a tall and dignified woman, with an elegance of figure which Longstaff felt a diva should have; it did not resemble Melba's much.

For some reason none of the many artists who painted Melba ever did an entirely acceptable portrait of her. Some captured a physical likeness, but missed her personality; others captured her personality, but missed a physical likeness; nobody succeeded in combining the two elements. The Australian, Rupert Bunny, did a full-length portrait which is now owned by J. C. Williamson Limited. This is a fine painting and brilliantly depicts Melba's imperious spirit; but lacking the nameplate it would not be recognizable as a portrait of her.

She was too hard-headed to be able to make herself believe in the 1920s that she was not ageing fast; the signs were all too plentiful and all too ominous. And then, one April day in 1925, she had to face the fact that not only age but death comes, soon or late, even to the immortals of grand opera. She was in Paris. Her old friend Herman Bemberg had lent her his luxurious apartment in the Avenue Victor-Hugo while he was on a visit to Algeria, and there they brought her the news that Jean de Reszke was dead. She, who rarely shed tears, turned away and wept. Most of the tears were for 'dear Jean', whom she had revered above all other singers, but a few were for herself. He was eleven years older than Melba, but they had been so closely identified in their professional lives, they had so often triumphed on the same stage together, that they were for practical purposes contemporaries, and when he died, like any songless commoner, a little of Nellie Melba died also.

Jean de Reszke had retired from the grand opera stage in 1902, and for many years before his death lived as a singing teacher in Nice. He died there, on 3 April, but they brought his body to Paris for burial, and Melba was one of the mourners who followed him to his tomb in the Montparnasse cemetery.

For two reigning monarchs of the grand opera world, the untroubled nature of their friendship was all but unique. After his retirement they kept in touch by letter, and saw one another at intervals whenever Melba visited Nice. Neither ever betrayed a romantic interest in the other (which does something to account for the abiding quality of their regard), and at no time did he show the smallest envy of Melba's success with an audience, nor did Melba of his. Their friendship did not quite embrace Jean's younger brother, Edouard, one of the greatest bass singers of the time and a man of rollicking likeability. For some years in the early period of their association as singers, the two de Reszkes and Melba were unwavering friends as well as artists who often appeared together at Covent Garden and in other great opera houses, but Edouard and she clashed later. They were singing together in Boston, in April 1901, and his friends wanted to celebrate the twenty-fifth anniversary of his grand opera début by flooding the stage with flowers at the end of *Faust*, in which he was the Mephistopheles. Melba, the Marguerite, flatly forbade it – any flowers passed across the footlights, she insisted, must come to her. Not wishing to force a crisis, Edouard gave in, but he did not forgive Melba. Some years later he lost a New York engagement, at the opening of Oscar Hammerstein's Manhattan Opera House, and told a friend that 'that jealous Nellie' had worked to keep him out 'so she would have the stage to herself'. No shadow ever touched Melba's friendship with Jean de Reszke, however, and, her *Melodies and Memories* being nearly ready for the publishers when he died, she seized the chance of paying a last tribute to him. Beverley Nichols was summoned and bidden to end the book with a couple of appropriate paragraphs. The passage is extraordinary, even as a specimen of prima donna autobiography. It goes thus:

'For twenty years Jean had not sung. The golden voice had been silent, and his days had been spent in giving the fruits of his experience to others. But towards the end he was forced to stay in bed, and as he sank lower and lower, his voice died away almost to a whisper. And then, suddenly, in his delirium, a miracle was worked. His breathing became clearer and clearer; his youth seemed, as it were, to come back to him, like a flowing tide; he sat up in bed crying, "Enfin, j'ai retrouvé ma voix!" And he sang.

'For three days in that house of death Jean sang, and the whole house rang and echoed with his golden notes pouring out with all their former loveliness. He was dying every minute, and yet the song still poured on, role after role in which he had once been so superb. I suppose it was uncanny and incredible, yet to me it was only beautiful. It is how I should like, when my time comes, to die myself.'

The picture of Jean de Reszke sitting up on his death-bed giving a three-day recital of the great arias with which he once enchanted multitudes is, as Melba was diffident enough to say, 'uncanny and incredible'. It is also untrue. The less dramatic facts are that Jean de Reszke was brought to bed with pneumonia on a day near the end of March 1925. In his delirium a day or two later he sang some snatches of the music from *Tristan*. Then his illness became worse, and he fell silent. In the hope of rallying him a specialist gave him an injection. He responded for a few moments and sang a chromatic scale. Then the tired body sank back, defeated. He died three days later without having uttered another sound.

Melba did not sing at Covent Garden that year, but it was not distress over Jean de Reszke's death that kept her away. The summer season in 1924 had resulted in a heavy financial loss and the Syndicate, taking fright, had decided not to put on a season in 1925. Then Mrs Samuel Courtauld, backed by her millionaire husband, formed a new syndicate, and announced in March that Covent Garden was to have a season after all. Even though the Courtauld syndicate had to work in a hurry it assembled a good company;

this included some of the young singers who had strengthened their reputations in the Melba-Williamson Australian season, notably Toti Dal Monte and Dino Borgioli. But Melba had made other commitments and was not available.

Such talented sopranos as Lotte Lehmann, Elisabeth Schumann, Maria Jeritza and Margaret Sheridan were at Covent Garden that year, but Melba was missed. Even if she could no longer work those miracles with her voice which she had once done as a matter of course she was still an unequalled draw. Her popularity as a recitalist was also undiminished; the size of her audiences in 1925, on a concert tour she made of England and Scotland, testified to that.

A year or two earlier this matter had become an issue between Melba and Lionel Powell, the London agent, who had for many years managed her tours in the British Isles. Powell told her he believed her name had lost some of its magic for British audiences and proposed that she should lower her fee. She wanted to go on being the highest-paid concert singer in the world, and, having told Powell she would not cut her fee by a penny, she dismissed him and summoned her old friend, Landon Ronald. Ronald heard her story and suggested he should telephone another London concert agency, Ibbs and Tillett. She agreed, and Ronald got busy on the telephone.

After a short conversation he put his hand over the mouthpiece and said, 'Bob Ibbs is quite willing to come over and see you, but he's worried because he isn't wearing his morning suit. Do you mind?'

'Tell him,' said Melba, 'that I don't care if he comes in his night-shirt.'

Ibbs arrived by taxicab, and when he left everything had been arranged. He made no demur about Melba's fee, and the commercial results of their partnership justified his judgement.

For the fancier of fine singing the Melba of the post-war years was a more satisfying recitalist than she had ever been, because the standard of her programmes improved. When she died a London critic, Robin H. Legge, noted: 'She had the power to make the poorest shop-ballad sound well by her skill as a singer, and the impression remains that her cup of happiness was as full on such an occasion as when she had triumphed as Mimi or Juliet.' It is true that for the first thirty-odd years of her singing life she sang the showpiece opera arias and won storms of applause with such beloved, if musically trivial, ballads as *Good-bye!*, *Comin' thro' the Rye*, and *Home, sweet home*, adding for good measure a flashy novelty such as *Lo, here the gentle lark*. But just after the war she started the experiment of introducing into her programmes works by some modern French composers, such as Duparc, Debussy, and Chausson. Her public responded well and always after that she sang a few songs of that genre in nearly every concert.

Melba did not adopt the French composers unprompted; her accompanist of the time, Frank St Ledger, urged their merits on her and she tried them rather hesitantly, seeming at first—which was astonishing for her—almost afraid of her ability to manage in public a type of music different from anything she had ever sung before to a mass audience. As a recitalist her musical taste had never erred on the side of subtlety, but once started she was presently singing to her audiences such songs as Chausson's *Le temps des lilas* and Debussy's *Noël des enfants* with no less pleasure than she took in singing to them the Jewel Song and *John Anderson, my Jo*.

Lindley Evans, who travelled as her accompanist for some years after World War I, recalled, 'She was happiest singing modern French songs, so you can imagine how she'd feel when some unsteady voice from the gallery would cry, "*Home, sweet home*, Nellie!"' It happened all the time.' But, in fact, she did not brood too much when her audiences, attentive and respectful in response to Duparc, greeted her with volleys of applause when she gave them Tosti. She was no missionary who felt driven to elevate public taste in music. John Brownlee, the Australian-born baritone, has put it thus:

'I well remember how much Melba was criticized for singing so many popular songs and cheap ballads, which she always included in her concert programs along with the operatic fare. The operatic arias provided the fireworks for the glorious voice and singer, and by that time, having the audience in the palm of her hands, she would caress them with the songs they loved to hear. She did not have to plumb the depths of lieder. Her public paid, and paid well, to hear what they wanted, and Melba gave it to them. Don't forget that she was a great showman who could make the simplest song seem like a big event. . . . Let us not forget the great singers of that era were all on very high pedestals with their audiences, and stout indeed would be the heart of one who set about loosening those pedestals.'

In 1925 she was acclaimed wherever she gave a recital, and she loved it; she never lost her appetite for adulation, and the clapping, the stamping, the cries of 'Brava!' were still, for her, the best wine of all.

She was sorry to have missed Covent Garden that year. Opera—the intoxicating music, the absurd melodramatic stories, the surging flow of the orchestra, the tiers of seats stretching up and away into the darkness, the rich and enchanting make-believe of it all—was then as always the thing nearest to her heart. But she knew that soon she would have to turn her back on it, not because she wanted to but because her time was running out, and sing her farewell to Covent Garden, even though that would be the most painful act of her professional life.

She put it off for as long as she could; then she had to decide. One day toward the end of 1925 Lieutenant-Colonel Eustace Blois, managing director of the Courtauld syndicate, suggested she should make her Covent Garden farewell the next year. When she put her name to the contract she must have felt like a queen signing her own death-warrant.

13

It was the end of Melba's reign at Covent Garden, but she made the most of it. She leased a lovely old house at Hatfield, in Hertfordshire, for the duration of the summer season from May to June. There, with her son George and his wife and daughter, and surrounded by old and new friends, she acted the part of an empress among her courtiers.

She chose to make her farewell not in a single opera but in excerpts from three operas—the balcony scene from *Roméo et Juliette*, the prayer scene from *Otello*, and Acts III and IV of *Bohème*. She wanted three Australians, the tenor Browning Mummery, the bass-baritone Frederick Collier, and the baritone John Brownlee, to be among the principals in *Bohème*. Mummery and Collier had respectable reputations in London, but at that time Brownlee was unknown, although he was to go on to make a bigger name than either of the others. He was twenty-six and, having gone to Paris in 1923 on Melba's advice, was studying with Dinh Gilly, and had made a few appearances in 1925 and 1926 at the Trianon-Lyrique, a French opera house in Montmartre which was a training-ground for the Paris Opéra. Melba heard him there and was impressed by his voice, his musicianship and his stage bearing, but Colonel Blois looked blank when she pressed Brownlee's name on him. Who was Brownlee? Of course, if Dame Nellie had a high opinion of this young man, then his fitness to take part in her Farewell would be considered, but whether Mrs Courtauld and her syndicate would choose to sponsor him was by no means sure. After all, there were three or four baritones of established reputation on the 1926 roster, and any one of them could be counted on to sing Marcello's music with distinction. Was there any certainty that this John Brownlee would be able to maintain the high standards which Covent Garden audiences expected? Melba listened with, for her, astonishing patience, but at the end she told Blois she wanted Brownlee, that she intended to have Brownlee, and that was that.

Blois, a man of sound musical education and good taste, was rather upset. As the Courtauld syndicate's managing director he was uneasy at the thought that an unknown and virtually untried Australian baritone was to be thrust on the stage to sing Marcello on the night of Melba's Farewell. It might be disastrous, and he could not afford to take the risk on that night of all nights when, with the King and Queen in the Royal box and the house packed with distinguished subscribers, Covent Garden would bear a strong resemblance, if one allowed for post-war laxities, to its appearance on the Melba Nights and Caruso Nights of twenty years before.

Browning Mummery walked into the foyer one day and came face to face with Blois. They talked for a few moments, then Blois grunted, 'That old bitch wants to put Brownlee on! I don't want him.'

Melba knew Blois was trying to foil her. Sitting near her in the stalls at a rehearsal, Mummery overheard her say to a companion, 'That man is trying to block me from putting John on. I won't let him!' Mummery reflected that the episode indicated a change from the days when Melba's word was law at Covent Garden. But the ending of it showed she was still Melba. She had her way: Brownlee sang.

Her Farewell was on Tuesday 8 June 1926, and the reserved seats were all sold weeks in advance. When Browning Mummery, who was at Covent Garden the night before, came out he saw the queue already forming for the Farewell performance next night;

people were squatting on their little stools, muffled up against the night chill, undismayed by the prospect of waiting nearly twenty-four hours. He strolled back to his hotel, thinking himself lucky to have been chosen to help write this particular page of Covent Garden history.

There could never again be another night like that one. Melba had outlasted all her contemporaries and now she stood in the afterglow of the Golden Age, watching the dark come down. That was her only Covent Garden appearance in 1926, and for the first time since her early years there she did not have her usual dressing-room; Jeritza, the Czech prima donna, was using it, and Melba agreed to dress in another room. There was something symbolic about that.

The *Roméo et Juliette* excerpt, in which Charles Hackett, the American tenor, sang opposite her, came first, and the *Otello* excerpt next. *Bohème* came last. Nothing else would have been appropriate. Melba had forced *Bohème* on Covent Garden in the first place, in 1899, and had proved herself the greatest Mimi of all. This above all was what the packed house had come to hear, and this above all was what Melba had come to sing.

It would be absurd to say she had never sung Mimi's music better than she sang it that night. She was sixty-five, thirty years older than Mummery, her Rodolfo, and forty years older than Brownlee, her Marcello, and the witchery of her voice had faded a little. Yet the applause which rolled and thundered about her at the final curtain was a tribute not only to the singer she had been but also to the singer she still was. Next morning's *Daily Telegraph* reported that Covent Garden had heard 'a glorious exhibition of the noble art of singing as singing should be'. Some of the flavour of the night is preserved for all time in gramophone recordings which His Master's Voice took inside Covent Garden. The whole performance was recorded, and, although not all of it was perfectly captured, the feat was a technical triumph at a time when microphone recording was in its infancy.

The last scene when Melba, in Mimi's costume, stood in the centre of a stage overflowing with flowers was unforgettable. Her voice broke as she made her farewell speech, but she took hold of herself, picked up the words where she had faltered, and went on to the end. She had no need to call on her histrionic skill that night; the catch in her throat was not simulated. Legend—naturally —insists that even in those last moments she was the complete showman in full control of herself, and missed no chance to gild the emotional lily. Marjorie Lawrence, the Australian dramatic soprano, who sang at Covent Garden in 1946, reported in her autobiography that a Covent Garden attendant told her: 'We could see that Melba was weeping as she took her bows—dozens of them. She seemed distressed, as she walked back into the wings, and, fearing she might collapse, I signalled my colleague to hold the curtains together and not to reopen them. I was standing with him when Melba, in a flash, made a complete recovery although there were tears on her cheeks and hissed at us, "Pull back those bloody curtains." We did, and she was out before the audience bowing and sobbing again.'

Sydney Cheney, who joined the Covent Garden staff in 1919, gave a less sensational but more convincing account of that episode in an interview with the London magazine *Music and Musicians*, which published some of his memories in its May 1961 issue, on the centenary of Melba's birth. Cheney was on the stage working the curtain on Melba's Farewell night. He was a few yards from her when she finished making her speech, with tears streaming down her face. Seeing she was on the verge of breaking down altogether, Cheney lowered the curtain and held it down until he was sure she had recovered. Then he took it up again, acting on his own initiative. Nobody told him what to do, and least of all Melba. She was, he said, too stricken by emotion to tell anyone to do anything.

No experience of her life equalled that last Covent Garden night for both anguish and rapture; by contrast, any of her subsequent acts of public leave-taking were to fall rather flat. She was disappointed when sickness kept her from travelling to Brussels later in the year, for a farewell appearance on 30 November at the Monnaie, where she had become a prima donna in 1887, but even that would have been an anti-climax. Nothing else counted alongside the parting from Covent Garden, the theatre she loved above all others. In December she sang in opera once again in London—this time at the Old Vic, in a performance to help raise money to save Sadler's Wells. But, no matter what came after it, the Covent Garden Farewell marked the real end of her career as an opera singer.

Something of Melba stayed behind in Covent Garden. Something of her will always stay there, so long as the Royal Opera House stands. No singer can grace an opera house for nearly forty years, as she did, treading its stage, standing in triumph as the applause surges about her, giving the immortal part of herself in performance after performance, and not leave a lasting impress of her personality on her surroundings.

Melba did that at Covent Garden, and she left also a tangible memorial of herself. This was a marble bust, sculpted by her old friend and fellow Australian, Sir Bertram Mackennal, which stood for many years on a pedestal on one side of the landing of the Grand Staircase; a like bust of Adelina Patti stood on a pedestal on the other side. One day, a decade or more after Melba's retirement, an aristocratic-looking lady came to Covent Garden and studied the busts long and thoughtfully through her lorgnette. Unable to identify either subject, she asked a charwoman who was scrubbing away nearby, 'Tell me, please, whom are these busts of?'

'I don't know, I'm sure, Mum,' the charwoman replied. 'We calls 'em Gert and Daisy.'

NIGHTFALL

1926–1931

1

'GOODBYE is of all words the saddest, the most difficult to say,' Melba told her Farewell audience at Covent Garden. Nobody can say she was not sincere; on the contrary, she went on saying goodbye for too long and said it too often. Beverley Nichols overstated the matter when he wrote: 'If Melba gave one Farewell she must have given fifty,' but it was a pardonable exaggeration.

She arrived in Australia in January 1927 with preparations in hand for a farewell concert tour, beginning early in March. This tour lasted nearly three months and took her as far as the Queensland sugar country; but not to Mackay. It was organized by her faithful John Lemmone, who was also the flute soloist and obbligatist; the other assisting artists were the pianist Lindley Evans and the South African-born bass-baritone Stuart Robertson.

Melba was always nervous before a concert or an opera performance, in her last singing years no less than her first. One Saturday morning in Sydney she telephoned Lindley Evans, and told him she wanted to go driving to soothe her nerves. He called for her and they started out, but they had not gone far when she decided that after all she would rather be resting. She told her chauffeur to stop near the Hotel Australia to put Evans down, and as he was getting out she handed him a portmanteau and said, 'Give that to the man at the Australia.' He was walking along to the hotel to check the bag into the luggage room when an old friend hailed him. They stood by the kerb for ten or fifteen minutes chatting, with the portmanteau at their feet, while the Saturday morning crowds swirled back and forth past them along Castlereagh Street. When they parted Evans picked up the portmanteau and went along to the Hotel Australia; having checked the bag in there, paid twopence and collected a ticket, he thought no more about it until he arrived at the Sydney town hall that evening for the concert.

'You're a bright one,' Melba greeted him.

He had been travelling with her off and on for years and knew her well enough to take what she said as it came, so he replied, 'Why? What have I done this time?'

'Do you know what was in that bag I gave you today?' she asked.

'I haven't the vaguest idea,' he said. 'What was in it?'

'Oh, nothing much!' she told him. 'Only these,' and she pointed to the diamond bracelet on her wrist, the diamond necklace at her throat and the diamond tiara on her head.

Evans turned cold as he remembered how he had stood at the kerb in Castlereagh Street with the portmanteau and its cargo of jewels, probably £40,000 worth or more, dumped at his feet like a sack of potatoes. He also marvelled that a woman with Melba's strong sense of the value of possessions should have let him entrust that precious portmanteau to an hotel luggage-room for a fee of twopence.

That 1927 tour was both a financial and a personal success for Melba, but the success was not unalloyed. Sometimes the quality of her voice was noticeably below the Melba standard; but she still sang with her accustomed mastery of phrase, and occasionally she seemed to rise above the years and sing almost as bewitchingly as she had done when she was a young woman. Even when she was below form the newspaper critics, remembering her old glory, managed not to say so. At least most of them were charitable but John Norton's old newspaper, *Truth*, was an exception. Norton had been eleven years dead, and his inheritors were kinder to Melba than he had been, but a front-page article, splashed under bold two-column headlines, in which *Truth* reported on her Sydney concert of 9 April was blunt. The writer said, in part:

'Sunset is one of the most brilliant pageants of the skies, but a pageant infinitely sad. The departing Sun God gathers his magnificence round him in one last effort of glory. Yet the pomp of his triumphal dying cannot achieve the fresh beauty of the dawn—for the one symbolizes birth, the other death. . . .

'Melba appeared three times on the programme. It was a great effort considering the fatigue of it to a lady of her years, though she looked startlingly young—last night. . . .

'Her antics were certainly droll if a little alarming. She made eyes and acted with the coquetry of a girl in her teens, finally showering kisses over the audience. There were polite suppressions of amusement, but generally the laugh was audible.

'Melba impresses by reason of her perfect taste in frocking, and her excitedly youthful mannerisms, but she impresses, too, as a personality, though the quality of the renowned voice is passing. It is more than a pity that she did not leave the world only memories of her voice in its truly golden prime. Last night she was showered with beautiful bouquets and greeted with much applause. But those who had the privilege of hearing her ten or fifteen years ago know that now is the Sunset.

'It sounds like sacrilege to say these things for critics the world over even now spend themselves in superlatives when speaking of the Voice. It is probably done out of a sense of kindness; a fear of offending the Singer. But that time has passed. The truth is now due. Melba charges fancy prices for her concerts and on that scale she must be judged on her merits. It's a pity to say it and pity 'tis true, but today Melba's voice is but the echo of departed glories. Her farewell concert should have been given many moons ago.'

If Melba read the *Truth* article—and she almost certainly did, for she was an avid reader of anything printed about her, although she never kept press-cutting books or even specimens of her gala programmes—she did not let it trouble her for long. Printed or spoken taunts could stir her to raging anger for a while, but she had wonderful powers of recovery and never sat brooding in a corner. The *Truth* writer's words left no permanent scar. Soon after the end of her 1927 tour she arrived at the Albert Street Conservatorium one morning to take a class. Escorted by Fritz Hart, she strode into a first-floor gallery in which her singing girls were assembled and announced, 'Well, I'm sixty-six today!'—it was 19 May. A babble of voices assured her that she did not look it, to which she replied, 'I certainly don't feel it', then tossed the subject aside and swept on with the lesson. To her singing girls she bore none of the appearance of a prima donna in retirement, and they were right; although she had just finished a farewell tour her career as a public singer was by no means ended, whether for good or for ill.

Her refusal to retreat into a chimney-corner, and in due time to subside slowly and gracefully into an honoured grave, did not make her unique among prima donnas. Some of the great prima donnas, having begun to feel the weight of the years, have gone into retirement and resolutely stayed there, but just as many, having taken leave of their dear public with brave smiles shining through the tears, have thought better of it and come back, not once but many times. A few of these—Tetrazzini, for example—were driven back to the platform by the stark need to earn money, but rather more have been drawn back by an irresistible desire to look out over a packed concert-hall, to sing into the rapt silence, and then to hear the plaudits breaking about them. Melba was one who kept coming back not because she needed the money but because she needed the adulation as an addict needs his drug. In that she was no different from many other ageing celebrities of the theatre.

As early as October 1924, on the eve of what was announced as her Australian Farewell to grand opera, she had given an interview to a Melbourne *Herald* writer, Frank A. Russell. Russell quoted her as saying: 'The greatest trouble of the artist who is nearing the close of her career is to secure a graceful exit. It is tragic to wait till the audience have clattered out, and the electrician begins to snap off the lights. I prefer to say farewell while people can still find pleasure in what I can do; to leave them with a recollection that does justice to me and to them.' Those who took the words at face-value, supposing them to mean exactly what they said, did not know Melba and her capacity for acting in a way which contradicted any of her considered opinions if it suited her to do so.

Many of her friends were sorry she went on having farewells, but she should not be judged too harshly. To win and keep success as a singer had been the motive of her life; all her actions had been directed to that end, and for that she had even rejected her marriage. She loved the bright and opulent world in which she stood supreme, and she was a woman who had to stand supreme. It was not as if her mind and body had reached a state of weariness where she wanted or needed to sit back and rest. The years had taken some toll of her vitality, but even when she was in the middle sixties her physical endurance was equal to that of a healthy woman twenty years younger, and her brain was as sharp and vigorous as ever. Although she had large business interests in Europe, America and Australia, the management of these with the running of Coombe Cottage and the entertaining of her friends absorbed only the lesser part of her energies. Some other outlet was indispensable, and singing was the natural thing.

She realized in those last years that her emotional life was incomplete. About that time a close friend asked her what she had missed most in her life and she answered, 'That I've never had the love of a good man.' The woman who asked the question knew Melba well; the two were sitting alone at Coombe Cottage, and

Melba spoke quietly, making no effort to dramatize the words or give them anything but their due. Perhaps in those last years she sometimes thought back to that long-ago interlude at Mackay.

She heard of Charles Armstrong now and then from relatives and friends who, on visits to America, made a point of going or returning by way of Canada so they could break the journey at Victoria, on Vancouver Island, and see him. Armstrong lived quietly on his tiny farm, on the western shore of Shawnigan Lake, a narrow wedge-shaped body of water about five miles long. The lake (whose name, derived from an Indian legend, means 'Abode of evil spirits') lies about twenty-five miles north of Victoria and is surrounded by heavily timbered hills. Even when Armstrong bought his piece of land and settled there just before World War I Shawnigan Lake was becoming a popular summer resort, known as a good place for boating and fishing, but for most of the year it attracted few visitors and was ideal for a man wanting solitude.

Armstrong lived in a cottage built of cedar shingles, and kept house for himself, doing his own cooking, even baking his own bread, and spending his spare time fishing, hunting and cultivating a fine vegetable garden. In his first years at the lake he was hard-pressed to make ends meet, but then legacies, and other help from near relatives, improved his financial position. After that such farming as he did was a pastime, not a means of livelihood, and his small private income, which he supplemented by selling the milk his cows gave and the eggs his hens laid, was adequate for his simple needs.

A post-office and Koenig's store lay diagonally opposite his place, separated from it by a mile or so of water, and nearly every day he would either row across in a boat (which he later fitted with an outboard motor) or sometimes in a hard winter make his way over the ice on snowshoes. On one ice-crossing a weak patch of the frozen lake surface gave way under him; he was carrying a large can of milk and wearing a rucksack, and was lucky to escape with nothing worse than a dousing in the icy water.

Except when he was snowed-in he spent most of his time in the open air. Whether jackarooing or growing sugar in Australia, farming in England, ranching in Texas, Oregon and California, running a commercial fishery in the Gulf of Mexico from New Orleans, or operating an estate and land agency in British Columbia, he had always been an outdoor man and neither wanted to nor could change his ways. He stayed mentally and physically alert, as he showed one evening when he got back from fishing in the lake to find a big cougar among his chickens. Although he was over seventy his nerves were steady, and he got a rifle from the cottage and fired. The wounded animal sprang at him, raging and snarling, but he fired again and the cougar died.

He had no near neighbours but never seemed to be lonely. He was a handsome man and always immaculately dressed – for instance, in summer he would put on white trousers, white shirt, white shoes and a blue reefer jacket for his daily trip across the lake to get his letters and buy anything he needed at Koenig's store. He made many friends on Vancouver Island. Their homes were always open to him, and in return his home was open to them so long as they were willing to take pot luck.

Charles Armstrong had long since come to terms with life, and the bitterness which had once surged in him when he heard Melba's name rarely showed itself in the thirty-odd years he lived at Shawnigan Lake. He did not advertise the relationship, nor did he wish to be reminded of it. He was once visiting a house when someone put a record of Melba's on the gramophone, and he got up and left. But he did not always respond so edgily to reminders of his dead marriage. In the later years of his life he was a member of the exclusive Union Club in Victoria. He was lunching there one day when the waitress made some passing mention of Melba Toast and Pêche Melba, both of which had been named in honour of Melba. Armstrong, who was eighty-five or eighty-six at the time but fit, rosy-cheeked, and physically and mentally lively, responded by telling the girl about his early life in Australia, and of how he fell in love with Nellie Mitchell and married her, and ultimately divorced her. He rarely volunteered such information about himself, however, and few of his friends on Vancouver Island remembered that he was Melba's ex-husband, if they had ever known it. They liked him for himself. Some addressed him as Uncle Charlie, some as Cap, and some as Mr Armstrong, and a few of his friends spoke of him, for no clear reason, as The Wicked Uncle, but nobody ever took liberties with him; he had a dignity which forbade familiarity. Women admired his spare good looks and natural courtliness. Men liked his masculinity, and many of them envied his command in times of stress of the flower of fine old Anglo-Saxon oaths; he once told a friend he had acquired this fluency while sailing as an apprentice before the mast.

Old friends from Australia, England, and the USA were always welcome to visit him at Shawnigan Lake, and he would cheerfully put them up in his cottage if they did not mind roughing it a little in cramped quarters. His son and daughter-in-law, George and Evie Armstrong, stayed with him from time to time (and in September 1939, a few weeks after World War II broke out, their daughter, Pamela, was to marry the second Lord Vestey's only son, William Vestey, in St Mary's Church, Oak Bay, Victoria). According to a piece of folklore of the Shawnigan Lake region, Melba herself once went to her ex-husband's cottage and stayed there, but this was untrue; if Charles and Nellie Armstrong had tried to spend a night under the same roof, even after thirty years or more of separation, the resultant explosion would have been stupendous.

So perhaps Melba in her last years knew regrets for her lost marriage, but it is unlikely that they bothered her for any longer than a little cloud takes to pass over the sun's face. There had never really been room in her life for a husband; she had never needed a man's shoulder to lean on, and her self-reliance did not lessen with the years.

She talked of entering Australian politics to crusade against Communism; she possibly had visions of emulating a man she had known for nearly forty years and always greatly admired, Paderewski, who in 1919 temporarily forsook the piano to become Premier of Poland. She did not pursue the idea, and this was lucky for the electorate as well as for her, because she could never have functioned in politics except as a dictator. She also talked of buying a racehorse and winning the Melbourne Cup, but this project also came to nothing. In fact her life seemed to be full without politics and racehorses; whether travelling (and her hunger for the urbanities of Europe took her away for some months every year) or living at Coombe Cottage she never had an idle moment. In what she called retirement her name did not fade. She saw to that. Not only in Australia but abroad also she loomed nearly as large as ever. Her name still had its magic quality wherever she went, and no door she wished to enter stayed shut against her, for her personality was still irresistible when she chose to use it.

Her life was rich in nearly all the things she valued, although she probably repented sometimes that she had formally abdicated from Covent Garden and by the same decisive act made it impossible for herself to undertake regular concert tours. The situation was bearable, however. When her craving for the adulation of a great

audience became too strong to be borne she could always subli-
mate it—temporarily at any rate—by giving another farewell performance for some deserving charitable cause. If she had not been
able to do that she would have curled up and died long before she
did.

2

IN 1928 Melba joined J. C. Williamson Limited in running another
opera season. Cynics wagged their heads and offered long odds
that when the company was formed Melba would head the list of
singers. They were wrong; the eight sopranos included Toti Dal
Monte, Lina Scavizzi and Hina Spani, and Melba was not among
them. The cynics had something on their side, however; Melba
took the opportunity to sing in grand opera in Sydney and Melbourne
for the last time—this really was the last time—at the end of the
season. In Sydney, on 7 August, she gave an evening performance,
singing in three acts of *Bohème* and the Prayer Scene from *Otello*,
and in Melbourne, at a matinee on 27 September she gave a shorter
programme, consisting of the third and fourth acts of *Bohème* and
the same *Otello* excerpt. As at her Covent Garden Farewell she
had the Australians, Browning Mummery and John Brownlee,
with her in *Bohème*, both in Sydney and Melbourne.

The Melbourne matinee was the last time Melba sang in a production of grand opera. His Majesty's Theatre was packed at high
prices, and profits went to charity. Many of the seats were taken
by society people, some of whom could not have distinguished a
Middle C from a High E or a piccolo from a bassoon, but many
music-lovers went also; after all, they told themselves, if this
should really turn out to be Melba's last appearance in opera it
would be a unique event, something to talk of to one's grandchildren.
Most of those who heard her did not know that she, the veteran
prima donna, was painfully nervous until the curtain went up.
She saw a friend, Harry Davies, before lunch and told him, 'Harry,
as usual I'm quite nervous.' Yet, also as usual, her tremors went
when she sang the first note.

The rehearsals, let alone the performance itself, were a heavy strain for a woman of Melba's age, but she saw them through without faltering. She was still the perfectionist. At a rehearsal she walked onstage for the *Otello* excerpt and noticed a scarlet cushion on Desdemona's bed. 'Who put that bloody thing there?' she demanded and pitched the cushion into the wings, then knelt and sang the Willow Song with ineffable purity.

Some of those surrounding her believed they detected signs that she was feeling her years, but mentally she was as alert as she had ever been. And she was still singing well; sometimes she sang better than well. The performance was largely produced by an Australian tenor singer and teacher, Charles Bradley, who recalled nearly forty years later that Melba's voice was 'as fresh and pure as a young girl's (or perhaps as a boy soprano's), and none of the magic quality had gone out of it.' Bradley wrote in a private letter: 'She simply "spoke on a melody" with that unforgettable virginal purity of tone that was yet so womanly. At a rehearsal she was seated on stage, talking to Elena Danieli, the Musetta. Her cue came up and she just turned her head to the front and sang. There was no change but that of pitch, and variation of the length of vowel sounds. It was a most wonderful example of the true art of singing.'

It would not have been grand opera of course if all had run smoothly. When the performance came to an end with Act IV of *Bohème* some of the audience guessed that something was amiss on the other side of the footlights, but they had no way of knowing what the trouble was. Melba, who had played the autocrat too long to be able to change, had told Browning Mummery, the Rodolfo, that she and Brownlee, the Marcello, would take the first curtain call alone. Mummery told her that he intended sharing in the curtain call—as Rodolfo he was the leading man in *Bohème*, he reminded her, and Marcello was a lesser figure. Her eyes flashed and she repeated that she and Brownlee would take the first curtain call without him, but Mummery was determined. When the curtain call came he walked upstage, while she walked downstage with Brownlee. All three took their bows and the curtain came down. Melba walked across to Mummery, gave him a light and playful slap on the cheek, and said, 'You brute!' That was the end of it. There was no lasting ill-will. She probably respected Mummery for asserting his rights; she herself always fought for what she wanted and held in secret contempt anyone who let himself be browbeaten, even by her.

Melba worked hard for the success of the 1928 opera season; she was never satisfied to lend her name to some venture and then sit back as a figurehead. She always wanted a voice in the running of her opera seasons—if possible a louder voice than anyone else, and for preference the last word on any and every matter of importance. The management of J. C. Williamson Limited would not give her carte blanche, but they allowed her a reasonably free hand, not only on the music side but on other aspects of the season also, and found no reason to regret it. She revelled in the successes, the setbacks, the battles, the victories. She did not however revel in one explosion which occurred while the season was at its height. She knew exactly how to deal with temperamental outbursts of principals or chorus members, but this one was outside her experience and she had to improvise ways and means of meeting it.

The cause was a short passage in a book *Clara Butt: Her Life-story*, by Winifred Ponder, which the London publishing house of Harrap issued about the middle of 1928. Dame Clara Butt, the English contralto, and Melba, although never close friends, had been for many years on terms of cordial acquaintanceship. Their good feeling for each other survived at least one test. Melba was making a concert tour of Canada at the same time as Clara Butt and her husband, the baritone Kennerley Rumford, and by an unhappy coincidence their concerts in Calgary were fixed for the same night. The two women made the best of the situation, holding a joint press reception, then going together to a joint supper reception arranged by one of the women's clubs. Those Calgary citizens familiar with the enmity which is apt to lie just behind the cooing endearments exchanged by women singers were astonished at the warmth the two dames showed for each other. They could afford to smile on one another because they were not direct competitors; one was a soprano and the other a contralto, and while Clara Butt was primarily a recitalist Melba was primarily a grand opera prima donna. At all events there was no shadow between them until copies of Winifred Ponder's biography of Clara Butt reached Australia some weeks after it was published in London.

Melba was staying in Sydney where the opera company was then playing. A newspaper reporter called on her with a copy of the book and told her he wanted her to look at a passage in it. He opened the book at page 137, and she began to read a description of a command performance at Windsor Castle just after Edward VII had become king. As the book told it, Melba and Clara Butt had gone down to sing, Fritz Kreisler to play the violin, and Tosti, the prolific composer of sentimental popular ballads, as accompanist. The concert over, the four started back for London, and then, the book related:

'At this time the Rumfords' first Australian tour was being mooted, and the subject was discussed by the artists in the special train returning to town. Melba naturally, being Australian, was particularly interested.

' "So you're going to Australia?" she said. "Well, *I* made twenty thousand pounds on my tour there, but of course *that* will never be done again. Still, it's a wonderful country, and you'll have a good time. What are you going to sing? All I can say is—sing 'em muck! It's all they can understand!" '

Melba read the words once; then she read them again. It was no hallucination! It was really there, printed in black-and-white, for all the world to see! Oh, the monstrousness of it! It was preposterous, outrageous, unthinkable for Clara Butt to say she had ever offered such advice as that: 'All I can say is—sing 'em muck! It's all they can understand!' Even if she had said such a thing it was intolerable that those words should come whirling out of the past, like a malign spirit from its grave, to haunt and torment her twenty-seven years later.

She snapped the book shut and handed it back to the reporter. Yes, he should have his statement. She had never said anything of the kind to Clara Butt or anyone else. Would he please give the story in the book an unqualified denial? All her life she had spent working for the cause of art in Australia and to improve Australian standards of appreciation. Surely the Melba-Williamson opera season then in progress was answer enough to such a statement. She could not understand the origin of it. She would send a cablegram to Dame Clara Butt at once.

When Clara Butt received Melba's cablegram she went billowing along to the offices of George C. Harrap and Company, the publisher, asking them to rescue her from this morass into which, all of a sudden, a few words in a book had plunged her. Harrap acted at once. They realized that if Melba cared to press this matter in the courts they might have to pay her substantial damages. To believe she had said the words was one thing, but to find legal proof was quite another. They had printed the book in a first edition of 3,000 copies; 2,000 of these were earmarked for sale in England and 1,000 for export to Australia. It was too late to change anything in 1,000 of the English copies and, as Harrap learned after cabling their Australian agent, in 150 of the Australian; these had already been sold with the 'sing 'em muck!' passage intact. The remaining 1,850 copies were subjected to editorial surgery. This was a fairly costly process; four pages had to be cut from every copy and four new pages inserted, eliminating any words which suggested that Melba had ever questioned the musical taste of her fellow Australians.

The news of the affair having been cabled all over the world and published under prominent headlines in every English-speaking country and many other countries also, potential buyers clamoured for the book, but not for the expurgated edition. 'We want the "muck" edition,' they said, and here and there a high price was paid for one of the 1,150 copies which had gone out into circulation before the shouting began.

The chief sufferer was Clara Butt's biographer, Winifred Ponder. Mrs Ponder, an English woman who had settled in Australia before World War I, had been a professional contralto singer in England, where she had trained at the Royal College of Music under Henry Blower, Clara Butt's old singing master. All through her student years Clara Butt was her idol. They met when Clara Butt and Kennerley Rumford toured Australia in 1925, and this was the start of a friendship which lasted until the upheavals over the book led to a temporary estrangement.

Mrs Ponder, on a visit to Malaya, was in Singapore when the book came out. Having read in the *Straits Times* an item of cable news from London, reporting that the King had accepted a presentation copy of her book, she went happily off to spend a few days on a remote rubber plantation and knew nothing of the crisis until she arrived back in Singapore. Cablegrams from Clara Butt and the publishers were awaiting her at the Adelphi Hotel. There were also messages from many of her friends in Singapore, for the news had been splashed there as elsewhere. Newspaper reporters came to her with questions. Who had told her the 'muck' story? Did she believe Melba had really said those words? If so, could she prove it? She answered their questions, and then, with head whirling, shut herself in her room and tried to think.

She wondered uneasily if her budding reputation as a writer would be hurt. She had published one earlier book and had ideas for other books,* and she had looked to the biography of Clara Butt to strengthen her name; now it seemed likely to do the opposite. She had also expected to make some hundreds of pounds from the book, but there seemed likely to be no royalties worth collecting by the time the clamour ended.

Mrs Ponder clearly remembered the circumstances in which Clara Butt had told her the 'muck' story. All she had done was to note down the facts, then weave them into the narrative at the appropriate point. It had come up while they were staying at Rhyl, a North Wales seaside resort. They had gone down there for a month while she worked on the book, trying to put more fire into it. After seeing an early draft the manager of Harrap had said, 'Can't you possibly get some spicy stories into it? This is too much milk-and-water.' One reason for this insipidity was that Clara Butt, in the best tradition of eminent women singers incubating their memoirs and supported by her husband, forbade the inclusion of any anecdote implying that this is not the best of all possible worlds populated by the best of all possible people. Then one Sunday W. H. Squire, the cellist, came to lunch, and heard of the book's need of lively anecdotes.

'What was that story about you and Melba?' he asked Clara Butt.

She remembered it then, and told it to Mrs Ponder as it was later to appear in the book. When Mrs Ponder put the anecdote down on paper and showed it to Harrap, the manager exclaimed, 'That's the thing! That will make headlines.' His forecast was amply fulfilled.

In Singapore Mrs Ponder resigned herself to the thought that she could do nothing but accept the situation, and after a week or two the public fuss subsided. Melba was mollified by the deletion of the words which she insisted she had not said, and Clara Butt made a public statement explaining that she had not seen the proofs of the book before publication and that only when Melba protested did she scrutinize the offending passage and realize that her biographer had 'misunderstood' her. Mrs Ponder knew she had misunderstood nothing, and presently she received a long letter from Clara Butt, full of contrition, and saying she knew her dear friend would understand. Her dear friend must have understood many

---

* As well as the Clara Butt biography Winifred Ponder's published books are: *An Idler in the Islands* (Sydney, Angus and Robertson, 1924); *Java Pageant* (London, Seeley Service, 1934); *Cambodian Glory* (London, Thornton Butterworth, 1938); *Javanese Panorama* (London, Seeley Service, 1942) and *In Javanese Waters* (London, Seeley Service, 1944).

things, notably that great singers will behave as meanly as any other human being when they find themselves in a corner with an action for damages hanging over them.

Melba's indignation was puzzling. She often publicly criticized Australia's cultural deficiencies in strong terms. Not a year before she had told a Melbourne *Herald* reporter and seen her words prominently published: 'It is time someone – one of themselves – told Australians some of their shortcomings. A visitor will not hurt their feelings by telling the truth; a foreigner they will not listen to. Well, they shall listen to me. . . . It hurts me, it shames me, for my fellow Australians to see a man like Zimbalist* or Friedman† come here, both men who never play but to packed, enthusiastic audiences, and to have them realize that our musical appreciation is only a myth. We have been so fortunate in hearing the world's best, but how long can we expect such men and women to travel all this way to coldness and neglect? It is scandalous. It is part of the slackness that is getting hold of this country. I will have more to say about it – no, not just now, but soon. I owe so much to this country that I owe it also to her to have the courage to speak out, even if the truth hurts. If more of us big people – yes, I can say that – dared to speak out, it would do a great deal of good. I love my country too much to be silent.' That statement seems to be no less strong than 'Sing 'em muck!', so perhaps it was the terminology in Mrs Ponder's book, not the sentiment, that riled Melba.

'Sing 'em muck!' lives on as an Australian colloquialism. Few Australians know its origin but many of them use it as a derisory epithet if anyone tries to palm off any kind of shoddy merchandise, ideas, services, anything, under the pretence that he is selling good quality. Whether or not Melba did tell Clara Butt to 'sing 'em muck!' can never be proved, but the words have an earthy forcefulness which some students of Melba's life, character and utterances find as unmistakable as the way she sang. So the dispute added to Australian English a phrase which shows no sign of ever becoming obsolete. That part of the affair at least would have pleased Melba.

* Efrem Zimbalist, see page 231.
† Ignaz Friedman, the Polish pianist.

3

DAVID MITCHELL bequeathed a strong constitution to his daughter Nellie, along with a share of his earthly wealth. When she was past sixty an American physician examined her and said, 'Of course, there's no reason why you should ever die at all. There is absolutely nothing the matter with you. I have looked, and I have searched my darnedest, but you are just one hundred per cent sound.' She liked telling that story. She drew comfort from saying the words aloud and thinking about them, because she hated to admit that some day she would die.

She was a remarkably robust woman, and for many years before her last illness never suffered any ailment worse than a feverish cold or an ache or a pain lasting a few hours. She needed glasses for reading, but she had her own teeth (an indispensable part of a singer's physical equipment, she said) and kept them strong, white and serviceable to the end of her life. Yet her terror of illness was more than the fear of colds which haunts all professional singers; it bordered on the morbid. A girl collapsed with a seizure in a singing class at the Albert Street Conservatorium one day; Melba turned away and rushed from the room, leaving the class to do what they could for the sick girl. It was not callousness, but a failure of nerve, a panic surrender to an irresistible impulse to escape. Yet she could be uncommonly kind to sick people. She put herself out time and again to ease the trials of Fritz Hart's son, Basil, whose spine was severely hurt in a shooting accident when he was fifteen. Young Hart was forced to lie in bed for five years, with frequent trips to hospital for surgical operations, and was unable to live a normal life until he reached manhood. Melba saw to it that his wheel-chair was always in the best place when she gave a concert in Melbourne, and in the interval or at the end of a performance she would demand, 'Where's the boy? Why hasn't he been brought round to see me?'

Her shrinking from anything related to serious illness and the satisfaction she took in feeling well were perhaps part of her subconscious defence against the onslaught of age. Even though she had so often helped to depict on the stage the fate suffered by Faust when he clutched at youth she would probably have hesitated toward the end of her life to reject a like deal with Mephistopheles on her own account. Not that she was unique in her desire to go on living; many ageing men and women feel much as she did. And for her the stake was larger – she had so much in the worldly sense to lose.

It is true that now and then she wrote – or, to be precise, put her name to – a newspaper article purporting to give her thoughts on death and the hereafter. In such an article, first published in a London Sunday newspaper in 1925 and widely quoted in Australian newspapers, she proffered this passage:

'I always instinctively believed in life after death. I cannot believe that God, who painted the rose, hung the stars in the summer night and breathed eternal music into the sea, is capable of mocking His creatures by denying immortality.

'. . . I know the best in me will live and the worst die. There may be fires to pass, tempests to face, but there is something that fire cannot burn nor storm quench. Call it soul, ego, astral body – what you will. I call it the true eternal me.'

Perhaps Melba with her own hand put those splendid sentiments down on paper, but they sound oddly unlike anything she ever said. She was usually too busy with mortal affairs to have time to worry over her immortal soul, or even to worry too much whether her name would live on when she was dead. When she did think of the survival of her name she must have known that her gramophone records would make it endure, if nothing else did; and this although the recording apparatus never did full justice to her voice, as she knew better than anyone else.

She began regular recording in 1904. Some of the recordings she made were never published, but she earned a large fortune from the hundred-odd that were issued. Many of her recordings are entrancing, but the element which made her unique among sopranos is to be found in none of them; it is rather as if Leonardo had painted Mona Lisa with a veil over the mouth. Melba was not the only great singer whose voice lost something in reaching the gramophone; Lillian Nordica, for example, was only one among many others whose recordings were disappointing and are of interest today as historic relics rather than as examples of fine singing.

Melba made four recordings at His Master's Voice studios in 1926, after her Covent Garden Farewell. Two are duets with John Brownlee, *Dite alla giovine*, from *Traviata*, and *Un ange est venu* (Bemberg), and two are solos, *Clair de lune* (Szulc) and *Swing low, sweet chariot* (arr. Burleigh). All four are excellent specimens of improved recording technique. But in 1926 Melba was sixty-five, and although she was still a great singer the quality which had been hers alone was gone. In the words of F. W. Gaisberg, for many years recording manager of HMV, these recordings 'show but a glimmer of the precious Melba timbre'.

Seeing how much money the gramophone was to earn for Melba it is ironic that at first she should have refused to have anything to do with it. Perhaps her standoffishness was an expression of her Scottish caution toward anything untried. In the first years of this century a few bold pioneers glimpsed the gramophone's possibilities, but Melba would not let herself be used, as she saw it, to boost something which might turn out to be a mere passing fad. Some of the finest singers of the day, including Caruso, Tamagno, Calvé, Plançon, Van Rooy, Scotti and Battistini, were recording while Melba was holding back. Then at last she yielded to the combined persuasions of Landon Ronald, who was the HMV musical adviser at that time, and Gaisberg. Gaisberg said later that a descriptive recording, made during the Boer War, of a troopship leaving for South Africa 'brought tears to the eyes of thousands, among them those of Melba, who declared in my presence that this record influenced her to make gramophone records more than anything else'. Let it be said that no tears blurred her eyes when she signed her first contract with the company; this prescribed that her records should sell at a guinea each, which was a shilling more than the price of any other singer's records, and should bear a distinctive mauve label.

Melba's approval of the gramophone did probably more than anything else to establish it. An English journalist, Filson Young, writing in 1908, said: 'I fear that the gramophone, like the motor car, has come to stay. There is hardly a country house in England, in which, straying unsuspectingly into some tapestried gallery, or some vaulted hall, you are not liable to be confronted by the sight of a monstrous trumpet, sitting on a table and emitting, after initial rasp and buzz, the loud nasal travesty of Melba's heavenly voice. It is true, however, that there are few singers or performers of any great eminence who have not sung or played into the gramophone, and in doing so have not committed the sin of blasphemy, but I think that no one has done so much to make that deadly instrument popular as Melba has done, and therefore she is the greatest sinner.'

Once converted to the gramophone Melba never wavered in her enthusiasm for it. She not only made a handsome income from her records for the rest of her life, but also spent hours playing over and studying every recording she made, in an effort to improve her singing. In her last years she must have taken some satisfaction in listening to the recordings that her younger self had made, whatever their technical deficiencies; she must also have felt depressed when she heard her own recorded voice doing things it was no longer quite able to do. She did not parade her discontent, however. Her vitality never diminished much—in public at any rate—until she went down with the illness which ended her life. But there were times when she felt the growing weight of her years and groaned under the burden when she was safe from the gaze of strangers, with only an intimate friend or two at hand to see. After one of her farewell concerts at Sydney, in 1927, an old friend went round to her dressing-room. Melba, a *peignoir* draped about her, was standing in front of the glass, taking off her make-up. She seemed tired, old, shrunken; her friend found it hard to believe that this was the woman who had stood on the platform twenty minutes earlier, holding the audience enraptured with her voice and her personality. They talked desultorily until Melba threw an evening wrap about her and led the way out. A crowd thronged the street outside the stage-door. At sight of them Melba stiffened and raised her chin; she seemed to gain inches in height. The cheers rolled about her and she smiled, bowing her acknowledgements, the monarch in every movement of face and figure, dominating the street and the people in it by a sudden assertion of personality. She strode to her car, and she and her friend got in. The chauffeur drew the laprug over their knees and closed the door. As the car moved away the mask that Melba had worn for those few moments as she left the hall crumpled and vanished, and she slumped back in her seat. Once more she was a weary old woman. A party of friends were waiting at her hotel to share supper with her, but she asked to be excused, bade them good-night, and went to bed.

Ever since girlhood her body had met every demand she had made upon it. Now, although the spirit burned as fiercely as ever, the flesh was beginning to weaken. She resented and hated the lengthening shadow of age, and rarely mentioned the inevitability of her own death except in a spirit of self-dramatization, perhaps hoping to hear some listener protest that *she* could never die.

When, as sometimes happened, her wish to keep thoughts of her death pushed away in a dark corner came into collision with her business interests, business won; she had too much respect for orderly business methods to ignore them even to maintain an illusion which ministered to her peace of mind. So when she decided in 1928 that she must prepare for her death by making a new will she did not temporize but plunged into the task.

A will she had made while visiting America many years before was obsolete. She discussed her ideas for a new will with Victor G. Watson, manager of a Melbourne trustee company which managed her father's estate, and he and William Stawell, a leading Melbourne solicitor, undertook to draft it. The task was demanding. Melba was a wealthy woman with large assets in Europe and the USA as well as Australia, and, although losses on foreign securities in World War I heavily diminished the value of her estate, she left £181,000. To complicate matters, for most of the time that Watson and Stawell were working on her will she was out of Melbourne, travelling with the Melba-Williamson opera company in other states and keeping a close eye on the performances and on her own substantial interest in the profits. She bombarded Watson and Stawell with letters of two or three or more pages, dashed off in her strong handwriting, detailing bequests she wished to make. She wanted to ensure that certain of her intimate personal possessions would pass into sympathetic hands, and her letters of instruction particularized item after item in unmistakable terms – to her sister Dora 'my diamond and pearl ring (which is the first jewel purchased by me after I became Melba)', to her brother Charles a silver cup presented to her by the Boston Symphony Orchestra, to her niece Nellie Patterson 'my Marguerite in diamonds with chain', and so on. There were also legacies to old friends and old servants scattered all over the world, such as £500 to Lady Susan Birch, of London, £100 to Miss Janet O'Connor, of Brisbane, who had been with the young Nellie Mitchell at Leigh House school, in Richmond, nearly sixty years before, £50 to a Covent Garden old retainer, one Eales. The will named fifty-five separate legatees, apart from institutions. There were six life annuitants; one was John Lemmone, with an annuity of £260.

Rather surprisingly, she did not bequeath her voice-box to a school of anatomical research. When younger she had talked of doing this, but was either persuaded to change her mind or perhaps rebelled against the idea as she grew older. It is to be doubted

277

anyway that the most skilled and searching physiological examination of her vocal mechanism would have revealed any of the secrets of her powers. A distinguished laryngologist has put it thus: 'You could no more tell anything of value about a singer's voice by looking at his vocal cords than you could tell anything about a runner by looking at his leg muscles. The vocal cords are only one element; so much else comes into singing as well as the voice. It is not so much what one gets out of the larynx as what happens when the sound reaches the head. The larynx contributes the pitch and volume; the timbre is acquired by the voice after it leaves the larynx. It is the resonating mechanism of the skull that contributes the timbre and overtones. You could tell something by examining the resonating mechanism of a singer with a large voice like Chaliapin, in whom the upper cavities were greatly developed, but little by a physiological examination of a singer like Melba.'

It is most unlikely that Melba meant to bequeath her voice-box to the anatomists and forgot to do so. At all events she forgot nothing else. Her letters of instruction came in, sometimes at the rate of two or three a week, from wherever the opera company happened to be playing, and Watson and Stawell knew they dared not skip the smallest point she made; if they did she would remember it and damn them as unjust stewards. But they liked dealing with her. As business men they particularly liked her passion for punctuality; by long-established custom she always arrived two minutes before the time of an appointment and would let nobody keep her waiting. If either Watson or Stawell was engaged when she arrived for an appointment he knew he must either dismiss his other caller at once or suffer Melba's wrath.

If she was haunted by secret fears that her life was running out she was determined to squeeze everything she could from the time left to her, and as soon as all the loose ends from the opera season were trimmed off she took ship for Europe, announcing that she would be away for two years. She was to give several charity concerts in England in the next year or two, but Australia was never to hear her sing again.

She travelled to Europe for what was to be her last visit with her protégée, Elena Danieli. They were walking on the deck of the RMS *Chitral* one day when Melba suddenly stopped and gripped Miss Danieli's hand.

'Helen,' she said, using her companion's baptismal name, as she always did, 'Helen, I cannot bear the thought of never being able to sing again. It is my life!'

That was one of the few times she ever let any eyes but her own see the ghost that she most feared rise up and terrify her.

4

FRIENDS of Melba were puzzled to understand why she should have decided to leave Australia in November, with the hot northerlies already starting to blow, and arrive in England as the long cold winter was setting in. The reason was that she felt she had been away from Europe too long; she could wait no longer to satisfy her yearning for a sight of people and places she knew.

She had sold her house in Great Cumberland Place some years before but had rented a house with a full staff awaiting her in Cadogan Square, and London fulfilled all her best expectations. It was nearly Christmas, and she plunged into a round of entertaining and being entertained, of lunches, dinners and suppers, of concert-going and theatre-going, with every minute of her waking hours filled. Many a younger woman would have become over-tired, and a few weeks after reaching London Melba went down with pneumonia. She was in a nursing home for a while, and when the doctors let her go back to Cadogan Square they warned her to walk carefully until she regained her strength.

She was fit again by the time the summer season opened at Covent Garden in April, and when she went back there they received her like a royal personage ushering her to her box almost with obeisances. The audience applauded when she appeared and, looking out on the auditorium, she knew she was still one of the great figures. She sat listening to Rosetta Pampanini singing *Bohème* and told herself that she could have outsung this girl once, good as Pampanini was; in fact, she believed she could outsing Pampanini still, making up with art whatever time had stolen from her voice. She demonstrated that she could still sing by giving a charity concert at the Brighton Hippodrome on 5 October; but, although well patronized, it was an interesting social occasion rather than an important musical event.

She crossed to Paris when the Covent Garden season ended and set up house in an apartment in the Boulevard de La Tour-Maubourg, on the Left Bank, spending freely to have the place furnished and decorated to her taste. There was one drawback; the building had an old-fashioned lift which often refused to work, and then Melba and her guests had to toil up the stairs, muttering their irritation. But to her the view over Paris from her windows on a misty evening was worth any trouble. She must have thought often then of those faraway years when she had gone for her lesson to the Ecole Marchesi in the Rue Jouffroy, walking all the way from her pension because she had to save the bus fare. Now, in the same city where she had once had to look at every sou twice before spending it, she was able to live as she pleased.

Her big black Cadillac was always at call with her nephew, Tom Patterson, Belle's youngest boy, to drive it. Tom was a personable young man in the early twenties, and she had brought him from Australia with her because he drove well, and also because he was good company. She was interested in antique furniture and objets d'art; she liked to prowl about the dealers' shops, rummaging in dark corners until she chanced on some good piece, and, after a suitable period of haggling, buy it as a bargain and carry it off in triumph. Tom Patterson drove her on many such forays, mostly in Paris itself but now and then as far as Versailles, and her collection of antique pieces steadily grew.

She had a good staff at the Boulevard de La Tour-Maubourg, and there was never any problem about putting on a dinner for ten or twelve people at short notice. John Brownlee, who had become a star of the Paris Opéra, and his wife, the former Contessa Carla Oddone di Feletto, were often bidden to dinner. So also was an old friend of Melba's, Tommy Cochrane, a middle-aged Australian man-about-town, who supplemented his private means by writing intimate social gossip for Australian newspapers and magazines. Cochrane, a perennial bachelor, spent much of his time travelling in Europe and knew his way about most of the great cities; he was a man with a bright eye and a quick tongue, and Melba found him a stimulating companion. He could make her laugh when things went wrong. She called him her Court Jester and treated him with affectionate irreverence; he responded by treating her with unawed admiration.

Time had not dulled her liking for helping young and talented people who were struggling for recognition, and in Paris on that visit she won the lasting regard of a young Australian pianist, Roy Shepherd. He was studying in Paris, and an Australian friend, Lady Tallis, the wife of an Australian theatre magnate, took him one night to Melba's apartment. He told Melba he had begun his pianoforte studies at the Albert Street Conservatorium and recalled one of her visits in 1924; she was to sing Mimi that night, and Shepherd was one of a group of students to whom she handed gallery tickets so they could hear her. He diplomatically refrained from reminding her that after distributing the tickets she gave the recipients a lesson in clapping, showing them how to hollow the palms of the hands to produce more noise. She made them demonstrate their proficiency and then left, having told them to clap 'until you are exhausted'. Melba liked friends to hear her sing; being a realist, she also liked friends to register their approval of her singing with all possible efficiency.

In Paris young Shepherd had no money to spend except on necessaries, and Melba gave him many glimpses of the city as the rich and privileged saw it. She asked him to dine a number of times; once or twice he was invited on formal occasions when the guests ate off gold plate; he enjoyed those nights but suffered agonies trying to cut his food and not let the knife squeal on the metal surface.

One night she took him and a party to hear Brownlee at the Paris Opéra. She swept into her box with a diamond tiara glittering on her head. At her entrance the audience began clapping. Melba bowed regally, and Shepherd saw a faint flush of pleasure rise in her cheeks. So they still remembered her! Shepherd was grateful that she did not know the clapping was for a young prima donna who had simultaneously appeared in a neighbouring box.

He saw enough of Melba in Paris to form the opinion that she was at times a lonely woman, even though she could at will surround herself with gay and brilliant people; he was never able to do much to repay the kindnesses she showed him, and the warmth of her response when he made any small gesture he could afford, such as sending her a Christmas card, made him realize that she was hungry for friendship.

A spirit of restlessness would take hold of Melba from time to time, and when this happened she would summon Tom Patterson and the Cadillac and escape from Paris for a few days. They went once to Biarritz and stayed for a fortnight. Two of her English friends, a banker and his wife, were also on holiday there, and one day she picked them up in the Cadillac to drive to San Sebastian in Spain, just across the frontier. They lunched there, then went to a bullfight. Melba disliked the blood and cruelty, and left after three bulls were killed, not bothering to hide from the bullfight *aficionados* her feeling that the whole thing was disgusting, sadistic and barbarous. She and the others were nearly out of the stadium when she found she had left her parasol behind. She sent Patterson for it and as, red-faced, he groped his way back to their seats to retrieve it he was enthusiastically hissed by the *aficionados* who evidently suspected him of sharing the blasphemous anti-bullfighting views of the English dowager duchess or whatever she might be.

Melba also made a sentimental pilgrimage to Brussels. She seemed to know she would not travel these paths again, because she turned aside here and there to linger for a while in places she had known and loved. In Chartres she and Tommy Cochrane went to evensong in the cathedral. They knelt, listening to the choir-boys' voices soaring to the vaulted roof, while the dying sun struck through the windows and splashed the floors and pews with great patches of jewelled light, and she whispered, 'I hate these boys. At thirteen they are doing what it took me years and years to do. And I don't know that they're not doing it better.'

In Brussels they called at the Monnaie. It was daytime and she went in and stood, alone, in the middle of the stage, looking out over the unpeopled stalls and up into the dusk shrouding the galleries. She stood there for perhaps fifteen or twenty seconds, and then raised her chin and sang a few phrases of *Caro Nome*, Gilda's aria in Act I of *Rigoletto*; it was the opera in which she had made her début at the Monnaie in 1887. The notes floated out into the empty silence and died away. Melba turned and walked back to the wings where Cochrane waited. She touched his arm and like that, with no word spoken, she left the Monnaie for the last time.

5

ONE thing that troubled her as she grew older was any long period of cold weather. She had always been a sun-lover, but the European winter did not bother her much until old age settled on her; then when she looked out on the bleak pavements of London or the snowy rooftops of Paris in mid-winter she would give an inward shiver and find herself longing for a hot blue Australian summer day, even for a burning north wind carrying a whiff of bush-fire smoke down from the ranges to Coombe Cottage.

She was miserable when winter gripped Paris in 1929 and snow filled the cobbled ways with slush and gave the wind a hard cutting edge. She knew she must escape to some warmer place, if only for a month or two, and one day a friend suggested Egypt. For some reason she had never thought of Egypt as a sanctuary from the European winter; to her it had never been more than a country one passed through on the trip from Europe to Australia, and she knew it only as tourists do—the gulli-gulli men of Port Said, the Muski bazaar in Cairo, the Pyramids and the Sphinx at Mena. As well as offering a retreat from the winter, Egypt might be interesting to see at leisure, she decided. The more she thought about it the more the suggestion commended itself, not only to her thin-flowing blood but also to her curiosity, and she booked a passage for Port Said.

She was away two months or so, and spring was returning to Europe when she left Egypt and went back to Paris. Her apartment was waiting just as she had left it, and she moved back into it with a sense of gratitude. She had been ill in Egypt with a fever which came and went, making her depressed and listless. The Egyptian doctors had been able to do little to help her, but she felt sure a few weeks of clean European air would put her right. She supposed she had picked up a germ of some kind in Port Said or Cairo and that her recovery was only a matter of patience and reasonable care. After all, she had always been able to defeat any ills of the flesh in the past, and she was confident she could defeat this one.

Paris rekindled her spirits and almost at once she felt better. A few days after getting back she gave a dinner at the Boulevard de La Tour-Maubourg in honour of her friends, the Prince and Princess Christopher of Greece. Some of the leading figures of the international smart set and a scatter of diplomats were among her guests. After dinner she sang to them, and several of those who heard her gave it as their view that she could walk back into Covent Garden or the Paris Opéra that very night and put the best of the young prima donnas to shame. That kind of praise fell sweet on her ears, but when the guests left and she was alone she knew it was not true; she still sang beautifully, but the thing that had once lifted her singing from the terrestrial to the ethereal was no more.

She thought her sickness was passing, as spring warmèd the boulevards and brought the colour flooding back into the Bois de Boulogne and the Tuileries Gardens, and she was even well enough to cross the Channel and sing at a semi-public charity entertainment at the Hyde Park Hotel, in London. But presently she sickened again, and found herself struggling once more against her desperate lassitude, her lack of appetite, her uncharacteristic apathy to what went on about her. She consulted doctors in Paris and in London. Then she went to Germany to see a specialist at Baden, a clever man whom she had met in Egypt when she first fell ill there; he had told her he would always be at her service and she went to his clinic, hoping for relief. He did everything in his power, but the relief he gave her did not last.

As the summer wore on her thoughts turned to Australia. She had sometimes been ill there but never for long; the air at Coldstream was pure and bracing, and she told herself the hot summer sun would burn away the germs which had somehow managed to invade her system. Her doctors, baffled to prescribe for her, told her a long sea trip might help her; anyway it could do her no harm. Another argument weighed with her also; the people she loved— her son and his wife and their daughter, and her sisters and brothers, nephews and nieces—were in Australia, and something told her to go to them. So she decided to make for home.

Una Bourne and a friend, Mona McCaughey, were in Bayreuth that year for the Wagner Festival, from 22 July to 21 August. They did not know Melba was there until they met her in the street one day by chance. She told them she was booked for Australia in the RMS *Cathay*, leaving England about two months later. They thought she looked ill, but did not dream when they shook hands at parting that this was to be their last meeting with her.

Sick as she was, Melba could not bring herself to leave Europe without paying a visit to Covent Garden. She went to see Colonel Blois by appointment and sat in his office, talking business. She was entirely self-possessed until suddenly her control slipped. 'This place is full of ghosts,' she said. 'Harry Higgins, Gladys Ripon, Caruso, Neil Forsyth! They have all gone and I shall never be here again!' She burst into tears and Blois could not comfort her.

Before taking ship for Australia Melba had one important engagement to keep in Paris; this was to be present at the christening of John Brownlee's first child, a daughter, at the church of Notre

Dame d'Auteuil on Saturday 20 September. She had agreed to be one of the godmothers of the child, Isobel Delphina Nellie, and on that day, perhaps under the stimulus of excitement, she seemed astonishingly well; looking at her, nobody would have supposed she had been ailing off and on for months.

Among Brownlee's Australian friends at the ceremony was a young man from Melbourne, Archie Longden, who was later to make his mark as a concert manager in Australia. Longden was living in Paris and had met Melba there two or three times, but their acquaintanceship was slight; he had good reason to remember her, however, for a kindness she had once done him which had altogether passed from her memory. When the 1924 Melba-Williamson opera season was playing in Australia he was a £2-a-week bank clerk in Melbourne, but managed by practising rigid self-denial to hear quite a number of performances from the five-shilling gallery seats. One night every seat was sold, and he was standing outside the theatre looking disconsolate when Melba came down the stairs into the foyer.

She glanced at Longden, whom she had never seen before, and said, 'Why so sad, young man?'

'Well, Dame Nellie,' he told her, 'I've missed out on a seat for tonight after waiting in the queue for four hours.'

'Never mind,' she said. 'Come with me.'

She led him upstairs and put him in a seat in her own box, and then, apologizing for not being able to stay, left him there.

Now in Paris he was face to face with her again, outside the church of Notre Dame d'Auteuil. He had a small and inexpensive folding camera, and when he saw Melba standing on the steps of the church after the christening ceremony, looking regal in a chinchilla coat and close-fitting hat, he screwed up his courage and asked her if he might take a picture of her. After reaching middle-age Melba was never eager to be photographed except by some skilled and obliging professional whom she could trust to edit any pictures of her before letting other eyes see them; she never pretended that she did not want the camera to lie on her behalf and cheerfully boasted to friends that she particularly liked the work of a certain photographer who could be relied on to make 'all necessary alterations'. So that day in Paris she looked at young Longden and his camera and shook her head.

'I don't think I want to be photographed today,' she said. Then, noticing that he was wearing a Boy Scout's small fleur de lis badge in his buttonhole, she said, 'Ah, I see you are a Scout! I have my own Boy Scout troop in Melbourne. It's called Dame Nellie Melba's Own.'

'Yes, Dame Nellie,' he replied. 'It's the 1st Camberwell Troop. I was a member of its Rover crew.'

She beamed and stepped closer to her co-godmother, Mrs Brownlee's sister, who was nursing the baby. 'Take your photo, Boy Scout,' she said.

He aimed his camera and clicked the shutter and thus took what is believed to be the last photograph taken of Melba. Even while he was focusing, he was thinking how well she looked. That must have been one of the days when, as sometimes happened, she rose above the pestilent Mediterranean fever which had attacked her and was, if only for a little while, her old self. Archie Longden at any rate believed that if outward appearances meant anything she had many years of life before her.

Melba left Paris a fortnight or so later to join her ship at Marseilles, and Longden went down to the train with prints of the snapshot. She was delighted with it, and asked him to have some larger prints made and to send one to the leading newspaper in each of the Australian state capital cities at her expense. He did so, and airmailed a note of the cost to catch her at Suez on her way home. Her note of thanks and a cheque came back by return mail. She was always punctilious about paying her dues, no less than about seeing that she was paid whatever was due to her.

6

THE sea trip home did not help her. Her health became worse, and for some days before the *Cathay* reached Australia she was in bed in her own suite. Newspapermen came on board at Fremantle but she, who had always revelled in giving press interviews, was too ill to see them. In Melbourne her doctor had an ambulance waiting when the *Cathay* docked, and she was carried ashore and driven to a hospital. It was 10 November, just two years and four days since, looking hale enough to live for another twenty years at least, she had sailed for Europe.

She gained a little strength in the next few weeks, and her doctor let her leave hospital and go home to Coombe Cottage for Christmas. She sent out hundreds of personal Christmas cards as usual. One went to her old friend, Dr Floyd, the organist, and on it she scribbled in pencil, in a hand only slightly unsteady, 'With my love, Nellie Melba. Please may I come and hear you one day—still very ill.' Some weeks later, when she was dying in Sydney, she sent Floyd several word-of-mouth messages. In one she said, 'Will you please play for me on the cathedral organ when I come back?'

She was worrying about some business loose ends, and after the Christmas celebrations were over she found enough strength to have herself driven to Melbourne. She stayed at the Quamby Club for two or three days while putting these small affairs in order but avoided friends and out of doors hid her face behind a heavy veil. One afternoon in Collins Street she came face to face with Cyril Dillon. They talked for only a minute or two, and he parted from her with one sentence she had spoken dinning in his ears; 'Fancy this happening to me!' It was a cry of despair by a woman who, having always imagined herself to be above incurable human ills, suddenly discovers that she is as vulnerable as everyone else.

She went back to Coombe Cottage and watched the Coldstream and Lilydale paddocks turn from green to light brown under the fiery heat of January. Now and then she went for a drive, but could never stay out for long without becoming tired. One afternoon her brother Charlie was driving her.

'I'd like you to do something for me, Charlie,' she said. 'I want to be buried on Mount Mary.'

Mount Mary, a shallow hill on Coombe Farm, lies a mile or two from Coombe Cottage. It rises perhaps 150 to 200 feet above the level of the surrounding country, with Stringybark Creek curling round its foot. Melba had some years before conceived the idea that she would like her tomb to be placed on top of Mount Mary, and in her will she recorded her wish to be buried there, but she was to change her mind in the last week or two of her life. It is a pity she had second thoughts about it. Mount Mary, which overlooks the highway linking Coldstream with Healesville, is in the heart of 'the Melba country'. A tomb on its summit, perhaps with a light burning constantly overhead, would be visible for many miles and an effective monument to her memory.

A few days after her drive with Charlie Mitchell she told her personal maid to pack her things; they were going to Sydney.

She was running a high temperature, but her decision was not the caprice of a delirious woman. She wanted to see her sister, Annie Box, who was living in the New South Wales country town of Moss Vale, and she also hoped to get better medical care in Sydney, because her daughter-in-law's brother, Dr W. O. Doyle, was practising there.

She reached Sydney but could not go on to Moss Vale; she was too ill. Dr Doyle ordered her into St Vincent's private hospital, in Darlinghurst and he and the consultants he called fought with all their skill; but it was hopeless. They found she was suffering from paratyphoid, complicated by the assaults of bacteria which had entered her bloodstream through a rash on her shoulders. Fifteen or twenty years later penicillin or some other so-called wonder drug might have saved her, but in 1931 medical science was impotent.

Yet she clung tenaciously to life. She went into hospital on 20 January, and nearly a month later was still living. The doctors, unable to arrest the progress of the infection in her blood, could not get her temperature down, and it hovered all the while around 102 degrees. Her spirit fired up at times, though. She had always worn her pearls – to keep them alive, as she put it – and when any well-meaning Sister of Mercy or nursing sister, thinking to make her more comfortable, wanted to take them from round her throat she would gasp, 'Leave them alone!', in a tone which nobody dared defy.

Only close relations and John Lemmone were allowed to see her, and even they could not stay for more than a few minutes at a time; they sat on the veranda outside her room while she dozed. Sometimes she gave a visitor a smile, and sometimes even muttered a few words. A caller, wanting to cheer her, told her she would soon be well again, and the old light flashed out of her sunken eyes as she said: 'Don't tell me lies! I'm dying, and you know it.'

Lemmone did not try to soothe her with words; he knew her too well for that. Her surrender frightened him. Ever since their first meeting, on that far-off day of 1884 when they had appeared together in the Melbourne Liedertafel's benefit concert for old Elsasser, she had been a fighter, but now her spirit seemed to be flickering out.

The thing that bothered her was that she was such an unconscionable time dying.

'John,' she asked Lemmone, 'why must I die a lingering death?'

He brushed her hand with his fingertips and left it at that.

At times she found strength and spoke out of a mind momentarily as lucid and imperious as it had ever been. Once it was to say she did not wish to be buried on Mount Mary after all, but in the Lilydale cemetery, beside the grave in which her father and mother lay with three of their children, James, Margaret and Vere. At another time she said, 'Let me be buried under bells, so that music will always be near me'—a wish that was not granted to her. She seemed to want to make sure that the arrangements surrounding her in death, like those which had surrounded her in life, would be orderly and correct.

In the early hours of 23 February she asked for a clergyman. They prayed together, and soon afterwards she became unconscious. Once, as the day wore on, she stirred and sang a few notes, which some of her listeners thought were a bar or two of Gounod's *Ave Maria*. That was all. Perhaps she was disappointed that she did not go down to death singing as she had liked to believe Jean de Reszke had done, but it could not have troubled her much in those last hours.

She died at five that evening, and the news went out to the world. In London, New York, Paris, Rome, and other world capitals editorial writers searched for phrases to match the occasion. The *New York Times* probably went as close as any other newspaper when it said, 'Fortunate the generation that heard her, for we shall never hear her like again.'

In Sydney they put Melba's coffin on the Melbourne express twenty-four hours after she died and took her home to the city of her birth. Marie Bremner, who had been one of her singing girls, was starring in *Lilac Time* in Sydney, and she sent flowers and went down to the central railway station to watch the train leave. The coffin was in a coach which had been specially fitted with a large plate-glass window and, standing among the silent watching crowd, Miss Bremner saw that her flowers – tuberoses and red roses – were lying all by themselves on the flag-draped coffin.

Melba's own city of Melbourne said its farewell to her at a service in Scots Church, the church her father had built; it was jammed to the doors and thousands of people waited in the streets outside and stood to watch the long cortege set out on the twenty-three-mile journey to Lilydale. It was evening with black clouds piling up in the sky before Nellie Melba, having made her last journey down the long hill sweeping past her father's limestone quarries, came to her grave. She lies under a stone bearing Mimi's words,

'*Addio, senza rancore,*' 'Farewell, without bitterness'. The grave is surrounded by a cypress hedge, and sometimes when the wind blows a listener standing there can fancy he hears the far sound of a woman singing.

ACKNOWLEDGEMENTS

ACKNOWLEDGMENTS

General Acknowledgements

THIS book was written with the help of a Commonwealth Literary Fund fellowship. I wish to thank the CLF, and the sponsors of my application for the fellowship: Professor Sir Bernard Heinze, Professor A. R. Chisholm; Mr Gavin Long, and Mr Frank Dalby Davison; I also have to thank Professor Heinze and Professor Chisholm for supplying information which is included in the book. I am grateful to the Secretary of the CLF, Mr A. L. Moore, and the former Secretary, Mr J. McCusker, who were unfailingly patient and considerate whenever I asked for procedural guidance.

I thank the Board of David Syme and Company, Melbourne, proprietor of the *Age*, and the then Editor of the *Age*, Mr Keith Sinclair, for granting me leave of absence to complete the book, and for generously allowing me unrestricted use of library, pictorial, and other company facilities.

Custodians of public and private collections of books and manuscripts were most helpful, in particular: Mr Harold L. White, Librarian, National Library of Australia, Canberra, A.C.T.; Mr Phil Garrett, former Chief Research Officer of the State Library of Victoria, and his successor, Miss Patricia Reynolds, now Deputy Librarian of the La Trobe Library; the staff of the Public Library of New South Wales and the Mitchell Library, Sydney; Mr G. L. Fischer, Archivist, Public Library of South Australia, Adelaide; Mr Willard B. Ireland, Provincial Librarian and Archivist, Victoria, B.C., Canada; Mr Horace Chisholm, Chief Librarian of the Melbourne *Age*; and Mr Roy Weston, Chief Librarian of the Melbourne *Herald*, and his assistant, Mr Col. Dawson.

I frequently asked the Australian News and Information Bureau, Canberra, for help in finding information and photographs and never in vain. I thank in particular the Director, Mr Kevin Murphy, and three members of his staff, Mr S. S. Brown, Mr Mel. Pratt, and Mr Hugh Murphy, who went far beyond the line of duty to get what I needed.

I also wish to make special mention of Mr L. Hevingham-Root, of Melbourne, who put at my disposal his unsurpassed knowledge of Melba as a recording artist; of British Broadcasting Corporation representatives in Australia, Mr Humphrey Fisher and Mr S. H. Gordon-Box, who obtained for me permission to draw for publication on a variety of BBC material; and of the *Daily Colonist* newspaper, Victoria, B.C., Canada, and the *Vancouver Province* newspaper, Vancouver, B.C., for publicizing my interest in Charles

Armstrong and bringing me letters from many people who knew him in the long years of his retirement at Shawnigan Lake, B.C.

I thank my late wife for her help in reading and criticizing early drafts of the book; I am specially indebted to her for offering a suggestion whose adoption greatly sharpened and strengthened my account of Nellie Mitchell's youth.

My debt to those men and women who knew Melba and gave me their memories and impressions of her personality is heavy. Miss Nellie Patterson, of Melbourne, stands out among them. Miss Patterson, a niece of Melba, encouraged many people who had known her aunt to talk frankly with me, while she herself, in twenty or more meetings, armed me with knowledge lacking which I could not have penetrated and dispelled the mist of fable and apocrypha that surrounded Melba and hid, or distorted, her personality. Miss Patterson tried as hard to steer me to the truth as some other people tried to steer me away from it. Nothing I say here should be interpreted to mean that she approves all my findings; I believe she would endorse some of them, but I know she would reject others.

I also thank the following for help, either in giving or guiding me to essential information or in supplying illustrations for the first edition: Mrs I. F. Abercromby; Mrs Enid Alexander; Mr Peter Alston; Mr Geoff Allan; Mr John Amadio; Mrs R. Anketell-Jones; Mr Arthur Anton; Madame Florence Austral (Mrs John Amadio); Mr Harold Badger; Dr David M. Baillie; Miss Wilma Barnard; Mr Herbert Barth (Bayreuth); Mr A. C. Bartleman; Mrs Winifred de Beaurepaire; Mrs Beatrice Bell; Mrs Elva Bell; Mr John Bennetts; Mr William Beresford; Mr George Blaikie; Mr Leo J. Bloxom; Mr Alfred Blundell; Dr G. C. Bolton; Miss Enid M. Botterill; Miss Una Bourne; Mrs Edward Boydell; Miss Vera Bradford; Mr Charles Bradley; Mr F. Maxwell Bradshaw; Mr Sydney Bradshaw; Mr Douglas Brass; Mr T. C. Bray; Mr M. S. Brennan, secretary of the Melbourne General Cemetery; Mr G. V. Briggs; Mr C. H. Bright, QC; Dame Mabel Brookes; Mrs Nina Brown; Mr P. K. Brown; Mr John Brownlee; Mr Hugh Bryn-Jones; Mr George Burns, editor of the *Christchurch Star*; Mrs F. Massy Burnside; Mr H. H. Burton; Mr W. B. Campbell, QC; Mr Alan Carmichael; Mr George Castles; Mr Jack Cato; Mrs Ewart Chapple (Marie Bremner); Mr Alec Chisholm; Miss Edith Clark; Mr R. F. M. Clark; Mr John L. Coad; Mr T. Hazelton Cochrane; Mr Gervase John Coles; Mr Frederick Collier; Miss Violet Concanen; Mr Norbert Coulehan; Mr Noel Counihan; Mrs Lorna Cowell; Mr Harry Cox; Miss Vera Crellin; Mrs R. H. Croll; Dr C. E. Crooke; Mrs E. M. Cryer; Madame Toti Dal Monte; Mr Harry Davies; Mr Herbert Davis; Mr Allan Dawes; Mr William S. Day; Dr C. H. Dickson; Mr Cyril Dillon; Mr Franklin Dixon; Mr Frank J. Doolan; Mr Ray Dougan; Mr Hume Dow; Mr David B. Doyle; Mr Harold W. Eather; Mrs Malcolm Elliott; Miss Patience Empson; Miss Grace Evans; Mr Lindley Evans; Mr Charles

C. Eyres, Town Clerk, Richmond; Mr Max Fatchen; Mr Paull Fiddian; Mr Phil. Finkelstein; Dr A. E. Floyd; Dr Michael S. Forrest; Mr. R. H. Fowler; Mr C. Homer Fraser; Mr E. A. Fullalove; Dr Engenio Gara; Mr J. H. H. Gaute, editor, George G. Harrap and Company, London; Mr Leon Gellert; Mrs Eric G. Gibson; Mr R. Glenister, Secretary to the Law Department, Melbourne; Signor Apollo Granforte; Dr Lyle Gray; Mrs J. S. Grice; Mr Alf Guest; Miss M. Gunn, Organizing Secretary of the Sydney Eisteddfod; Mrs D. Gunning; Mr Keith Halliday; Dr Mary Ham; the Reverend Ian Hamilton; Mr Edward Harrington; Mr E. C. Harris; Mr R. L. Harry, CBE, Australian Ambassador to the Belgians; Mr Basil Hart; Mrs G. Helm; Mr Robert N. C. Hemberow; Dr Raymond Hennessy; Mrs My Henry; Mr Kurt Hensel, Consul of the Federal Republic of Germany at Melbourne; Mr Edric Henty; Mr Arthur Heymanson; Mr Rudolf Himmer; Mr Cavan Hogue; Mrs F. R. Holland; Mr Charles E. Howlett; Mr Noel de Hugard; Mr Dennis Mason Hurley; Mr Bruce Hutchison; Mrs Inez Hutchison; Mr Geoffrey Hutton; Mrs E. R. Jackson; Mr Eric Jackson; Mr Frank Jenkins; Miss Gertrude Johnson, OBE; Mrs Stanley C. Johnson (Elena Danieli); Mrs Linda Kauffmann; Mr Jack Kelly; the Reverend Eric D. Kent; Colonel E. G. Keogh, MBE, ED; Mrs B. Kingsley-Newell; Mr Claude Kingston, OBE; Mrs Olive Kloeden; Sir Robert Knox; Mr George Knupfer; Miss Ruth Ladd; Mr Robin Latreille; Mrs Eliza J. Lawlor; Miss Jeanette Lemmone; Mrs Mabel Lemmone; Mrs Malcolm Letts; Dr Zdzislaw Libera (Warsaw); Sir Daryl and Lady Lindsay; Mr Norman Lindsay; Mrs Robert Lindsay; Mr A. D. M. Longden; Mr Ron Lovitt; Mr Peter Lucreyne; Lord Lurgan; Mr R. A. Lyons; Mr John McCallum; Mr C. A. McCormick; Miss Sheila McCubbin; Dr Colin Macdonald, senior; Mr D. G. McFarling; Mr Claude McKay; Sister Clyne Mackay; Mr A. H. McLachlan; Miss Madelina Main; Mr John Malone; Mrs Kathleen Mangan; Mr George Martin; Mrs E. N. Matthews; Mr Sydney May; Mr Alan D. Mickle; Mr H. S. Mishael; Miss Blanche Mitchell; Mr David Mitchell; Mrs J. Mitchell; Mrs Jennie Mitchell; Mr Ray Mitchell; Mr Tom Mitchell; Mrs F. Monk; Mr John H. Moores; Mr William Mortill; Mr Tom Muir; Mr and Mrs Browning Mummery; Miss Stella Murray; Mrs Frank Murphy; Mrs Louis Nelken; Miss B. C. Newton; Mr George Nicholls; Mr Beverley Nichols; Mr Charles Nicol, Director of Public Relations, Australian Army; Miss E. B. Norcross; Mr L. de Noskowski (who not only supplied me with much information from his expert and intimate knowledge of grand opera in Australia, but also specially translated for me substantial passages from the autobiography of Madame Janina Korolewicz-Wayda, the Polish soprano); Mr Nicholas O'Donohue; Miss Annie Oliver; Mr Albert J. Oostergetel, Consul of Belgium at Melbourne; Mrs John O'Reilly; Mr F. P. O'Grady, Director-General of the Australian Postmaster-General's Department; Mrs William O'Rourke (Stella Power); Professor W. A. Osborne; Mrs O. Oxlee;

Mrs A. H. Panet; Mrs Dorothy M. Parkin; Mr Tom Parrington; Mrs Geraldine Paterson; Mr Ambrose McC. Patterson; Mr Douglas A. Patterson; Mr Gerald Patterson; Miss Mary Patterson; Mr Tom Patterson; the Reverend P. W. Pearson; Mrs Kathleen Peat; Professor Willard Pederick; Sir Charles Petrie; Mr Mort Pettigrove; Professor Stuart Piggott; Mrs Constance Pilkington; Dr V. Politi; Mrs Winifred Ponder; Mrs Floretta S. Posner; Mr Colin Preece; Mrs Katharine Susannah Prichard; Miss Dorothy Propsting; Mr R. J. Prowse, Chief Australian Film Censor; Mrs Beatrice Pym; Mr Lloyd Rees; Lady Rich; Mr Colin Rigg; Mr Ken Roberts; Mrs Jessie M. Robertson; Mr Philip Robertson; Mr F. H. Rogan, Town Clerk, Melbourne; Mrs Sonia Rose; Mr Newman Rosenthal; Mr Leslie Ross; Mr Reginald Ross Williamson, former Regional Director, British Information Services, Melbourne; Mrs C. Rymer; Mr David Saunders; Miss Ida Scott; Miss Olive Sebire; Mr Clement Semmler; Mr Roy Shepherd; Mrs Joyce Sherek; Mr N. D. Sinclair; Dr Bernard Smith; Mr David Smith, Town Clerk, Kirriemuir; Mr H. F. Smith; Mrs Karl Smith; Mrs H. Macpherson Smith; Mr Jascha Spivakovsky; Mr Alfred Stirling, CBE, Australian Ambassador to Italy; Mrs Reg. Stock; Mrs John Summons; Miss K. A. Syme; Sir Frank Tait; Mr Ivan Tait; Mr John Tallis; Mr Edgar Tanner, MP; Mr J. R. C. Taylor; the Very Reverend T. W. Thomas; Mr Wilfrid Thomas; Mr John Thompson; Mr Gordon Thomson, Deputy Director, National Gallery of Victoria, Melbourne; Miss Aggie Todd; Mr Hec Tonkin; Mr Peter Townend, Editor, Burke's Peerage; Mrs Valerie Tredinnick; Mr Eric S. Vance; Mr Willy Van Cauwenberg, Ambassador of Belgium at Canberra; Miss Dorothy Vollugi; Mrs Rowley Walker; Mr Judah Waten; Mr Hartley P. Watson; Mr V. G. Watson; Mr Eric Westbrook, Director, National Gallery of Victoria, Melbourne; Mrs F. Williams; Mr Merv Williams; Mr Ross Wilson; Sir Henry Winneke; Mrs Keith Wood; Professor R. Douglas Wright.

Copyright Material

I thank the following for permission to quote from copyright material: The Trustees Executors and Agency Co. Ltd, of Melbourne, and Mr George Armstrong, for letters written by Dame Nellie Melba; Thornton Butterworth Ltd, for *Melodies and Memories* by Nellie Melba, and *The Passing Show* by Henry Russell; George Allen and Unwin Ltd, for *The Romantic World of Music* by William Armstrong; Angus and Robertson Ltd, for *Music for Pleasure* by Neville Cardus, *This is the Life* by Claude McKay, *The Hill of Content* by A. H. Spencer, and *Child of the Hurricane* by Katharine Susannah Prichard; Dr Ruffo Titta, of Rome, for *La Mia Parabola* by Titta Ruffo;* Jonathan Cape Ltd, for *Evensong* and *All I Could Never Be* by Beverley Nichols; William Collins Ltd, for *Joan Sutherland* by Russell Braddon; J. M. Dent and Sons Ltd, for *Till I End My Song* by Robert Gibbings; Robert Hale Ltd, for *Music on Record* by F. W. Gaisberg; Hamish Hamilton Ltd, for *Am I Too Loud?* by Gerald Moore; Hutchinson Publishing Group Ltd, for *A Mingled Chime* by Sir Thomas Beecham, bart, and *The Autobiography of Felix Semon, KCVO, MD, FRCP*; Jacaranda Press Pty Ltd, for *A Thousand Miles Away* by G. C. Bolton; Lansdowne Press Pty Ltd, for *On Lips of Living Men* by John Thompson; Methuen and Co. Ltd, for *Recital* by Eleanor Gerhardt, *Overture and Beginners* by Eugene Goossens, and *The Life of Oscar Wilde* by Hesketh Pearson; The Oakwood Press, for *The Golden Age Recorded* by P. G. Hurst; W. H. Allen and Co., for *Wild Men of Sydney* by Cyril Pearl; Putnam and Co. Ltd, for *Two Centuries of Opera at Covent Garden* by Harold Rosenthal; the Public Trustee and the Society of Authors, London, for *Music in London* by Bernard Shaw, and *London Music in 1888–89*, as heard by Corno di Bassetto (later known as Bernard Shaw); Union-Fidelity Trustee Co. of Australia, for *Much Besides Music* by Thorold Waters; Weidenfeld and Nicolson Ltd, for *The Amazing Oscar Hammerstein* by Vincent Sheean; Grayson and Grayson Ltd, for *Melba* by Percy Colson; James T. White and Co., for *The Secrets of Svengali* by J. H. Duval; Michael Joseph Ltd, for *Low's Autobiography* by David Low, and *London Has a Garden* by Clemence Dane; Simon and Schuster Inc., for *Mary Garden's Story* by Mary Garden and Louis Biancolli; Routledge and Kegan Paul Ltd, for *The Golden Age of Opera* by Herman Klein; George G. Harrap and Co. Ltd, for *Clara Butt: Her life-story* by Winifred Ponder; Chatto and Windus Ltd, for *Melba* by Agnes Murphy;

* As a singer, Ruffo Titta, senior, used his given and family names in reverse order.

Frederick Muller Ltd, for *The Savoy* by Stanley Jackson, and *That Was Yvette* by Bettina Knapp and Myra Chipman; Alfred A. Knopf Inc., for *With Strings Attached* by Joseph Szigeti; the Richards Press, for *Singer's Pilgrimage* by Blanche Marchesi; Howell-North Books, for *20th Century* by Lucius Beebe; Falcon Press, London, and Invincible Press, Sydney, for *Interrupted Melody* by Marjorie Lawrence; Sampson Low, Marston and Co. Ltd, for *Myself and Others* by Sir Landon Ronald.

I thank the following for permission to reproduce illustrations in their possession: the Australian News and Information Bureau for photographs of the portrait of Melba by Rupert Bunny, Melba and her son, Marchesi and Nellie Armstrong, Melba as Marguerite, Melba as Lakmé, Melba as Aida; the Raymond Mander & Joe Mitchenson Theatre Collection, London, for photographs of Enrico Caruso, Jean de Reszke, Luisa Tetrazzini, Melba in London in the 1890's, Melba as Rosina; the *Radio Times* Hulton Picture Library, London, for the photograph of Louis Philippe, Duke of Orleans; Punch Publications Ltd for the cartoon of Melba and Caruso which originally appeared in *Punch* on 8 June 1904.

Chief Printed Sources

Books

Armstrong, William, *The Romantic World of Music*, London: George Allen & Unwin, 1923

Baily, Leslie, *Scrapbook 1900-14*, London: Muller, 1957

Beebe, Lucius, *20th Century*, Berkeley, California: Howell-North, 1962

Beecham, Sir Thomas, *A Mingled Chime*, London: Hutchinson, 1944

Benson, E. F., *As We Were*, London: Longmans, Green, 1930

Bispham, David, *A Quaker Singer's Recollections*, New York: Macmillan, 1920

Bolton, G. C., *A Thousand Miles Away: A history of North Queensland to 1920*, Brisbane: Jacaranda Press, in association with the Australian National University, 1963

Braddon, Russell, *Joan Sutherland*, London: Collins, 1962

Brockway, Wallace, and Herbert Weinstock, *The World of Opera*, London: Methuen, 1963.

Brookes, Dame Mabel, *Crowded Galleries*, London: Heinemann, 1956

Calvé, Emma, *My Life*, New York: D. Appleton, 1922

Cardus, Neville, *Music for Pleasure*, Sydney: Angus & Robertson, 1942

Colson, Percy, *Melba: An unconventional biography*, London: Grayson & Grayson, 1932

Cowles, Virginia, *The Kaiser*, London: Collins, 1963

Dane, Clemence, *London Has A Garden*, London: Michael Joseph, 1964

Dawson, Peter, *Fifty Years of Song*, London: Hutchinson, 1951

Duval, J. H., *The Secrets of Svengali*, New York: James T. White, 1922

Finck, Henry T., *My Adventures in the Golden Age of Music*, New York: Funk and Wagnalls, 1926

Finck, Henry T., *Success in Music*, New York: Charles Scribner's Sons, 1926

Gaisberg, F. W., *Music on Record*, London: Robert Hale, 1946

Garden, Mary, and Louis Biancolli, *Mary Garden's Story*, London: Michael Joseph, 1952

Gelatt, Roland, *The Fabulous Phonograph*, London: Cassell, 1956

Gerhardt, Eleanor, *Recital*, London: Methuen, 1953

Gibbings, Robert, *Till I End My Song*, London: J. M. Dent, 1957

Goossens, Eugene, *Overture and Beginners: A musical autobiography*, London: Methuen, 1951

Hurst, P. G., *The Age of Jean de Reszke*, London: Christopher Johnson, 1958

Hurst, P. G., *The Golden Age Recorded*, London: The Oakwood Press, 1963

Jackson, Stanley, *The Savoy*, London: Muller, 1964

Key, Pierre V. R. in collaboration with Bruno Zirato, *Enrico Caruso: A biography*, London: Hurst & Blackett, 1923

Klein, Herman, *Thirty Years of Musical Life in London 1870–1900*, London: William Heinemann, 1903

Klein, Herman, *Musicians and Mummers*, London: Cassell, 1925

Klein, Herman, *The Golden Age of Opera*, London: George Routledge, 1933

Kolodin, Irving, *The Metropolitan Opera 1883–1939*, New York: Oxford University Press, 1940

Korolewicz-Wayda, Janina, *My Memoirs*, Wroclaw (Breslau): National Ossolineum Institute, 1958

Lahee, Henry C., *Grand Opera Singers of Today*, Boston: Page, Revised edition, 1922

Lawrence, Marjorie, *Interrupted Melody*, Sydney: Invincible Press, 1949; London: Falcon Press, 1952

Lawton, Mary, *Schumann-Heink: The last of the Titans*, New York: Macmillan, 1940

Leiser, Clara, *Jean de Reszke and the Great Days of Opera*, London: Gerald Howe, 1933

Le Massena, C. E., *Galli-Curci's Life of Song*, New York: Paebar, 1945

Leslie, Seymour, *The Jerome Connexion*, London: John Murray, 1964

Lindsay, Joan, *Time Without Clocks*, Melbourne: Cheshire, 1962

Low, David, *Low's Autobiography*, London: Michael Joseph, 1956

McKay, Claude, *This is the Life*, Sydney: Angus & Robertson, 1961

Magnus, Philip, *King Edward the Seventh*, London: John Murray, 1964

Marchesi, Blanche, *Singer's Pilgrimage*, London: Grant Richards, 1923

Marchesi, Mathilde, *Marchesi and Music: Passages from the life of a famous singing teacher*, New York and London: Harper & Brothers, 1898

Melba, Nellie, *Melodies and Memories*, London: Thornton Butterworth, 1925

Meudell, George, *The Pleasant Career of a Spendthrift*, London: Routledge, 1929

Moore, Gerald, *Am I Too Loud?* London: Hamish Hamilton, 1962

Morton, Frederic, *The Rothschilds*, London: Secker & Warburg, 1962

Murdoch, Nina, *Portrait in Youth*, Sydney: Angus & Robertson, 1948

Murphy, Agnes, *Melba: A biography*, London: Chatto & Windus, 1909

Nichols, Beverley, *Twenty-Five*, London: Jonathan Cape, 1926

Nichols, Beverley, *Are They the Same at Home?*, London: Jonathan Cape, 1927

Nichols, Beverley, *Evensong*, London: Jonathan Cape, 1932

Nichols, Beverley, *All I Could Never Be*, London: Jonathan Cape, 1949

Orchard, W. Arundel, *Music in Australia*, Melbourne: Georgian House, 1952

Pearl, Cyril, *Wild Men of Sydney*, London: W. H. Allen, 1958

Pearson, Hesketh, *The Life of Oscar Wilde*, London: Methuen, 1946; Penguin Books, 1960

Ponder, Winifred, *Clara Butt: Her life-story*, London: Harrap, 1928

Pound, Reginald, *Gillies: Surgeon Extraordinary*, London: Michael Joseph, 1964

Prichard, Katharine Susannah, *Child of the Hurricane*, Sydney: Angus & Robertson, 1963

Reid, M. O., *The Ladies Came to Stay: A study of the education of girls at the Presbyterian Ladies' College, Melbourne 1875–1960*, Melbourne: The Council of the College, 1960

Roberts, Kenneth, *Captain of the Push*, Melbourne: Lansdowne, 1963

Ronald, Sir Landon, *Myself and Others*, London: Sampson Low, Marston, 1931

Rosenthal, Harold, *Two Centuries of Opera at Covent Garden*, London: Putnam, 1958

Rosenthal, Harold, and John Warrack, *Concise Oxford Dictionary of Opera*, London: Oxford University Press, 1964

Ruffo, Titta, *La Mia Parabola*, Milano: Editore Treves, 1937

Russell, Henry, *The Passing Show*, London: Thornton Butterworth, 1926

Scholes, Percy A., *Concise Oxford Dictionary of Music*, London: Oxford University Press, 1952

Scott, Ernest, *A History of the University of Melbourne*, Melbourne University Press, in association with Oxford University Press, 1936

Selby, Isaac, *The Memorial History of Victoria*, Melbourne: Old Pioneers' Memorial Fund, 1924

Seltsam, William H. (compiler), *Metropolitan Opera Annals*, New York: H. W. Wilson, 1947

Semon, Felix, *The Autobiography of Felix Semon, KCVO, MD, FRCP*, London: Jarrolds, 1926

Shaw, Bernard, *Music in London 1890–4:* Criticisms contributed week by week to *The World*, 3 vols, London: Constable, 1931

Shaw, Bernard, *London Music in 1888–89* as heard by Corno di Bassetto (later known as Bernard Shaw), London: Constable, 1937

Sheean, Vincent, *The Amazing Oscar Hammerstein*, London: Weidenfeld & Nicolson, 1956

Spencer, A. H., *The Hill of Content*, Sydney: Angus & Robertson, 1959

Szigeti, Joseph, *With Strings Attached: Reminiscences and reflections*, New York: Alfred A. Knopf, 1947

Tertis, Lionel, *Cinderella No More*, London: Peter Nevill, 1953

Tetrazzini, Madama (Luisa), *My Life of Song*, London: Cassell, 1921

Thompson, John, *On Lips of Living Men*, Melbourne: Lansdowne, 1962

Waters, Thorold, *Much Besides Music*, Melbourne: Georgian House, 1951

Wechsberg, Joseph, *Red Plush and Black Velvet*, Boston: Little, Brown, 1961

Wood, Henry J., *My Life of Music*, London: Gollancz, 1938

Newspapers and Magazines

It is impracticable to name all those daily newspapers and periodical publications, from about 1850 up to the present day, which contributed something to the author's knowledge of Melba's career and his understanding of her character. This is a list of the most substantial of such sources:

Australia

Herald, Melbourne, *The Merry, Merry Pipes of Pan*, by John Lemmone, 7 June 1924

Herald, Melbourne, *Melba Looks Back* (Interview by Frank A. Russell), 13 October 1924

Herald, Melbourne, *Melba on Life After Death*, 26 October 1925

Herald, Melbourne, *Melba's Indictment: 'Our Musical Reputation a Myth'* (news-page interview), 5 September 1927

Herald, Melbourne, *Where Is Happiness? Is It in Fame?* by Dame Nellie Melba (No. 2 of a series of articles, written 'by famous happy people'), 10 September 1927

Illustrated Australian News, Melbourne, *Lilydale and District*, by 'The Vagabond', 1 February 1894

Lone Hand, Sydney, *Music As a Profession: Some Personal Advice*, by Nellie Melba, 1 February 1909

Table Talk, Melbourne, *Signor Pietro Cecchi*, 6 December 1889

Truth, Sydney, *Concerning Her Champagne Capers, Breaches of Public Faith, Outrages Against Good Manners, and Insults to Australian Citizens!* by John Norton, 28 March 1903

Truth, Sydney, *Sunset? The Pathetic Fading of Melba*, 10 April 1927

Woman's Day, Melbourne, *Sneezes, Songs and Melba*, by Gladys Moncrieff, 23 January 1950

Britain

Chambers's Journal, London, *About Melba*, by Sir Landon Ronald, 22 April 1922

Chambers's Journal, London, *More About Melba*, by Sir Landon Ronald, 29 April 1922

Listener, London, *I Knew Melba*, by Ivor Newton, 29 September 1938

Monthly Musical Record, London, *Melba: 1861–1931*, by William Murdoch, 1 April 1931

Music and Musicians, London, *What Melba Did to Help Me*, by Elena Danieli, May 1961

Musical Times, London, *Melba: An Appreciation*, by Herman Klein, 1 April 1931

Saturday Review, London, *Melba*, by Robin H. Legge, 28 February 1931

Spectator, London, *Melba*, by Basil Maine, 28 February 1931

Strand, London, *Madame Melba*, by Percy Cross Standing, January 1899

Sunday Referee, London, *Melba, Dictator of Song, Suffered No Rivals*, by Constance Vaughan (interview with Blanche Marchesi), 19 January 1936

USA

Century Magazine, New York, *The Gift of Song*, by Nellie Melba, June 1907

Lippincott's Monthly Magazine, Philadelphia, *Grand Opera*, by Nellie Melba, April 1895

Saturday Review, New York, *Melba and I*, by John Brownlee, 25 December 1954

Index